11/1/2012

Advance Praise for Patricia Aburdene's

Conscious Money

"*Conscious Money* does for individuals what Conscious Capitalism did for corporations: it articulates a simple, brilliant framework for achieving sustainable financial results, while espousing the highest ideals. Read it, get inspired, and prosper."

—**John Mackey**, coCEO and cofounder of Whole Foods Market

"Perfect timing. In an era when most of us question 'economics as usual,' *Conscious Money* charts a personalized strategy for embracing human values as the cornerstone of sustainable finance. This is a rare and winning blend of inspiration, information, and wisdom. Bravo Patricia Aburdene."

—**Amy Domini**, founder and CEO of Domini Social Investments

"Anything Patricia Aburdene writes is of immediate interest to me. In *Conscious Money*, she shows us why we should reject conventional economic wisdom (greed is good) and grow prosperity by recognizing values like trust and integrity as our greatest financial assets. Passionate and persuasive; read it to make a difference, find fulfillment, and grow 'conscious' wealth."

—**Stephen M. R. Covey**, bestselling author of *The Speed of Trust* and *Smart Trust*

"*Conscious Money* translates the profitable business model of Conscious Capitalism into a blueprint for personal finance. Read it, change the way you see, and engage with the world of business, and personally prosper by honoring your values."

—**Kip Tindell**, chairman and CEO of
The Container Store

"This profound and eminently practical book is pure genius when it comes to money and consciousness. It is not only a superb guide to the release of our money sickness but gives us transformative skills that lead us towards clarity and abundance while enlightening our mind and spirit."

—**Jean Houston, PhD**, author of
A Passion for the Possible

"We can have a new economic era now—where sustainable values and the genius of human consciousness outperform fear and greed. *Conscious Money* imagines it, presents the evidence for it, and creates a blueprint for achieving it. Nothing could be a more significant contribution to our personal and global healing."

—**Marianne Williamson**, author of *Return to Love*

"Fundamentally, our inner relationship with our money—how we feel about our prosperity and the paths we've chosen to reach it—is one of the truest definitions of fulfillment and security. Patricia Aburdene's insightful, delightful work carefully and accessibly explores these truths and provides pioneering counsel on reaching our goals. Reading her book is a deeply satisfying and enriching experience."

—**Jack Canfield**, author of *The Success Principles*,
The Golden Motorcycle Gang, and
co-creator *The Chicken Soup for the Soul*

Conscious
Money

Conscious Money

Living, Creating, and Investing with Your
Values for a Sustainable New Prosperity

Patricia Aburdene

ATRIA PAPERBACK
New York London Toronto Sydney New Delhi

BEYOND WORDS
Hillsboro, Oregon

ATRIA PAPERBACK
A Division of Simon & Schuster, Inc.
1230 Avenue of the Americas
New York, NY 10020

BEYOND WORDS
20827 N.W. Cornell Road, Suite 500
Hillsboro, Oregon 97124-9808
503-531-8700 / 503-531-8773 fax
www.beyondword.com

Managing editor: Lindsay S. Brown
Editors: Anna Noak, Carolyn Bond, and Dan Frost
Copyeditor: Henry Covey
Design: Devon Smith
Proofreader: Linda M. Meyer
Composition: William H. Brunson Typography Services

First Atria Books/Beyond Words hardcover edition September 2012

ATRIA PAPERBACK and colophon are trademarks of Simon & Schuster, Inc.
Beyond Words Publishing is an imprint of Simon & Schuster, Inc. and the Beyond Words logo is a registered trademark of Beyond Words Publishing, Inc.

For more information about special discounts for bulk purchases, please contact Simon & Schuster Special Sales at 1-866-506-1949 or business@simonandschuster.com.

The Simon & Schuster Speakers Bureau can bring authors to your live event. For more information or to book an event, contact the Simon & Schuster Speakers Bureau at 1-866-248-3049 or visit our website at www.simonspeakers.com.

Manufactured in the United States of America

10 9 8 7 6 5 4 3 2 1

Library of Congress Cataloging-in-Publication Data

Aburdene, Patricia.
    Conscious money : living, creating, and investing with your values for a sustainable new prosperity / Patricia Aburdene.
       p. cm.
    1. Finance, Personal—Psychological aspects.   2. Investments—Psychological aspects.   I. Title.
    HG179.A254   2012
    332.024—dc23
                                                                                    2012016157

ISBN: 978-1-58270-292-6
ISBN: 978-1-4516-2315-4 (ebook)

The corporate mission of Beyond Words Publishing, Inc.: *Inspire to Integrity*

For Alain Boléa, with love and appreciation

Contents

Acknowledgments

This book was born when I realized there was a lot more I wanted to say about consciousness and finance. In time the words and ideas began to flow. The new creation announced itself in a conversation with my agent Bill Gladstone of Waterside Productions. "The word 'money' belongs in the title," he said definitively. That felt right to me. "Well then it must be *Conscious Money*," I replied. Thank you, Bill, for always "getting" my work and for your unfailing support.

I have always wanted to speak in a more personal way about the spiritual journey we all share. The more I wrote, the clearer it became that this book was for people who wanted their money life to better reflect the values espoused in their personal and spiritual lives. In Beyond Words, Bill and I found a publisher that heartily endorsed that approach. I believe that great partnerships evolve when people possess complementary, rather than similar, skill sets. The expertise of Beyond Words in the self-help genre artfully balances my own very different strengths. With the help of Kenneth Kales, we learned how to merge the categories of trend-tracking, business, and advice into a new approach to personal finance. Thank you, Cynthia Black, for your vision of what this book could be and your willingness to see it through.

At Beyond Words, Dan Frost, among his many other contributions, often voiced the energetic perspective of a younger generation with whom I feel great kinship. So did Emily Han. Good fortune shined upon *Conscious Money* and me the day Beyond Words assigned Carolyn Bond to the project. Never have I worked with a more committed, brilliant, and tireless editor. Carolyn, I could never have done this without you.

Early in the project my former assistant Trude Irons morphed into a plucky researcher, charming many a reluctant source into spilling the beans (some of them coffee beans). Even after moving on in her own editorial career, Trude cheerfully tracked down the stray clipping and note. It has been a complete pleasure to renew my association with my Megatrends researcher Joy Molony (formerly Van Elderen) after we both showed up in Boulder, Colorado. I've never worked with anyone else who better understands exactly what I need and how to find it. Thank you, Joy, from the bottom of my heart.

Anna Noak helped transition the manuscript toward production. It was a little embarrassing when I assured managing editor Lindsay Brown she needn't worry about fact checking since I always do that. Lindsay and Henry Covey did an absolutely amazing job copyediting, even managing to convince me that I am not the world's most flawless fact checker after all. Thank you all for shepherding *Conscious Money* from manuscript to book. I am grateful for the Beyond Words sales and publicity teams who took over then, and special thanks go to Georgie Lewis, Whitney Quon, Leah Brown, and Jessica Sturges. I've had the pleasure of meeting almost everyone at Beyond Words and many of its authors as well. Thank you, Cynthia Black and Richard Cohn, for creating a community.

I am indebted to many people who generously shared their lives, work, and stories for this book. Thank you Cliff Feigenbaum, Nana Naisbitt, Srikumar Rao, Byron Stock, Jason Apollo Voss, Jeff Klein, Amy Foster, Cindy Wigglesworth, Callie Micek, Elizabeth Culter, Lynne Sausele, Gail McMeekin, Lawler Kang, Carolyn Long, Paul Rice, Karen Gross, Bennett

Dorrance, Jack Robinson, Matt Patsky, Angel Rich, Janet Zhou, Sharon Shuteran, and Alison Hall.

Numerous others helped my team and I assemble the information that gives this endeavor its factual backbone. They include Claire Montaut, Sandy Yusen, Dean Cyclone, Joshua Onysko, Leyla Steele, Remy Bolea, and Katie Barrow.

My team of conscious investment experts—Steve Schueth, Michael Kramer, Gary Moore, Matt Patsky, and Jason Voss—provided many insights, much clarification, and lots of good advice. Thanks to all of my colleagues in Conscious Capitalism: John Mackey, Jeff Klein, Raj Sisodia, Rand Stagen, Randy Eisenman, Sunny Vanderbeck, and Roy Spence. There have been many Conscious Capitalist gatherings, but the first public event, to which I refer in chapter 4, provided such an in-depth focus on the basic concepts that I wanted to introduce our movement to a general audience. I am especially grateful to the speakers at that event whose words of wisdom I have enthusiastically shared with my readers.

As we went to press, I received the heartbreaking news that my friend Sharon Shuteran, whose story of volunteer adventure is described on pages 245–246, passed away unexpectedly. To keep the focus on her commitment and to honor her spirit, I have kept the story in the present tense. The concluding sentence states, "Sharon and her entire team will be back next year." I am certain that she will be there in spirit.

As this project draws to a close, I look forward to spending time with my inner circle of beloved friends Carolyn Long, Donna Coombs, Lynne Sausele, Kathleen Loughery, and Sousan Abadian. Thanks for your love and understanding. To my immediate family, Barbara Jones and Phil Harter; Chris and Hunter Jones; Jennifer, David, and Nathan Smallwood; Nana Naisbitt and her children, Rory, Lily, and Jake Sullivan, I give thanks for our wonderful times together and for your steadfast support. Thanks to Geoff Hoppe and Linda Benyo for supporting my work, birthing me as a journaling teacher, for your own devotion to your mission, and for all the fun we've had.

Thank you, Kathleen Loughery, Guidance Energy, and Green Ray for being in my life, getting me through all the bumps along the way, and for your certainty that this book would see the light of day and reach the people who sought its message.

Most of all I thank my partner in life and love, Alain Boléa, for our shared values and commitment to conscious business, for your companionship, devotion, and for the joy I take in and the laughter I cherish in your presence.

Introduction

Today's headlines tell a story of economic turbulence: OCCUPY WALL STREET. EUROPEAN MONETARY CRISIS. MORE AMERICANS IN POVERTY THAN EVER. US JOB CREATION "FRUSTRATINGLY SLOW." Business, once confined to the financial pages, is now big news on Main Street. Most people believe corporate greed plays a major role in today's economic trouble and that human values are woefully lacking in business policy and action. A 2011 NBC News/*Wall Street Journal* poll found 76 percent of respondents agree the US economic structure is "out of balance."[1] Millions have lost their homes, jobs, or savings and feel they may never recover. Many more are paralyzed about making financial decisions.

There is a reason why money tops the worry lists of so many people. The antiquated financial structures of yesteryear are crashing all around us. But if you're willing to look beneath the surface, I will show you evidence that a holistic, values-based economic transformation is well underway, opening the door to a new era that can bring you fulfillment and prosperity.

I call this emerging megatrend Conscious Money.

Conscious Money is a growing movement of people who draw on values, creativity, and the power of human consciousness to clarify and guide their financial choices. I use the term "values" to mean the transcendent ideals that connect us with our soul's wisdom. When values also guide our financial decisions, our choices are grounded in the deepest part of ourselves. Being creative allows you to see things in a new way and to generate new possibilities. But creativity requires higher consciousness—and then the willingness to act on your insights. Higher consciousness links us to a state of awareness or presence. To be conscious is to be present—in one's work, with a person, or in a situation—without preconceived notions, emotional blocks, or mental fixations.

Together, creativity and conscious presence are powerful tools for growing Conscious Money. In fact, today, because of the economic shift I'll soon describe, these inner resources constitute the primary economic drivers behind success and wealth creation. Conscious people are awake, aware, and living in what spiritual teacher Eckhart Tolle calls "the Now," the present moment. The ability to experience the Now by choice, and the capacity to resolve issues and challenges in a creative way, form the core of a new economic age.

Up till now, people have viewed economic history in terms of three commercial eras: agriculture, industry, and information. The Age of Information began sometime in the mid-to-late 1970s, when more people and more companies created new wealth and new jobs through information rather than through industry.

But today we have entered what I call the New Economy of Consciousness. In this exciting new era, we create value not by sifting, mining, or manipulating information but by creatively expressing the genius of human consciousness. As this new age progresses, most of us will earn our income through conscious creativity. In fact, experts agree that creativity will be a very important talent to nurture for this new era, no matter what your career, profession, or job might be.

Consciousness and values go hand in hand today. In this new economic era, the emerging megatrend of Conscious Money connects the outer world of money with the inner realm of human values and higher consciousness. Even as we witness the old economic order falling under the weight of its profound unconsciousness and lack of values, a new economic operating system is already coming forth to replace it.

For many people, money and values are incompatible. They believe that decisions about money—the practical, earthy, and external symbol of economic exchange—ought to be decided apart from their inner selves, the seat of transcendence and the spirit. And certainly the commonplace world of money and finance is almost exclusively devoted to the mind-set of making as much money, as fast as possible, by any means necessary. In such a mind-set, it matters not how unconsciously a person earns money, because he or she can be (or appear to be) highly conscious by giving some of it away to a worthy cause. These types of contributions can be beneficial, but when we follow such a path, we set up a personal dynamic that divides us in half and saps our power. As Cliff Feigenbaum, publisher of *Green Money Journal*, says, "That's like profiting from tobacco stocks during the day and contributing to the American Cancer Society at night."[2]

Conscious Money flips this flawed assumption on its head. The truth is, your values can be a great financial asset. They can and should serve as guidelines in making choices about money matters, while you also respect sound financial principles.

This is something that I have discovered as a social forecaster and spiritual seeker. Early in my career, I worked for *Forbes* magazine (tagline: The Capitalist Tool). Later I became a number-one bestselling author. The megatrends books that I've cowritten have sold more than fourteen million copies worldwide. I've lectured about these megatrends throughout North and South America, Europe, Asia, and Australia. After the publication of my book *Megatrends 2010: The Rise of Conscious Capitalism*, I was named one of the "Top 100 Thought Leaders in Business Behavior" by Trust Across America in 2011 and 2012. I have also served as a Public Policy Fellow at Radcliffe College. For thirty years, I've helped individuals and businesses discover the opportunities of social and economic change.

For the past decade, as a trend tracker I have studied how the Conscious Money megatrend plays out in business through Conscious Capitalism, a humanistic, values-driven approach to free enterprise that honors employees, customers, suppliers, the community, and the environment, not just investors. Conscious Capitalism illustrates that human values and higher consciousness, when embodied in business, can generate success. In fact, I'll cite studies which demonstrate that Conscious Capitalism can financially outperform conventional capitalism, thus illustrating how effectively the combination of money and values can foster financial success.

Conscious Money can work at the individual level too. In these pages, I will share the lessons I've learned as a social forecaster, as well as the discoveries I've made on my own financial journey and as an individual committed to personal growth and spirituality.

Today, I feel confident and at peace about money. This is so even though my net worth is a good deal less than it once was. I feel good about money because my money is "conscious," which is to say, I make financial choices that reflect my values and awareness. As a result, I trust myself more and worry about money a lot less.

This was not the case fifteen years ago. Although I viewed myself as a spiritual person, my money life was worrisome and unfulfilling. I spent money and "gave to myself," yet I sometimes felt empty. My holiday gifts to others were excessive, stress inducing, and too often without joy. I also committed many financial errors while investing. My worst mistakes came when I sought to "make money" by investing in companies I did not believe in or followed the advice of others without checking to see how a decision felt within. I gave money and time to people and causes, but I often felt more obligation than inspiration. I longed to earn my income by being more creative, yet somehow felt stuck. Worst of all, I second-guessed my financial choices and propelled myself into a spiral of self-judgment.

Finally, I decided I wanted to heal my relationship with money. More of my deeper self, I sensed, had to be part of my financial life. So I vowed to consult my inner self whenever I faced a financial choice. Not sure of what to expect, I posed this budding awareness as a question: "What would I see or understand now if the right financial decision were also the right inner choice?" In other words, I held within myself the possibility of a positive resolution between inner and outer, even though I didn't yet know what that might look like. Gradually, I developed a "felt sense" that guided me to make choices that both felt good and made financial sense. These decisions satisfied both my heart and my head.

As my awareness grew, my financial life transformed. Overspending became ridiculous. Why engage the energy of excess, when spending consciously is so much more fulfilling? Investing was no longer a minefield of confusion but a great opportunity to make a difference while growing my portfolio and learning about conscious companies. As I came to trust myself, the doors of consciousness opened. Creativity and intuition infused naturally into my work, earning, spending, investing, and giving. I gave my time, money, and energy when it felt right and grew comfortable saying no and sending love and goodwill instead when it did not. Over time, I discovered the power, wisdom, and joy of Conscious Money.

In this book you will discover that when you make financial choices that honor your values, you can gracefully navigate the new economy in good times and bad. As a result, you'll experience greater satisfaction as you consciously and wisely spend, invest, earn, or contribute your financial resources. All of these lessons will move you closer to fulfilling the promise of Conscious Money.

You will learn about Conscious Money from the inside out, focusing first on its internal dimension. Part I of this book is designed to help you clarify your values and create a Conscious Money strategy based on those values. You will learn how to release the unconscious thoughts, feelings, or patterns that can block a healthy relationship with money. And you will develop what is perhaps the most important attribute of Conscious Money: the capacity to make conscious choices, which is the essence of self-mastery. This can be considered an essential money skill because almost every financial error imaginable can somehow be connected to a lack of self-mastery. The beauty of self-mastery, however, is that once you begin even a single self-mastery practice, it can inform your choices and make them more conscious.

You will gradually come to see that conscious choices are the result of cultivating mental, emotional, and spiritual self-mastery, and these choices will increasingly come naturally to you.

In Part II, we move into the outer dimension of Conscious Money: embodying these inner principles as we enter the marketplace. First, we look at the characteristics of Conscious Capitalism, so you can identify the conscious enterprises with which you want to engage. You will find tools for selecting products, companies, and financial partners that reflect your personal values. There is one chapter devoted to each of your roles as a consumer, earner, and investor. Finally, as a practitioner of Conscious Money, you are an active participant and contributor in both the local and global economies.

Throughout the book, there are interactive exercises to support you in practicing the new capacities that this book presents. At the end of each chapter, you'll find a list of options to choose from, or to use as inspiration, for creating your unique Conscious Money strategy, based on your personal choices. After the options phase, there is a closing affirmation embodying a key point explored in the chapter.

There is one last and very important element of Conscious Money to consider as we begin. The power of the individual lies in his or her capacity for choice. As a result, we wield great influence as a force for good in the economy. Conscious Money is about recognizing, embracing, and activating this personal power. With every conscious financial choice, you alter the collective economic reality by healing the sense of separation between the worldly (or external) quality of money and the spiritual (or internal) dimensions of values and higher consciousness. With each creative resolution, you are building the foundation for a new and conscious economy that will sustain the future of human evolution and transformation.

Part I

The Inner Dimension of Conscious Money

1

The Fundamentals of Conscious Money

Conscious Money begins with you. Not with your wallet, savings, home, possessions, or stock portfolio, but with *you*. It starts with *your* values, and with *your* state of consciousness about money. It is a journey that will lead you to explore your thoughts, feelings, and beliefs about money in greater depth. And the first step we will take on the path to Conscious Money is to focus on your values, the inner strength that grounds your Conscious Money strategy. Each individual is unique, and to a great extent, we express our individuality through our choices. Whether we know it or not, what we value is the guiding force behind those choices.

Because your Conscious Money practice is sourced from and anchored in a deeper part of yourself, the Conscious Money strategy that you will create is unique to you. And it involves developing the internal tools you'll need to make your money choices consciously.

People who seek to grow their money consciously, rather than by avidly pursuing money for its own sake, often create more sustainable finances. This is so for several reasons:

When your money choices are values-based, they require a more thoughtful approach and often a longer time horizon. Over time, these choices translate into better financial decisions. Practicing Conscious

Money brings you back to center again and again, steadying the way as you negotiate the inevitable bumps that come with money and life. Most of all, you embody a sense of goodwill that attracts the right people and right opportunities at the right time.

The objective of Conscious Money is not to "get rich" (and certainly not to get rich quick) but to earn, invest, and spend financial resources in ways that are congruent with your ideals and awareness. Yet even though Conscious Money is not about getting rich, there is good reason to expect that you'll grow your finances as you practice it. That's because there is already a well-established track record for making money through the powerful combination of values and higher consciousness. You'll discover this track record as you learn more about the megatrend of Conscious Capitalism.

Conscious Money and Conscious Capitalism are cut from the same financial cloth, in that they share the same economic operating principle: when values and greater awareness, in conjunction with solid monetary practices, inform a financial strategy, sustainable Conscious Money is the positive result. This is as true for individuals as it is for businesses.

As your money (your income, cash, savings, expenses, investments, and philanthropic contributions) becomes Conscious Money, that is, when your money is imbued with your values and consciousness, you in time create what I like to call Conscious Wealth. Some people might not feel comfortable with the term "wealth," but all it really means is the money that remains when you deduct expenses from income. Your Conscious Wealth might consist of fifty dollars or one million. It's not the amount but your intention about your money that matters most.

There is a very real difference between unconscious and conscious wealth. You might not see it in the figures of your bank account, but you will feel it in your heart.

Because Conscious Wealth is created from the inside out, it is anchored in what really matters to you: it is grounded in meaning.

In this chapter, we begin the journey toward Conscious Money by focusing on your values, and on the basics of a sound Conscious Money strategy. Then, we'll explore the capacity to make money choices consciously in chapters 2 and 3.

Values

It may appear that your values don't directly influence your financial well-being, but they do. It's difficult, however, to see a direct link between money and values because almost everyone is influenced by traditional money thinking, which is rooted in considerations like self-preservation or self-interest, which are valid—up to a point.

The trouble arises when we follow the mundane path of self-interest so exclusively that we shut down our higher, soulful instincts. If we sacrifice justice, truth, or compassion to promote our self-interest, we will suffer a profound sense of self-betrayal. Success feels empty because our self-serving actions fail to mirror our values or true spiritual identity.

As we explore topics like conscious investing and mindful spending, you will see that many of the best financial choices also powerfully validate your values. The path of Conscious Money might look like this:

You would seek a job that respects your values, taps into your creativity, or honors your desire to make a difference. And you wouldn't stop searching until you found it. Since you love your fulfilling work, you succeed in it and that boosts your income.

You'd spend mindfully on purchases that reflect your values. You might pay a bit more for local organic food, for example, if well-being were an important value for you—and you would cut back elsewhere in your budget. You'd certainly avoid the trap of overspending to "feel good about yourself," only to find yourself temporarily satisfied but increasingly in debt.

Once you grow enough Conscious Money to consider investing, your values, along with your consciousness and intuition, would help direct your research as you as consider companies and projects that fulfill your heart and satisfy your head. If your choices satisfy you both mentally and emotionally, it is likely such investments will also make good financial sense.

To walk the path of Conscious Money, however, it is essential that you first know exactly what your values are.

Your Unique Values

You possess a unique set of values made up of spiritual ideals like truth, justice, or compassion. These are your transcendent values. Most likely, you also embrace concrete standards like accountability, hard work, or simplicity. These are your practical values. Together, these intangible forces guide your choices, whether in finance, work, or relationships.

But few of us can instantly cite our top values; we have them all right, but they are often somewhat obscured and thus "unconscious." So let's uncover, identify, clarify, and reflect on our deeply held values.

Values clarification is a simple process, yet it requires a bit of thought. The exercise, "Choose Your Top Values," will help guide you through this process. The first step is to review a list of sample transcendent and practical values. Feel free to consider additional values that are meaningful for you. It is a good idea to take your time and get to know your most deeply held values, say your top three. Selecting a limited number of values may be challenging, but it tells you what you care about most. Over time, you may also want to choose your number one value, the one that is most meaningful for you. You will find the exercise an enlightening one that will greatly help you to focus in on the right Conscious Money choices for you.

Choose Your Top Values

Review the list of values that follows. It includes both spiritual and practical values. Note those values that are important to you but do not appear here.

- First, select the ten values from the list below that most deeply resonate with you.
- Reduce that list to your top five values, then to three, and then to two.
- Finally, select your most important value.
- Now, write down your top two or three values. Briefly describe why each is important for you. (I'll soon invite you to create a Conscious Money journal for collecting notes like these.)

There are no right or wrong answers about your values. You may find that practical values are as important to you as spiritual ones. When I did this exercise decades ago, I was a bit surprised to discover that my top value was a practical one: resilience. Later I thought, "That's right. How can I practice love or justice if I can't pick myself up off the floor after a big disappointment?"

Accountability	Freedom	Love	Security
Achievement	Friendship	Loyalty	Self-reliance
Adventure	Fun	Meaning	Self-respect
Beauty	Goodness	Openness	Service
Community	Hard work	Personal growth	Simplicity
Creativity	Harmony	Practicality	Success
Discipline	Hope	Privacy	Sustainability
Efficiency	Independence	Reliability	Tolerance
Excellency	Individuality	Resilience	Trust
Excitement	Integrity	Resourcefulness	Truth
Faith	Justice	Respect	Wisdom

How we hold our values powerfully influences our actions. If you honor integrity over success, you won't feel the need to lie in order to do well in life. But if you revere success first and foremost, you might lie, cheat, or steal to succeed (or you might not; it's just a possibility). When you know what you stand for, you possess the clarity to take steps, including financial steps, that are congruent with your values.

Well-being, justice, compassion, and other values influence your money choices. If sustainability is one of your top values, you will most likely choose to protect the environment by refusing to invest in a chemical manufacturing company whose factory runoff harms waterways or whose emissions pollute the air. If reliability rates high on your values list, you might well choose to pay a bit more for a car or a laptop with a reputation for rarely malfunctioning and needing service.

At the heart of Conscious Money is the desire to exemplify your carefully identified personal values in your financial interactions. As tremendously useful as values are for gauging your choices and making difficult decisions easier, they involve far more than practical considerations. Spiritual or transcendent values express humanity's greatest soul qualities. They're the imprints of Spirit that accompany you on the journey of life.

A Conscious Money Strategy

Conscious Money is both a mindful practice and a financial strategy. The choices you make while practicing Conscious Money set the stage for greater fulfillment and financial success. That is because Conscious Money enhances sound financial practice with the inner resources of values and consciousness. Together, these positive attributes foster sustainable financial resources in the long term.

A Fresh Take on Personal Finance

Conscious Money offers a powerful complement to traditional personal finance. This is because at its heart lies a potent truth: people make wiser money choices, and can grow money in a more sustainable manner, when their actions match their ideals and reflect their expanded awareness. Such decisions are generally more thoughtful and consistent

But even some thoughtful financial plans stop short of advocating values as a primary factor in financial decision making. Instead, they endorse the imperative of making money first and treat values as a secondary consideration, if at all. Such a stance, however, leaves us without an inner compass. Transcendent values, intuitive wisdom, and the expanded awareness of higher consciousness constitute a powerful guidance system, especially for navigating uncertain economic times.

Many personal finance plans are supposed to work for you whoever you are. While most of us agree that getting out of debt is usually a very good idea, in fact, that choice doesn't necessarily work for everyone.

For example, if you are in the prime earning years, your forties and fifties, and you are looking to pay off your mortgage in order to live debt free (as one financial plan advocates), you'd actually lose a valuable tax deduction. However, paying off your mortgage as you gear up for retirement, when income typically falls, could prove to be a wise move. The path of Conscious Money invites you to explore a range of options, eliminate those that do not work for you, remain true to your ideals, and exercise personal responsibility by selecting only those choices that are right for your unique personal circumstances.

Personal finance covers many different topics such as financial planning, budgeting, debt elimination, real estate, investing, estate planning, saving, financing education, wealth creation, and more. Conscious Money, in contrast, is an overall financial perspective and strategy. With the exception of investing, it is not within the scope of this book to address in detail these typical elements of money planning. For that kind of information you might explore the work of personal finance teachers such as Dave Ramsey, who focuses on how to get out of debt; Suze Orman, who offers a comprehensive approach to personal finance; or Vicki Robin, who helps people cut free of consumerist culture and move toward financial independence. Their websites appear in the resources listed in the chapter options.

Even though Conscious Money embraces a more values-based and customized approach to finance, a good Conscious Money strategy incorporates the basic principles of personal finance. Let's briefly review a few of the more important ones:

1. *Live below your means.* The old expression "live within your means" has given too many people permission to spend every dollar they earn. Result: a dearth of savings and a wealth of debt. Thank the Great Recession, however, for today's grassroots "cheap is chic" movement. It's a breath of fresh air.

   (The classic definition of a recession is two or more quarters when the economy fails to grow. But the Great Recession lasted much longer than most recessions. Furthermore, even after it ended, at least technically, the housing market remained weak and hiring was exasperatingly slow to recover. That is why for millions of people the recession still seemed to be going on, even after economists had declared it over.)

2. *Save—early and often.* That is exactly what many Europeans and Asians have famously done. Not so in the United States. But in 2010 and 2011, Americans started saving more. "Pay yourself first" is an old but excellent adage.

3. *Be fully conscious about your expenses.* Know what they are, and be certain that they reflect your values and priorities. Writing them down is a great way to begin. Then take time to reflect on your expenses and the motives behind them, as you will have a chance do in the exercise following this chapter.

4. *Create priorities and then make trade-offs.* When you know what matters most to you, it's easier to choose what you really want to do

and save elsewhere in your budget. Love going out for dinner? Be an expert on "value" restaurants. Crazy about movies? Skip the expensive theater tickets and download a frugal flick from iTunes or Amazon.

5. *Have a clear financial goal.* It is a lot easier to tackle a challenging financial issue, such as getting out of debt or building a sizable nest egg, when you can consistently draw on inspiration by invoking a clear image of what you desire. Find the needed discipline with a vivid picture of what you want and why you want it. Know your goals.

Integrate the practical power of sound financial principles with the wisdom of personal values and human consciousness. Because when you act in harmony with your truth, while observing the basic rules of finance, you make better and more satisfying financial choices.

Choosing Financial Goals

We all have goals, whether or not we are aware of them. I use the term "goal" as a statement of desire, intention, and choice. Vague and poorly defined goals or intentions do not get you where you want to go, nor are they conscious. At the same time, overly exact goals leave little to no room for the Universe to surprise you with a creative solution or with more than you've requested.

The key is to formulate clear but not excessively precise goals that are designed to make you feel great each time you articulate them. You might decide, "I want to own a beautiful house that I can easily afford." Or "My goal is to thrive financially, serving clients that I genuinely enjoy." Or "Next year, I will focus my thoughts and feelings on the freedom and joy I will feel as I eliminate my debts."

In many ways, the "granddaddy" of goal creation is Napoleon Hill, who wrote an enormously successful book about getting rich at a time when people were anything but. In 1937, in the belly of the Great Depression,

Napoleon Hill published *Think and Grow Rich*. The book is based on what Hill calls the secret of wealth creation, which, he says, was whispered into his ear by the wealthy and famous industrialist Andrew Carnegie.

Hill met the illustrious Carnegie as a reporter assigned to interview him. As Hill tells it, Carnegie "asked me if I would be willing to spend twenty years or more, preparing myself to take it [the secret] to men and women who, without the secret, might go through life as failures." Hill promised Carnegie—"that canny, lovable old Scotsman"—that he would do so and plunged himself into years of research on wealthy people.[1]

Hill did his homework, analyzing some five hundred exceedingly well-to-do individuals. One very important trait he discovered was that wealthy people create their great fortunes primarily with "Thought" and "Definite Major Purpose."[2] Today, we'd probably characterize these success elements as "goals."

Napoleon Hill has long since passed on, but you can still get a good feel for the man on YouTube, where you can watch the dapper Mr. Hill, a Harry Truman look-alike, deliver short lectures. Even in the autumn of his years, Hill appears ever confident, articulate, passionate, and practical.

Hill advises the would-be wealthy to buy themselves a good notebook. First, he says, write out "your idea of success" and "major financial desire." Your success, he emphasizes, depends on your "definiteness of purpose."[3]

Hill has much more to say about wealth creation. However, here I want to suggest using his advice about making organized plans, and having a definite purpose when it comes to goals.

Goals are essential to the practice of Conscious Money because they focus your energy and keep you motivated about what you want most. You may have heard that it is a good idea to set goals that are challenging, yet within your reach. This is good advice.

But "setting" goals might not be the best way to go about the process. For most of us, goal setting is primarily a mental exercise. There is nothing wrong with that. However, for a Conscious Money practitioner, a better approach may be to explore more deeply and *discover* which goals move you most. Instead of thinking in terms of setting goals, you might create the intention to *recognize* which goals you authentically desire. It is not a question of rejecting the mental dimension of your goals but of aligning heart and head. When you do, you liberate the greatest resource you possess for achieving those goals: the power of your will—which is naturally activated when heart and head are in harmony.

Building Your Conscious Money Strategy

As you progress through this book, I invite you to create a personalized overall Conscious Money strategy to guide your financial life. A strategy is a plan that gets you from where you are to where you want to go. Start by asking yourself, "Where am I right now?" Acknowledge where you currently stand, point *A*. Next, decide where you want to be at a later time, point *B*, by asking yourself, "Where do I want to be?" Also choose a time frame that makes sense for you. It might be six months, one year, or longer. In goal setting, it's important to have an end date, a "by when," because it gives you a framework for your subsequent choices.

To support building your Conscious Money strategy, I recommend creating a Conscious Money journal. In the journal, you can collect your insights from the numerous interactive exercises you'll find throughout this book. Your journal is also a place where you can capture ideas, make plans, and design your personal Conscious Money strategy.

For example, as you set goals and begin to strategize, you might say, "I have no savings right now. I want to have $500 in the bank six months from now." That statement covers points *A* and *B* and your timeline. It is not yet a strategy, but it defines where you want to go and when you want to get there.

Now let's apply this approach to a broader topic: your relationship with money. Open your journal and explain in a paragraph or two where you are right now in terms of money. Next take a visionary leap of faith and describe where want to be in your relationship with money at the time in the future that you choose. You've again clarified your personal points *A* and *B* and your timeline.

Your Conscious Money strategy comprises a set of specific money choices that create an overall framework for conducting your financial life. The objective of this book is to deliver the information, inspiration, and suggested options to help you build that strategy.

When it comes to finance, there are no one-size-fits-all solutions or formulas. For a host of reasons, such as your age, income, and many other factors, what works for you might not suit a person whose circumstances differ from your own. As you consider your financial options while honoring the principles of sound finance, notice how you feel. You will begin to observe that the best choices for you will make sense, feel good, and resonate.

Options alone do not constitute a strategy. You must transform an option into a choice. Begin by making an inner choice. Select the options that both feel good and help you achieve your goals and then gradually act on them. That will launch the customized strategy that advances you from where you are to where you want to be. At first you might take actions that represent relatively small steps. Then when you are ready, you can increase the size and substance of your commitments and actions.

Let's revisit the goal to save $500 in six months. Six months is about twenty-four weeks. So in theory, you need to average at least $20 per week in savings. To achieve your desire, you might entertain several possibilities. Two immediately come to mind: reduce your expenses by $20 per week or grow your income by the same amount. It would be a useful exercise to brainstorm three ways to cut costs, such as bringing your lunch to work, eliminating that daily latte, or skipping drinks with your colleagues after work. To boost your income, you could babysit, do lawn work, or take a job in a store or restaurant for a few hours each week. When you have clarified your goals, researched or brainstormed your options, and committed to acting on your choice or choices, you have a strategy.

But your comprehensive Conscious Money strategy will include a lot more inner work than the practical example illustrated above, however concrete and useful it may be.

Conscious Money Options

The list of Conscious Money options at the end of each chapter is designed to offer you possible choices, while also encouraging your own creative thinking. The options are grouped as reflections, resources, and right actions.

The **reflections** can support your commitment to cultivate the inner dimension of Conscious Money. Economic conditions and your personal situation will shift. In the face of change, you can return again and again to your inner compass of values and higher consciousness by reviewing the options labeled "reflections."

The **resources** are designed to expand your thinking and base of information. The journey toward Conscious Money need not be a lonely one. You need resources and will probably enjoy companionship. From websites and books to experts and trusted friends, from corporations to nonprofit associations, resources are your allies on the journey toward Conscious Money.

The **right actions** suggest the concrete steps that you can take to further your Conscious Money practice. Without action, you do not have a strategy; with right action, you have a conscious one. Inspired by reflection and informed by resources, you suffuse your actions with consciousness.

As you plot your Conscious Money strategy, select among the options those that genuinely resonate for you. Let the list also inspire your own ideas. Write your additional options in your journal. Remember also that a recommendation that does not ring true for you today might be a perfect fit three months from now.

When you pick your best, most resonant options, you will naturally want to assume responsibility for them and to take action too. Your personal choice is critical because it is your Conscious Money, and you must live with the consequences of your choices. So begin by taking a few small steps and observing how you feel about the choices you have made. Grow your confidence organically. When you feel ready, take a somewhat bigger step. Chapter by chapter, you will be selecting those steps or options, which, when acted upon, constitute the core of your Conscious Money strategy.

Following each options list is a declaration that describes a positive state of being related to the chapter's topic. Feel free to substitute your own words to describe the conscious financial life you want to live in the time frame you have chosen.

Your Money Life

Your money life is actually a complex, interpersonal web of affiliations, partnerships, and interactions. So you will be in a better position to thrive financially when you invest in positive, healthy relationships. The people in your money life have an interest or stake in your financial success or failure. They might include a child you hope to send to college, and a spouse (or former spouse) who is dependent on you, at least in part, as a breadwinner. Your money relationships also involve financial partners, like the enterprises you patronize, the companies into which you invest, the bank that holds your mortgage, or the charities and other worthy projects to which you contribute your Conscious Money.

It's worthwhile to commit to creating high-quality relationships with each of the people in your web of financial interactions. For example, take a moment to say hello to the manager of your local bank or grocery store. Should an issue arise, this person will be a good ally. Positive relationships make life a lot more pleasant.

Your money life also possesses an overall "feel." This is the atmosphere or emotional climate in which you conduct your finances. Notice how you feel while paying your bills or examining the balances of your checking, savings, or brokerage accounts. Some people might be in survival mode, while others feel confident. Many are simply overwhelmed. A state like scarcity or productive efficiency could characterize a person's money life.

As the emotional atmosphere of your money life reflects more of your purpose, values, and positive relationships, it will feel better. You will start to move out of old money patterns and begin to experience a sense of openness, poise, and flow. Your money choices will gradually be liberated from the pull of old, limiting patterns as you become aware of habitual thoughts and feelings. How to achieve this freedom is the topic of the next two chapters.

Exercises

Identify Your Conscious Wealth Goals

Take out your Conscious Money journal and write a simple statement that expresses your goal or intention about growing Conscious Wealth: for example, "I will save fifty dollars per month by depositing it into my savings account before cashing my paycheck," or, "This year I will explore ways to consciously invest my annual bonus." Do not overthink your goal. Let it emerge naturally. Just be certain it feels good to you.

Once a month or so, revisit this basic Conscious Wealth statement. You can add additional goals in the form of statements as your Conscious Money intentions reveal themselves to you. Clarify your goals by describing any further thoughts or ideas you have about them. Give them a timeline if that feels right for you. If your Conscious Money goals are slow to emerge, take heart; your journey has only just begun.

After you have refined these statements for a while and identified those that resonate most for you, choose a few that you want to continue working with. I suggest you limit yourself to two or three Conscious Money goals. If you choose more than that, you risk losing focus. Of course, once you achieve one of these goals, you can release it in appreciation and discover a new one.

Cultivating Consciousness about Your Expenses

To be truly conscious about money, it is essential to be fully aware of what you are spending. To shed the light on your expenses, it is a good idea to examine them systematically. You can get started with a simple exercise to review your expenses and observe your reactions to them.

Take a piece of paper. Make two columns. List your monthly expenses in the left column. Breathe deeply. Look at each item.

1. What do you feel? Write it down in the right column.
2. Notice any spending patterns. Where are you spending more money than you choose?
3. Review the feelings captured on the right side. What do they tell you?

Options

Reflections

- Consider your emotional reaction to the terms Conscious Money and Conscious Wealth. If the latter does not work for you, select a neutral term such as Conscious Nest Egg or Conscious Savings Account.

- Think of values and consciousness as your inner compass. When you make a financial choice, consult that compass and notice your feelings.
- Ask yourself these questions and write your answers in your Conscious Money journal:

  - Do I experience harmony between my values and my money?
  - Am I at ease or fearful of making money choices based on my values?
  - Am I attracted to quick and easy financial fixes?

- Tune in to the possibility of a new financial mind-set where values and consciousness ground everyday money choices.
- Assume personal responsibility for your financial life.

Resources

- Pick a Conscious Money partner, a trustworthy, like-minded friend with whom you can share your practice, successes, and challenges.
- Create your own board of financial advisors. They may be people in your life, like your accountant; deceased individuals, like your wise granddad; or luminaries, such as Warren Buffett or Suze Orman. Decide or intuit what advice each board member would give you.
- For more information on the personal finance teachers cited earlier, consult their websites: SuzeOrman.com, DaveRamsey.com, and Vicki Robin at ymoyl.wordpress.com.
- Assemble a list of people in your money network. It might be useful to organize them by category, such as personal, work, commercial, investment, and philanthropic. Describe each person's role in your money network. Your boss and coworkers, for example, might further your career, and therefore boost your income.
- Read or reread *Think and Grow Rich*. The Atria/Beyond Words edition contains a foreword by Napoleon Hill's grandson.

- Watch the Napoleon Hill video (cited in this chapter's notes) on YouTube. In your journal, follow his journaling directions, which appear on page 12.

Right Actions

- Describe your financial circumstances in your journal, noting your age, family status, occupation, income, savings, monthly expenses, debt, and other obligations. When reviewing the options at the end of each chapter, consider which ones are appropriate to your financial situation. Seek added input from a financial planner or advisor.
- Determine whether you need a financial planner. You might if you've had a child, received a large sum of money, or must roll over an IRA.
- Honor the basic principles of personal finance described on pages 10–11.
- To choose a certified financial planner you might consult the Certified Financial Planner Board of Standards, whose website is cfp.net. Or ask a financial or investment professional to recommend one who works with clients whose circumstances are similar to yours.
- Select a financial authority to follow on the Web, in magazines, on television, or via Twitter. The websites of three "money gurus" whose ideas are fairly compatible with a Conscious Money strategy are cited in the resources section on the previous page..
- Set up your Conscious Money journal in a format that works for you. Write in longhand or on the computer. Pick paper with or without lines. To collect your insights on the go, keep a small notebook with you or use the notes feature on your mobile device.
- Express your authentic truth in your journal for ten minutes per day or longer.
- Know your top human values and financial goals. Keep them handy. Write them in your journal, citing why they are important to you. Carry a short list of your values in your wallet or on your mobile device.

- Start to practice calling on your intuition as you examine the options that will constitute your Conscious Money strategy. True intuition feels good and makes sense.
- Review your favorite Conscious Wealth statement every three to six months; revise and update it, adding new good feeling details to keep it fresh and current.
- Open a new bank account the purpose of which is to be a sacred vessel for your Conscious Money. Deposit all of your new income into it.

Conscious Money Affirmation

I am getting clear on my Conscious Money values, goals, and strategy.

2

Making Conscious Money Choices:
Self-Mastery, Thoughts,
and Emotions

Perhaps the most essential characteristic of Conscious Money is the capacity to make conscious money choices. We make conscious choices when we cultivate self-mastery, the attribute that lies at the heart of the spiritual journey. Seekers in every tradition hold self-mastery in the highest regard as central to their quest for wisdom and enlightenment.

By self-mastery, I don't mean discipline or self-control, although that definition of the term typified the moralistic attitudes prevalent a century ago. In his 1898 Carnegie Hall lecture titled "The Art of Self-Mastery," ethics professor Felix Adler spoke of self-mastery as reining in our impulses, appetites, and passions.[1] This definition persisted well into the twentieth century. But contemporary seekers view self-mastery as a process of self-discovery and self-knowledge. In a way, we've come full circle, because so did the ancient Greeks. The motto "Know thyself" was frequently invoked by Plato and Socrates.

The way to acquire self-knowledge is through the spiritual practice of examining our thoughts and emotions, as well as our decisions. Those thoughts and feelings, however, can often be conditioned and negative. Conditioning refers to a person's unique bundle of habitual thoughts and emotions. These elements solidify into patterns that determine our behavior and our lives—even though we did not consciously choose for this to happen.

When conditioning is operating, as it is for most of us much of the time, we are rarely aware of it. We may wish to alter our behavior, but it is nearly impossible to change something we cannot recognize. Through self-observation, however, our conditioned thoughts and feelings become conscious, making it possible for us to change, albeit gradually and over time.

How can simple observation be the first step in making a change? Quantum theory and modern physics tell us that we alter something just by witnessing it. This is also true when it comes to what's going on with us internally.

By observing our thoughts and emotions as part of a dedicated practice, old patterns can begin to loosen and eventually start to dissolve. Then we can free ourselves to consciously choose new thoughts and emotions and to respond to current events in a fresh and open way, instead of in the same way that we've reacted to past events.

A key element in this process is self-acceptance—the willingness to observe ourselves without judging. When we do not accept ourselves as we are, here and now—when we judge what we see—we are in resistance to what is. And as one well-known saying states, "What resists persists." Self-acceptance means we are willing to allow ourselves, our thoughts, and our emotions to simply be in loving awareness, even as we continue to observe them.

As challenging as it may seem, developing self-mastery is at its core an uncomplicated mission: to build one's capacity for consistent conscious choice. If you could condense billions of moments over a lifetime of seeking self-mastery into a one-sentence story, it might read: "After what seemed like an endless journey, along many winding paths, I gradually learned to make better choices more often."

Self-mastery is the personal process that transforms us into masters. In this practice, we repeatedly make choices, observe the results of those choices, and make new choices until we quietly graduate to the next level of self-mastery. Mastery has no end goal. It is an ongoing practice. "We fail to realize that mastery is not about perfection," wrote the late George Leonard in his book *Mastery: The Keys to Success and Long-term Fulfillment.* "The master . . . is willing to try, and fail, and try again, for as long as he or she lives."[2]

We are often counseled to learn to love the journey rather than seek the destination. Nowhere is this wisdom more fitting or valuable than in the quest for self-mastery.

Self-Mastery and Money

Few of us link the virtue of self-mastery with money. We regard self-mastery as a spiritual practice and money management as a practical one. That is understandable. But if you separate self-mastery into the discrete abilities that it requires—mental self-observation, emotional awareness, and spiritual wisdom—you will discover some highly practical money skills. In this sense, self-mastery is your greatest financial asset.

In fact, virtually every money mistake you or I could ever make has at its source the failure of self-mastery. Conversely, self-mastery can save us from committing painful financial errors. A few examples of common money mistakes people make include the following:

Suppose a woman has diligently focused on climbing the career ladder to the exclusion of almost every other priority. But now the lucrative management position she's worked so hard to achieve is in jeopardy, because, when the boss offers constructive criticism, she reacts quite poorly.

Imagine an investor whose neighbor works for a software company that's "changing the face of technology," or so the neighbor says. Swayed by his insider perspective, this investor sinks his life savings into this company's stock. But one year later, the investment is as financially devastated as his neighbor's former employer.

A person has to "look the part" to succeed, so it makes sense to spend a lot of money on a sports car or a designer wardrobe, or so the thinking goes. Once he or she amasses $40,000 in debt, however, the monthly credit payments rival a frugal person's rent check.

As you gradually claim self-mastery, you avoid many common financial pitfalls, such as compulsive buying, unwise investments, debt accumulation, or a limiting money mind-set that keeps you stuck in poverty consciousness. The surest way to master your money is to master yourself.

Self-mastery involves working with many levels of ourselves. In this chapter, we discuss two of them: thoughts and emotions. When thoughts and emotions are unconscious, they create patterns in the deeper mind that are also unconscious. In chapter 3, we'll examine those, as well as our illuminating connection to higher consciousness.

Your commitment to Conscious Money, as well as your ability to grow it, begins with your thoughts and feelings about money. So let's start by looking at how your thoughts affect your money.

Cultivating Positive Money Thoughts

What is your "money mind-set"? Do you think money is "hard to come by?" Or do you expect it will flow to you easily? Are you tight-fisted? Generous? Do you feel guilty about the money you have? Do you experience negative thoughts about money? Does a statement from your childhood, like "Money doesn't grow on trees," keep echoing in your mind? Or do you genuinely think, "The money is always there when I need it"?

For centuries, if not millennia, sages have taught us that our beliefs and feelings about money determine our wealth.

From the Emerald Tablet cited in the bestseller *The Secret* to biblical sayings like "Ask and it is given" to Charles Haanel's legendary *The Master*

Key System, there is but one unifying idea: it is that *you*, not your job or the economy, possess from within the ability to influence how much money you possess.

During boom times, when there's lots of opportunity, an individual can easily assume that money comes from the external world. After all it is just common sense that when jobs are plentiful, most people earn more money. So it is easy to conclude that externalities—someone like an employer or something like a job—must exist in order for us to earn the funds to pay for the rent, car payment, health insurance, groceries, utilities, and gasoline. None of that can come from within—we think.

But when the economy contracts and the outer world yields fewer lucky breaks, we're compelled to fall back on our inner resources to make our financial way. Left to our own devices, some of us experiment with this notion of inner wealth. Hard times offer the perfect laboratory.

If you are easily discouraged or harbor resentment, it is easy to think things like, "I am never going to find a job," or, "Why did that blasted boss of mine let me go?" But when you allow yourself to indulge such negative thoughts, you put yourself at a distinct disadvantage when attempting to find a new job, recover from financial losses, or sell a home that's already been on the market for a while. Success in tough times requires an upbeat attitude, persistence, and goodwill. And constructive money thoughts serve to nurture these productive character traits.

The Wisdom of Abundance Thinking

Abundance thinking is positive thinking when it comes to money. It rests in the inner knowledge that there is always enough, no matter how much money you have or don't have. Because what you really need comes from your Being. This unique store of treasure is always at your disposal because it lies within. That profoundly spiritual statement is the antithesis of mundane money thinking.

When you grasp this meaning of abundance, that the true source of money lies within each of us, you recognize that money is energy and sometimes intangible. So, inner resources, which are potentially as real as money, might appear invisible, too. If what you are looking for is only dollar bills already in your wallet or sizable financial sums in your online banking statement, you may miss seeing the great possibilities right before your eyes. Abundance thinking unlocks the ability to recognize resources and money opportunities that otherwise lie unseen, as I learned from observing my stepdaughter Nana Naisbitt.[3]

Nana was a rising star in her hometown of Chicago. A creative entrepreneur and fashion retailer, she drifted into the lucrative field of corporate brand management to earn the high income needed to send her three children to college. That income, however, was seriously disrupted when she fell in love with Telluride, Colorado, where her dad and I then lived. In Telluride, with a population of only two thousand, Nana reasoned, the kids could play safely, enjoy living in a small community, and spend lots of time in the great outdoors. So she left an upscale lifestyle and found fulfillment creating a nonprofit that, among other good deeds, brought world-famous scientists to the local schools. As you might imagine, her income plummeted; she and the kids went without things everyone else had, like a television—and a car. To help out, the kids got after-school jobs and summer work.

As time passed, the children were devoted to their studies and grew into balanced, hard-working people. College beckoned. But there was no money for their higher educations. Or so we all thought. That is, except Nana.

She drew on all her creative and intellectual resources and became an expert on college admissions—scholarships, entrance essays, deferments. The fruits of her newly developed expertise and the initiative of her three great kids resulted in full scholarships to expensive, private colleges for all three. The total amount awarded came to approximately $475,000. Even if she had been working at a well-paying job all those years, she would have been hard pressed to sock away that much money for her kids' college funds.

I don't think my practical, resourceful stepdaughter considered herself an abundance type, yet that is exactly what she was because she never doubted that there was enough money available to send her kids to great colleges, and she pursued it. But it did not end there. She went on to share her know-how with the community as a college admissions coach specializing in scholarships and helped forty students win spots at prestigious schools including Stanford, Harvard, and Cambridge University.

When you think there is enough, your thoughts reflect an inner wisdom that agrees that there is indeed enough. With that insight, your money intentions veer toward positive, practical solutions and away from less productive pursuits. This wisdom can also help protect you from unsafe financial schemes, because you will be a lot less likely to put money at risk unnecessarily if you sense there is already enough.

Abundance thinking can be an excellent antidote to greed. One of the motivating forces behind greed is the inability to experience having enough. A need cannot be met unless the person who experienced it is able to feel satisfaction. For complex psychological reasons, some people fail to recognize that a need has been fulfilled and that they are free to feel a new and perhaps more satisfying need. The ill-fated urge to seek more and more, even though there is already plenty, leads to financial carelessness, from accumulating credit card debt to investing in real estate bubbles.

Abundance thinking is a powerful Conscious Money tool. It means recognizing that you already have everything you need. Yet even practiced abundance thinkers are susceptible to negative, self-limiting money thoughts. Such thoughts are common for many of us. The key is to know how to address and resolve them—and that brings us back to the topic of self-mastery.

Many people teach methods that are designed to help you change your thinking, especially your thoughts about money. Yet the only way to transform your thoughts deeply and permanently is by cultivating the power of self-mastery. One of the best people to teach you that is Srikumar Rao.

Mental Self-Mastery

Professor Srikumar Rao teaches people how to change their thoughts, not in an ashram, but at the world's most prestigious business schools. His course has won extensive coverage in *Time, Fortune, Bloomberg Businessweek*, the *Wall Street Journal*, the *New York Times*, and every major business publication in the United States and the United Kingdom.[4]

A few years ago, I attended a workshop Professor Rao offered at a conference. Then I discovered the audio version of his work, *The Personal Mastery Program*. In a thoughtful and lilting voice, he asks, "Consider this vision: you wake up in the morning, suffused with an ineffable feeling of joy, your blood sings at the thought of being who you are and doing what you do."[5] Your life will look a lot more like this, suggests Professor Rao, once you cultivate the power of personal mastery.

The Making of Rao

Srikumar Rao was born in Mumbai and earned a master of business administration in India and a doctorate in marketing at Columbia University Business School.[6] He achieved dazzling success in the world of business, but oscillated between feeling "somewhat down and downright miserable," as he put it somewhat humorously to me in an email once.[7] The only thing that gave him hope was reading mystical biographies and spiritual autobiographies.

Rao describes his mother as "a very spiritual lady" who was attracted to the teachings of many spiritual leaders, such as Maharishi Mahesh Yogi and the disciples of Sri Ramakrishna. Over time, he explains, the wisdom of these teachers "sank in by osmosis . . ." Then one day he thought, "if all of these concepts are useful only when you are quietly reading, then they aren't worth much."[8] With that realization, he decided to draft an academic road map for the study of personal mastery, drawing from many spiritual sources. The course that came out of that draft is the subject of two books, the most recent of which is titled *Happiness at Work*. Rao has taught it at business schools, including Long Island University, Columbia Business School, the University of California at Berkeley's Hass School of Business, and the London Business School.

Three Core Concepts

Professor Rao's work speaks to the issue of observing and shifting those thoughts that we do not wish to entertain. In particular, we can focus on three of his core concepts to do exactly that.[9] Each would serve us well in and of itself. But taken together, these concepts (presented here in the same order as the professor addresses them) constitute a thorough and practical method for transforming negative thoughts. I find it useful to view the three as steps in a process. But as with other such methods, bear in mind that "steps" like these can often overlap.

The first of these concepts is "mental models." These are the personal points of view we tend to interpret as "reality" or "the Truth." It's not; it's just one way of seeing it: ours. When we mistake a point of view for truth, says Rao, it can distort how we perceive our lives. The second is "mental chatter," an inner dialogue with ourselves that spins along inside our heads. The mental models and mental chatter of most people are generally negative.

These first two concepts, as I see them, are all about awareness. If we have harmful, self-limiting thoughts—and we all do, at least to some extent—we can't possibly release or transform them until we recognize them. Once we experience our mental chatter and mental models, and notice that they are flawed at best and probably downright false, we have the option to stop energizing them with belief. Maybe we will just say,

"Well there they are and they're just thoughts." No more, no less. Perhaps then the power of negative thinking slowly and gradually begins to fade.

Positive thoughts are a useful tool in this regard. This is where the third core concept comes in. Rao suggests replacing your old "reality" with a new one that you like better. This makes a lot of sense. Because negative thoughts, even those we have released, have a tendency to find their way back! That's why fortifying ourselves with positive thoughts that we have consciously nurtured is a powerful way to support ourselves.

These three concepts are useful in changing our money thoughts.

Concept One: Identify Mental Models

In his audio presentation, Professor Rao describes "mental models" as our ideas about "how the world works," as he puts it.[10] Although often inaccurate, they powerfully shape our life view. We all have these ideologies; that is not the issue. The problem comes, the professor says, when we accept them so completely that we think of them as reality.[11]

Here's one of the professor's examples of a mental model cited in one of his books: "My coworkers try to undermine me by being sarcastic . . . pretending not to hear me, boasting about their achievements while underplaying mine. They are always trying to use me."[12]

All of us, whether we know it or not, carry around similar mental models about money, investing, work, and other Conscious Money issues. Consider these examples:

"God doesn't want me to make money in the stock market."
"The kind of work I want to do just doesn't pay well."
"When the going gets tough, the tough go shopping."

All of these financial mental models, however, are nothing more than a viewpoint and most probably an inaccurate one. What they are not is "the Truth." When we take time to inspect our models, we can often see how flawed they are. Sometimes we can even collect insights about how they originated.

Concept Two: Notice Your Mental Chatter

In addition to mental models, most of us also harbor negative thoughts and judgments running in the back of our head. Professor Rao calls this "mental chatter." Here is my take on the difference between mental models and mental chatter: mental models are encapsulated notions of what we believe to be true. For example, "I'm never going to amount to anything because that is exactly what my mother told me as a child time and time again."

Mental chatter possesses a more rambling, stream-of-consciousness quality. Here's an example of what I would call mental chatter: "I can't believe it. Why haven't they called me back? I really wanted that job. Well, here we go again, another disappointment. I'm so tired of this stuff. Things are never going to get any better. I can't stand it anymore."

In combination with our mental models, this chatter "creates our reality," the professor says, echoing the metaphysical law that states: our thoughts, positive or negative, create our lives.[13]

But why would we create a reality we disdain? Rao explains that we create "a whole lot of stuff" we don't want, simply because we are not conscious of our mental chatter.[14]

Consider now a few of the many negative thoughts most of us have about money:

"Bills, bills, bills: all I get are bills. Do I ever get a check in the . . ."
"You just can't earn a buck these days. Why, I remember when . . ."
"Gold. I've got to buy gold. I said I was going to. But then I . . ."

Once we recognize negative chatter, why don't we simply suppress it or replace it with positive thoughts? Because it's not that easy. Mental chatter, Professor Rao warns, "won't go away. You're stuck with it."[15]

Besides, he adds, we're probably aware of "a tiny fraction of one percent" of our mental chatter.[16] So even if we could delete our negative chatter once we recognize it, there's no way to identify and replace all of it. The good news is that even a slight increase in awareness "will bring a quantum improvement in your life," he concludes.[17]

Concept Three: Replace Your Old Reality with a New One

In the end, self-observation and self-awareness deliver a wonderful payoff. They put you in a position to transform your life. If you created your reality in the first place, you possess, by definition, the power to change it. Now that you have observed your mental models and mental chatter, and understand that they are just that and not "the Truth," you are better equipped to transform your self-limiting or harmful thoughts, which in turn transforms your reality. You do it by replacing your old reality with a new one that feels better. This is exactly what the professor advises.

Suppose, Rao suggests, that you think your boss doesn't like you because he doesn't return your emails, meet with you, or appoint you to a key post. Now, Rao says, create a new reality, an alternative way of seeing the same situation, such as this one: "My boss really has my best interests at heart . . . and wants me to learn the ropes before I take on added responsibilities . . . As to not responding to my emails or meeting with him, everybody has more stuff on their plate than they can handle."[18]

Now let's apply this process to a Conscious Money issue. As an example, suppose your old reality is, "I despise paying my bills." After you've carefully observed and accepted this mental model and the mental chatter around it, you are in a better place to choose new thoughts and a new reality. Make it a gentle one, like, "I'm letting go a bit about bill paying. Money comes and goes. There's a flow to it. I'm going to go with the flow."

It's absolutely essential, the professor stresses, that your new reality be one that you believe is plausible.[19] Only you can know if it is so. Once you choose your new reality, the idea, he says, is to live as if this new reality were true. He concludes: "You'll be amazed to discover the number of occasions when your alternative reality does in fact become your new reality."[20]

That is what the professor's MBA students discovered. As they began to observe, accept, and start to shift their thoughts, they changed. At twenty-seven years old, Brandon Peele was a disillusioned investment banker at Merrill Lynch. "I wanted to make a lot of money, travel the world, sleep with a lot of women." During Dr. Rao's course, Brandon saw "there is much more out there than getting that big house." As a result he looked beyond investment banking to starting a television channel on corporate responsibility and personal growth. "You spend so much of your day working, you might as well be enjoying yourself," he adds.[21]

Professor Rao challenges your deeply held beliefs and tutors you to build a new universe—one that you consciously create. One of his favorite tools is journaling. A student of Rao's, Charles Marcus, who was then thirty-two years old and a Harvard graduate, had worked at a few start-ups. But then came the dot-com crash, during which he "was forced to fire people" and "squeeze clients for higher rates." He wrote in his journal: "Woke up one morning, late in 2000, and wondered whose life this was that I was living. I had been sucked into a greed machine."[22]

Creating a Mental Screen Saver

What Professor Rao calls a "mental screen saver" is an enjoyable and effective way to begin shaping the reality you want.[23] To invent this screen saver, you systematically focus on a joyful, satisfying experience. You then craft it into a lasting memory that you can call to mind whenever you wish. He reasons that since the mind is going to chatter away anyhow, why not choose to fill it with the happy experiences of your life?

Exactly. To my mind, mental screen savers are also an excellent antidote to mental chatter and mental models. First, they're positive instead of negative. Second, we design them consciously, unlike the unconscious way in which we create and energize mental chatter and mental models. Positive and conscious trumps negative and unconscious every time. Instead of allowing unconscious, negative thoughts to "run" us, we take a proactive stance and choose in favor of feeling good when we create a screen saver, load it into the computer of our brain, and turn it on any time our spirits need a lift.

I followed Professor Rao's screen saver instructions and decided to construct my screen saver based on a great experience I once had speaking in Berlin. As I answered his suggested questions and put it together one fortuitous detail at a time, I came to see that the Berlin event, which I describe below, was one of the best experiences of my professional life.

My Berlin Screen Saver

Where are you? Describe your surroundings. I'm in the sleek Commerzbank building at the center of what was once East Berlin, savoring a spectacular view of the Brandenburg Gate, a beautiful historic monument.

Who are the people around you? My German editor, Nadja Rosmann, who arranged my talk, sits in the front row beside our sponsor, Paul Kohtes, founder of the Identity Foundation. They smile encouragingly.

How do you feel? As the audience becomes engaged, I feel reassured. The young people there are quite fluent in English, and they laugh at my jokes.

What are the tastes and smells? There is the scent of strong coffee and aromatic breakfast pastries.

The energy kept building even after the event, as Nadja and I crossed the street for coffee at the historic Hotel Adlon. There, as we stood by the door, German Chancellor Angela Merkel strolled right by us, surrounded by a throng of serious-looking bodyguards. This delightful synchronicity marked the culmination of a perfect day.

Create your own screen saver by choosing any high point in your life and answering Professor Rao's questions, which I have italicized above.

To cultivate self-mastery is to cultivate the power to choose. As Professor Rao and other spiritual leaders teach us, however, we cannot truly choose until we have developed the ability to witness, experience, and only later transform our thoughts through the faculty of choice. In fact, we follow much the same path when it comes to our emotions, where choice is again essential.

Cultivating Positive Money Emotions

To practice Conscious Money, you must be keenly aware of your emotions. The failure to cultivate clear and positive emotions can defeat your desire to grow Conscious Wealth. Unfortunately, however, many emotions around money are neither conscious nor helpful. In fact, unconscious and negative feelings about money are almost inevitably wound into our financial issues.

For example, suppose someone you know receives a sizable inheritance. Excited about the new life this development promises, she decides to invest not just some but all of it for the down payment on what for her is an expensive dream house. The mortgage payment is a stretch (so are the maintenance costs), but she says that it is "doable," until she then loses her job and foreclosure threatens. In this unfortunate situation, chances are that your friend has been the victim of euphoria and denial.

Or perhaps someone complains that he can't afford health insurance but then treats his friends to dinner and drinks every Friday night, spending the equivalent of a monthly insurance payment on weekend outings with his pals—who themselves earn good salaries but do not return his generosity. It is a good bet that this type of financial behavior is motivated by feelings of loneliness and an attempt to "buy" friendship, which is rarely a good bargain.

There's little doubt that human emotions, such as low self-esteem, fear, and even an overzealous elation, can create serious errors in judgment and demoralizing loss. To bring these emotions to light we must boost our skills in Emotional Intelligence.

What Is Emotional Intelligence?

Emotional Intelligence (EI) is based on a simple idea with sizable consequences: people who are more aware of their emotions make better choices and thus create better results. Most people know EI through the work of Daniel Goleman, author of the benchmark book *Emotional Intelligence*. Dr. Goleman studied 188 companies and arrived at an extraordinary conclusion: 85 to 90 percent of the success of top executives is attributable to emotional competencies, not IQ or technical skills.[24] This realization expanded the executive skill set to include emotional awareness, and has served as a catalyst for more conscious business.

Enter Byron Stock, age sixty-five, who was inspired by Goleman's work to create and later teach what he calls "applied" Emotional Intelligence.[25] Byron calls himself a "recovering" engineer. He may have started out with a rational, scientific bias, but for eighteen years he has instructed executives at Fortune 1000 firms, nonprofits, and government agencies about emotions, as he has trained and coached them to achieve professional goals through the power of conscious emotions. Byron's experiential approach to the topic provides lots of interactive exercises that enable people to test their skills.

The power of Emotional Intelligence lies in this statement: Emotional awareness creates choices. If I know I'm angry, this emotional awareness increases my power to choose how and when to express my anger. I might decide to take a time out and revisit the situation later. Without that awareness, I might strike out unconsciously and suffer the unhappy results.

I met Byron through our mutual client, Herman Miller, Inc., and interviewed him to learn more about EI. At the time, he had just finished teaching EI skill building to sixty executives and managers. He shared with me later the results of his follow-up analysis of the group, which certainly illustrates the power of EI. Their productivity rose 34 percent and their mental clarity grew 39 percent. But it's the feedback from participants that shows how EI changes people's lives. One participant reported: "A colleague read my report and came up with nitpicky comments. I felt my blood pressure soar, but I practiced the techniques and calmed down. If I hadn't, she'd bump it up to the VP, and I'd get a black eye professionally."

The first step in applied EI, Byron explained to me, is to become aware of your emotions. This is a double challenge. Not only are many of us unaware of what we are feeling, the majority of us are unfamiliar with the full range and variety of our emotions. In one exercise, Byron gives participants one minute to list all of the emotions they can think of. "The men come up with maybe seven to ten," he says. "The women, with twelve or fifteen. I then ask them to turn to a page in their workbooks where there is a list of 244 emotions." Clearly, we are aware of a mere fraction of our emotions.

Emotional Intelligence also teaches us a great way to live in the present. Asking yourself "What emotion am I feeling right now?" Byron says, is the first step toward being in the moment.

Regularly checking-in with your emotions is an excellent practice. You might do so every time the phone rings or set specific times, like 8:00 AM, midmorning, after lunch, and so forth. Always check in on waking.

Corporations realize that Emotional Intelligence nurtures success. So they hire people like Byron to teach it. You and I can apply EI to grow more aware of the unconscious emotions that run and probably harm our money lives. We can get started with the exercise at the end of the chapter.

Emotional Intelligence is a prerequisite for self-mastery. Look at it this way: when you master your emotions, you master yourself; when you master yourself, you master your money.

Handling Fear regarding Money

When it comes to money, one very common feeling is fear. But it is very important to distinguish between fear and anxiety, says the author of *The Intuitive Investor*, Jason Apollo Voss, whose ideas we will visit in more depth in the chapter on investing.[26]

The symptoms of fear and anxiety, however, are so similar that it is easy to confuse them. What is the difference? Fear has a more distinct feel and warns of a present threat, says Jason. It is a fresh, unlearned reaction to a new situation. Anxiety, on the other hand, is more amorphous and pervasive. It usually occurs when an event in the present moment triggers an old response to a fearful situation in the past. Of the two, anxiety tends to be more destructive, contends Jason, because it can block intuition and cause inaction.

Most of the time "what masquerades as fear is anxiety," says Voss, and it was created during moments in the past when we felt "vulnerable and incapable."[27]

Jason's insight became very real to me once after I experienced a sort of anxiety attack about money. Just as he suggests, at first I was convinced I was feeling fear and had no idea that it was related to a financial upset in the past.

Walking the Talk

One day in June 2010, I checked my investment portfolio and felt sick to my stomach with fear (or I assumed it was fear). I had recently gotten back into the stock market after years of caution. At the time, I thought that while the economy might endure a tepid recovery, the worst had passed and some optimism was appropriate.

I had instructed my new investment team to put most of my funds in bonds, which are generally more stable than stocks. But that day in June, the value of my portfolio had dropped so precipitously that I felt wave after wave of terror watching it fall, and I started to think that my advisors had not followed my instructions about the bonds. (In fact they had, but I was so disturbed I could not think straight or see the obvious.) To help me calm down, I decided to try some of Voss's exercises from *The Intuitive Investor.*

There are several steps in Jason's method, but here I have chosen to focus on four key ones: recognize, transform, examine, and dismantle.[28] Let me explain what these terms mean and apply each step to the investment upset I've described above. In the italicized text, I share my feelings and the lesson I learned.

1. ***Recognize the emotion.*** Begin by identifying what you're feeling. Once you're aware of your feelings, your power grows. So do your options. With awareness come expanded choices. *I was feeling sheer terror; I couldn't even think. But once I realized that I was too shaken even to be productive at work that morning, I remembered to work with Jason's process. What I discovered: When we observe our feelings, instead of being run by them, we make better decisions. Awareness creates power.*

2. ***Transform the emotion into a thought.*** In the midst of anxiety or fear, one of the most powerful things you can do is to reach for a soothing thought. Assure yourself that you are okay and that things will somehow work out. Further calm yourself with a few deep breaths. *I reminded myself that I would probably not lose my entire IRA that day. Once I could actually think, I realized that much of my portfolio was in bonds. Good. What I discovered: Find the thoughts that can help you to feel better.*

3. ***Examine the emotion's source.*** Recall the first time you felt threatened by a similar situation. That event may be the original source of what you now feel—especially if you are really feeling anxiety but

think it is fear. At that time in the past, your fear was probably justi-fied, says Jason.[29] Be easy on yourself. You've solved bigger problems since that original event, he reminds us. It is time to move on. *That is certainly what happened to me. Back in the dot-com era when my stocks fell precipitously, I watched paralyzed, incapable of making a deci-sion, and failed to sell my stocks in an effort to preserve my assets. Before that time, others had managed my investments. But when I had to make the decisions myself, and the stakes were high, what did I do? I froze. What I discovered: The power of "Be here now." The dot-com crash is over. It is time for me to accept the past and move forward as an investor.*

4. ***Dismantle the emotion.*** Having recognized the emotion that is "running," it is now time to let it go. *As I followed this process, I dis-covered that it was anxiety, not fear, that had overwhelmed me. Then I had a huge breakthrough: My deepest worry was not market loss. I real-ized there would be ups and downs. It was that I would again freeze, even more than ten years later. So Jason was right—my anxiety was related to a trauma from the past. With that insight, I realized I am stronger, more capable, and better-informed now, so my reactions will probably be healthier. I regained my perspective and felt better. What I discovered: If I created it, I can change it.*

As Voss's second step illustrates, thoughts can be a powerful tool for working with negative feelings. And the tool's use is not limited to invest-ing; it works just as well with other financial issues. In the midst of money challenges that evoke difficult emotions, you can seek comforting thoughts, such as "I'm smart; I can figure this out," or "I have friends and family who love me and will help me through this." Or you can remind yourself of positive actions that you can choose, such as "There are free college courses I can take to improve my finances."

Choosing positive thoughts to calm raging negative emotions might sound simplistic. But do not underestimate the physiological changes that a strong negative emotion like anxiety creates in the body—or the power of a positive thought to change it. Anxiety literally disrupts the chemistry of your brain to block your powers of thought and intuition, as my story illustrates. It has been my experience that one calming thought that is carefully selected can break a downward emotional spiral for long enough to permit inspiration and hope to arise again.

You can try this too. Once you settle on your soothing thought, notice your reaction, even if it is just slightly better. Acknowledge that change. Then try to find another comforting thought.

By accepting your feelings, be they positive or negative, you gradually come to master them. Simply acknowledging them is the first step. The next time you experience an unpleasant emotion around money, like fear or dread, do not suppress it. Feel it. When you feel your feelings, they grow conscious. When you're aware of your feelings, that awareness gives you options. Use those options to make conscious choices in addressing all of your money issues.

The Law of Attraction and How It Works

An often-quoted biblical phrase that assures us God unhesitatingly answers our every prayer is "ask and it is given." Yet most of us have had the experience of asking for something we did not receive—from a pony to a BMW to a new house. Why didn't we get what we asked for? The answer lies in the workings of what's called the Law of Attraction, the "universal" law based on the principle that like attracts like. I recognize that some people can be skeptical about this concept, but I've seen how it works and now often have occasion to draw on my feelings to attract and call forth the circumstances I want to experience in life.

According to the Law of Attraction, to attract your heart's desire, you must be like it at the deepest level—in your essence. We become like our desire by matching its energetic vibration. Whether I want a million dollars or a great job, I must resonate at the same frequency as my desire *before* I receive it.

Penney Peirce, a pioneer in intuitive development and the author of *Frequency*, says each of us possesses a "personal vibration." It is "the frequency of energy you hold moment by moment in your body, emotions, and mind," and it is "the most important tool you have for creating and living your ideal life."

"If your energy frequency is high, fast, and clear," Penney continues, "life unfolds effortlessly and in alignment with your destiny, while a lower, slower, more distorted frequency begets a life of snags and disappointments."[30]

Vibrations are of course invisible. But we can measure them with some accuracy through our feelings because they radiate outward from our body: the better we feel, the higher our vibration. The feelings of joy and freedom are probably the highest vibrations known to humanity. Love, optimism, and happiness are up there as well. The emotion of powerlessness is the lowest vibration people can feel, says spiritual teacher Esther Hicks. It is lower than depression or anger. Anger, she repeatedly states, is a higher emotional state than powerlessness and can indicate that a person's vibration is actually getting higher.

Raising Your Vibration

To raise your vibration, feel better, and get what you want, start by observing your feelings. For some, this is a challenging prospect. If you are experiencing a negative feeling, you would probably rather not have to focus on it. That's fine—after you have honestly noted what you feel. There's a big difference between noticing your anger (saying, "Wow, I feel angry") then letting it be, and fanning the flames of what might be a passing state of anger until it becomes a violent outburst. Do not allow yourself to dwell on negative feelings, just acknowledge them. The payoff for doing so comes when you notice that you feel a little bit better.

The way you feel right now shapes your success or failure to attract what you want—be it wealth, health, or happiness. So check in often. Each day, describe how you feel in your journal and see how it changes as time goes forward. Every hour or so, especially if your work is sedentary, get up and move around for five minutes. This is the perfect time to ask yourself how you're feeling in the moment. How you feel is important. As you grow more aware of your feelings, you gain more ability to engage and lift them.

Feeling somewhat better is highly underrated. Find a little better feeling and build on it. Always acknowledge a feeling of well-being, even a modest one. Feeling a little better may not look like the road to happiness, but it can be a powerful step in the right direction, especially if you build on it. As you gradually feel better, you anchor a new and positive state into your Being, one that can be a lot more sustainable than experiencing a temporary high. People generally cannot move from feeling miserable to feeling happy in one giant leap, so it seems unwise to even try. Instead, feel better one step at a time.

A Virtuous Cycle

When we try too hard, we create resistance. There is no room for resistance in the Law of Attraction. To encourage the positive feelings that dissolve resistance, try replacing left-brain words like "objective" with right-brain words like "desire." The latter evokes feeling delighted, the former, determined. Since positive thoughts lead to positive emotions, more positive thoughts beget more positive emotions. This is called a virtuous cycle, and it's exactly what we want to launch if Conscious Wealth is our desire.

The Law of Attraction may be best known for helping people get what they want. But it is also an excellent way to practice nurturing positive feelings around money. Choose to be aware of your vibration or frequency, because it will trump your thoughts, important though they are, when it comes to attracting what you desire. Your vibration is clearer, more powerful, and more authentic than your thoughts, because it represents the power of your life energy.

I once thought I had a clear financial desire to earn higher lecture fees. But I soon realized my desire was clouded with doubt. Then something shifted, and I experienced a breakthrough. When I analyzed it later, I realized the shift had taken place in eight steps. I describe those steps and my process through them here. You can choose a financial desire and apply these steps to energize and attract it by moving through the same phases I did:

1. *Feel the desire.* Scan your awareness or review your journal notes for a recurring desire about money. Connect to the deep, genuine energy in your desire. Notice any emotional nuances it may hold. Create a simple statement of financial desire, including its good-feeling elements, such as "It will feel great to save money for my child's education," or "I want to be excited about planning for my retirement." Feeling good about your desire is essential, I discovered. *In my case, I created an ambitious goal that I thought was "reasonable." I wanted to earn higher speaking fees, yet the dollar amount I set did not feel good to me. That was an important clue. Eventually, it was feeling my desire, not attaching a number to it, that got me back on track.*

2. *Look for a reaction.* Observe your thoughts and look for any reaction to your statement, especially a critical one, like "Of course, I should have done this years ago." Acknowledge any negative thoughts. But do not try to change them at this point; just let them be. Remind yourself that you can tap into your creative power in this very instant. *In my case, I discovered that I had a recurrent, negative thought about which clients would pay my higher fee. My doubt trumped my logic, and I set up an inner contradiction.*

3. ***Release assumptions.*** Write down your assumptions on a piece of paper. Then to symbolize and aid in their release, shred the paper into tiny pieces and send it off to the recycling bin. *I thought only a corporation would pay my higher fee. Not so, I later learned when an association did so.*

4. ***Listen for a fresh statement to naturally emerge.*** To capture a more accurate and better-feeling statement of desire, tune in to the heart of what you want. Don't think about what you want. Feel it. Do not worry if it seems vague. Describe the "felt sense" of your desire in your journal. As you do, it may coalesce into the new statement of desire you seek. Consider creating a vision board of images depicting your new desire. Images shift your awareness into your heart. *In my case, I did not devise a new statement of desire. Instead this one came to me naturally: "I want to be well paid by clients who really want to hear my message." Wow! It felt great, much better than articulating any specific fee. For some people, my new statement of desire might seem a bit vague. But its power animated my good feeling and it was my excited and happy vibration that attracted the result I desired, not identifying some exact amount I wished to be paid. "I want to be well paid." That felt fabulous.*

5. ***Nurture your great-feeling desire.*** Let your new desire remain unspoken and share it sparingly. *I silently repeated my desire and wrote it in my journal. Only later did I share it with trusted people.*

6. ***Write down your expectations, and then burn them.*** As one famous self-help maxim states, "An expectation is an upset waiting to happen." Find a safe spot, like the living room fireplace or perhaps an outdoor fire pit of some sort. The burning process transforms your expectations into ashes and supports you to release their energy. Remember, positive feelings are a lot more powerful than expectations. Keep the faith. Don't second-guess yourself about whether or not you have the "right" statement.

Does it feel good? Well, then you have the right statement. *I did not wait for invitations to roll in. Instead I returned again and again to how good my new statement felt.*

7. ***Be patient.*** Be willing to "get rich slow." *It took six to eight months, but as I scheduled new events, my fee rose 30 percent, then 50 percent, and later 100 percent.*

8. ***Expect more blessings.*** Collect your blessings in appreciation; be sure to record them in your Conscious Money journal; and share them with your trusted friends. *My new clients were kindred spirits. I relaxed and spoke with ease, humor, and improvisation. In addition to being well paid, I was having a lot more fun.*

By observing your feelings, you can tap into the power of a natural statement of desire. That shift will raise your vibration, activate your powers of attraction, and create Conscious Wealth.

The journey toward mastering yourself, as I have often noted, is a challenging one. But you and I possess the power to make it beautiful and fulfilling. Begin by choosing to love and accept yourself. Remember, you are only witnessing those negative thoughts or emotions. Instead of judging yourself when one of them pops up, give yourself a pat on the back and say "Good catch" or select a phrase that works for you. Observe, gently accept, and then release.

When many of us feel desire, we focus on our current lack. That can be unproductive. As you move toward creating the reality you really want, explore the possibility of actually enjoying the experience of wanting something that you do not possess. Nourish thoughts of what you desire, like seeds planted in a lush and lovely garden. Instead of focusing on lack, encourage yourself to associate the feeling of desire and anticipation with pleasure: "It's going to be so great to feel good about money." As you engage the path of self-mastery, meditate on the abundance you already have: "Whether I experience it or not, I have enough right here, right now."

Exercises

Financial Self-Mastery: Just Feel It!

Choose a time when you will not be disturbed for twenty to thirty minutes. Relax, close your eyes, and take a few deep breaths. Ask yourself: Where in my financial life do I seek greater self-mastery?

Be patient. Take time to allow your response to emerge from within. If you're like most of us, the feelings that arise may not make you feel good or competent. Your challenge might be debt, poor credit, a recent loss, or the inability to make an important money decision.

Now take another deep breath and choose to create a safe space where you can allow any additional feelings to surface. It is possible that you might experience guilt, shame, grief, or another difficult emotion. Reassure yourself that this is a safe space: you are simply being present in the moment with what you experience. Give yourself permission to feel whatever you feel. Let it be. Take your time.

When you're ready and feel comfortable, ask yourself: "What would it take to receive inner guidance about my money issue and my feelings about it?" Be aware of any insights you receive and note them in your Conscious Money journal.

Identify Your Financial Mental Models

Review the description of mental models and examples of money models earlier in this chapter. Set the intention that at least one of your financial mental models will reveal itself to you.

For the next week, observe your thoughts about money. Pick one that you believe might be a financial mental model and describe it in your Conscious Money journal. Don't worry about whether it's the right model.

Once you do this exercise, you will likely become increasingly aware of other financial mental models. Also note these in your journal when they show up. That way, you have recorded them and can explore them more fully at a later date.

In time you will probably identify one or two financial mental models as those that influence you most in the present time. Later these may be replaced by new ones.

Be Aware of Your Money Chatter

Listen for your mental chatter about money. Do not judge it. But do allow it to become conscious.

Take out your Conscious Money journal and turn to a fresh sheet to which you can easily return, such as the final page. That way you'll collect all your mental chatter in one easily accessible place so that you will not have to leaf through many journal entries to find the last time you noted your mental chatter.

Do not judge the chatter; just record it. But do notice if it changes over time. Label this list something like "Mental Money Chatter That I Am Now Lovingly Releasing."

As you become aware of your mental chatter over the next days, weeks, and months, regularly commit your observations to this special page.

Getting in Touch with Positive Money Feelings

The emotional check-in exercise recommended by Byron Stock can be applied to emotions around money. Go inside. Breathe. Ask yourself:

How does "wealth," as you define it, feel?
How does being "conscious" about money feel?
How does being "debt free" feel?

In the intuitive, or "felt-sense," aspect of yourself, did these money scenarios feel good? Or did other feelings arise that surprised you?

Options

Reflections

- Describe your money mind-set in your journal. If it feels right to you, ask for some insight about the people and past experiences that influenced you to create that mind-set. Describe in your journal the new money mind-set you now choose for yourself.
- Ponder the true meaning of Abundance, as the divinely orchestrated gift of having "enough" no matter what your finances might be. Consider a financial issue or problem; what new insights does the wisdom of Abundance bring to the issue?
- Begin now to observe the subtle difference between a positive money attitude and a dangerous tendency toward euphoria or denial. We'll explore this more deeply in chapter 2.
- Faced with a money issue, like debt, investing, or unemployment:

  - Observe your thoughts: Is the "mental chatter" positive? Negative?
  - Check in with your emotions: How do you feel right now?
  - Identify a thought that helps you feel better. Keep invoking it.
  - Specifically and actively ask for spiritual guidance.

- Consider the possibility that a weak economy might be beneficial. Many highly successful initiatives got started when things looked worst.

Resources

- Live by the motto "My greatest resources are intangible: they are a sense of Abundance and thoughts that feel good."

- Watch Professor Rao's YouTube video, "Plug into your hardwired happiness," from the "Awesome Fest 2010 in Costa Rica," or his new video, *The Happiness Project*, distributed by Beyond Words.
- For fresh inspiration, follow Jason Voss and Byron Stock on their websites.
- Read a book on the Law of Attraction, such as *Ask and It Is Given* or *The Secret*. Discuss the insights from your reading with trusted friends.

Right Actions

- Activate the energy of Abundance with the color green. Place your financial records—statements, bills, documents—in green folders.
- Renew your commitment to Abundance with a seasonal ritual.
- Make your next bill-paying session an Abundance ritual. Buy flowers or light candles. Play relaxing music. Remind yourself: "Even if I feel fearful, the truth is that I am circulating wealth and that I am abundant."
- In your journal, define what self-mastery means to you.
- Recall a recurring money mistake. List one or two ways that the spiritual discipline of self-mastery might have prevented it.
- Create a description of what Dr. Rao calls your "mental model." Take a guess at how you created it.
- For one day, be alert to your mental chatter. Be sure to recognize any positive thoughts that arise. Note them in your journal with the date.
- Create a gentle, positive yet transformative statement about one aspect of your money life, such as savings, spending, investing, or giving. For the latter, you might say, "I give to others, and I give to myself as well."
- List every emotion you can think of in your Conscious Money journal.
- Determine the emotional climate in which you typically operate concerning money. Describe it in your Conscious Money journal.

- Test your Emotional IQ. Google the phrase "Emotional Intelligence test," and you will find several websites that offer free EQ (emotional quotient) tests online.
- Choose a financial area where you seek greater Emotional Intelligence.
- Notice how you experience fear and anxiety, as well as any physical sensations that accompany each feeling. Do fear and anxiety "show up" differently in your body?
- Recall a recent money upset. Work toward dissolving it as I did on pages 40–43. In your journal, note the insights received during each step of the way.
- Activate the Law of Attraction by:

  - Identifying a financial desire
  - Choosing to attract it
  - Focusing on the good feelings around manifesting your desire

- Tune in to the frequency or vibration of your desire. For example:

  - To save $1,000 might feel responsible or joyous.
  - To own a red sports car might feel playful or frivolous.
  - To pay off an old debt might feel liberating or call up resentment.

- Attract your desire using words and feelings that create a space for the manifestation to occur.

Conscious Money Affirmation

I choose to focus on positive money thoughts and emotions.

3

Money Shadows and Higher Consciousness

As you have now witnessed, observing your thoughts and emotions is an essential practice if you seek self-mastery. But there is another equally important step: nurturing your connection to higher consciousness, which links you to the wisest, most creative part of your Being, often called the Higher Self. Although most people associate the Higher Self with spiritual matters, it is also a great source for guidance and intuition in money matters. In this chapter, we'll explore how to cultivate our connection to this inner wisdom.

As our consciousness expands, however, it illuminates the parts of us that still remain unconscious. These are the patterns we have not yet brought to light, and many of them can pertain to money. Untangling those patterns, while nourishing the link to higher consciousness, powerfully serves your Conscious Money practice.

Do bear in mind, however, that with these profound topics we approach the realms of deep personal work and psychotherapy, both of which lie outside the scope of this book. Nevertheless, it is valuable to discuss such matters in a general and metaphorical, and rather than a clinical, manner. This is important because our patterns powerfully influence the practice of Conscious Money.

Untangling the Bonds of
Unconscious Patterns

We saw in chapter 2 that mastering the practice of Conscious Money means having a balanced, healthy sense about money, which is typically expressed in our thoughts and beliefs. Not every money thought or belief, however, is a helpful one. Nor are the actions that can follow. Sometimes we unwittingly block our best efforts at financial success. When we engage in a pattern of self-sabotage, it's a very good bet that negative and unconscious patterns are at work.

We create unconscious patterns with thoughts and feelings that we experience over and over again, until they can be said to be impressed on our psyche. As these "impressions" grow deeper and more entrenched, they become patterns that mold and influence our behavior. We, however, are unaware of the entire process—and can remain so unless we decide to investigate it. Fortunately, even a little attention can begin to yield sustainable benefits.

Our patterns or habitual ways of thinking often start early in life. By adulthood, we have grown so accustomed to these habits that we don't see or recognize them. They are like deep grooves in the road that are virtually invisible to us. Perhaps that is why we keep falling into our patterns again and again. Unconscious, self-limiting patterns defeat the practice of Conscious Money.

To become aware of our patterns, we take the same approach as we did with our thoughts and emotions: we simply observe them. This observation might reveal patterns like these:

"Whenever I have money in my pocket, I spend it."
"I tend to get stuck in well-paying jobs that are boring and uncreative."
"Every investment I make seems to fail."

But instead of bemoaning these seemingly negative patterns, we should simply be more aware of them. Eventually, this awareness reveals insights that can unveil for us the motives behind our patterns. In fact, the simple act of recognizing a pattern often begins to bring about a shift in perception or behavior.

The loving self-observation that is basic to self-mastery is essential when we seek to free up conditioning. Gentle attention can help reveal financial motives that may be murky and ambiguous. Reflect on these situations and the possible motives behind them:

Imagine that your friend, who earns an excellent salary, finds it strangely impossible to save for his child's education. You happen to know that your friend's own parents did not help educate him; he was required to "work his way" through school. Is it possible that the resentment he might feel about his own past is undermining his efforts to save funds for his child?

Consider the case of a young person starting her first job. She is not earning a large income. Nevertheless, she purchases a turquoise Coach purse for $600. It's a good bet that her motive is low self-esteem and that she seeks the admiration of her peers or coworkers.

Suppose you know a parent who cannot say no when his or her adult child asks for money again and again, never to pay it back. What would possess such a parent to keep making these handouts? Maybe the parent feels guilty about divorcing the former spouse and breaking up the family. Or perhaps the parent simply wants the grown child's love or protection.

When we avoid doing what we "know is right" about a money issue— or act in a way that is clearly unwise—there may be a truth we do not want to face.

The Money Shadow

There is a part of the self that is so thoroughly repressed that it remains entirely hidden or unconscious. Psychiatrist Carl Jung called it the shadow.

A subset of the shadow is the money shadow, the thoughts, beliefs, and attitudes about money that we refuse to confront or acknowledge.

In this money shadow are the deep, unconscious patterns we all possess about money. Like the shadow itself, these unconscious money patterns are invisible to the conscious mind. Think of the shadow as the dumping ground within each of us for the traits we can't accept in ourselves or others. Typically, we toss shortcomings such as egotism, weaknesses, or laziness into this psychological junkyard. But the shadow can also embody seemingly positive traits, like enthusiasm that has gone a bit overboard and become zeal.

There is one more key point to remember about the shadow: we reject the elements within it so unconsciously that we not only deny their existence in ourselves, but also refuse to acknowledge that we ever thought of or discarded them. That might sound dishonest or irresponsible, but we usually do it with good reason. We are trying to manage or cope with uncomfortable or threatening thoughts, feelings, or self-concepts that we are unprepared to look at or resolve at the time.

It is now widely believed that the shadow: (1) holds enormous creative energy, (2) weakens as we bring it to light, and (3) requires integration into the personality. But we must consciously choose to face and integrate the shadow. This inner work requires the self-examination and self-observation that defines self-mastery. It is, however, well worth the effort. Carl Jung believed welcoming the shadow into the personality was an essential step toward individuation, the journey toward our fullest human potential.

The same is true of the money shadow. As we become more conscious of what lies in our money shadow, we expand our capacity for making conscious, creative choices in regard to money matters.

Two of the most common and dangerous money shadow elements are arguably fear and greed. But the shadow can also embody seemingly positive traits, like optimism, which taken to extremes can explode into a toxic brand of denial or euphoria.

Because our shadow is unconscious, we often project it onto others: "Me greedy? Ha! You're the greedy one."

Ironically, people who label themselves "greedy and proud of it" are often, though not always, better equipped to recognize those individuals who would part them from their precious money. For one thing, such people are likely to be more suspicious. For another, the greedy among us heartily embrace their desire for money, for better or for worse. More altruistic people may feel the need to reject the idea of liking or loving money, which can mean that the trait gets consigned to their shadow.

Acceptance and Healing

Although you won't transform a money shadow with an exercise or two, such tools can help open your eyes; offer real insights; help you identify old, unconscious patterns; and motivate you to more deeply explore your inner life.

The paradox of the shadow is that it most likely represents the opposite of how you see yourself and how you present that self to the world. Experimenting with this principle more than a decade ago, my lifelong friend Donna Coombs and I made up the little quiz I now call the Shadow Game. "What is the most disturbing thing you could ever say about yourself?" we asked each other. We then made up a statement about it.

Having lived an independent, self-directed life (or at least thinking I had), mine was "Patricia is needy and confused." I felt nearly ill at the very thought—a good indication that these qualities were actually key shadow elements for me. (In creating a Shadow Game statement, I found it very powerful to voice my name, but you can simply say "I" if you prefer.)

Gradually over the course of perhaps five years or so, I came to honor both need and confusion as natural, lovable human attributes in others and myself. I also realized that need and confusion were powerful, unseen factors that shaped my money shadow, too. I did not have a clear money strategy at the time, and I tended to overly rely on the advice of experts. Not any more. As I gradually acknowledged the presence of these rejected emotions in my money shadow, I also cleared some negative money habits.

Similarly, imagine a kindly, impecunious person making a declaration like "I am selfish, and I love money." That statement itself sounds crude and may be off-putting to you as you read this, but because those words would probably shock and repulse the person who uttered them, there is a good chance that this characterization factors into the money shadow.

It is important to me to make this point because part of Conscious Money includes feeling comfortable liking money. People with a strong spiritual inclination in particular may have to work with their money shadow in order to discover that enjoying money does not automatically impair one's connection to God or the Higher Self.

Is it possible that liking or loving money might be a positive, healthy choice? We've all heard the stories of lottery winners who experience all sorts of problems or of wealthy people who are unhappy. So it all depends on the individual and his or her consciousness. But I believe there are many good reasons to like money that involve neither selfishness nor materialism. Money can bestow beauty, freedom, adventure, and ease. It puts you in a position to make the world a better place and nurture your well-being and that of others. Money can finance your creativity, your business, or your life purpose.

Liberating the Money Shadow in Four Steps

Facing, accepting, freeing, and integrating the shadow, or more specifically the money shadow, is a complex process best undertaken with patience and over a long period of time. I have attempted to differentiate the elements of this process and present them as "steps" along the way. But do not envision these as concrete steps. They can overlap and their sequence can vary, depending on the person.

1. *Allow.* Gently step off the spiritual pedestal and honestly invite your shadow or your money shadow to show itself. You'd be a rare person indeed were you to have no shortcomings. Decide to let this shadow out of its metaphorical closet. Suppose you have just discovered a place in yourself that is jealous, fearful, or "cheap" about money. If you feel embarrassed about acknowledging this particular trait, remember that there are very real benefits to shadow liberation: when you free your money shadow, you liberate the energy spent denying it. That precious resource can now be used to boost your creativity or to support you in growing your Conscious Money.

2. *Accept.* Gradually let yourself see that it is normal to periodically feel emotions that seem unappealing, such as selfishness, confusion, zealous enthusiasm, fear, or even greed. What is most important is your awareness and self-forgiveness.

3. *Heal.* Remind yourself that true healing requires honoring both sides of the psyche: shadow and light. Know that doing so allows us to be fully human.

4. *Explore.* Play the Shadow Game—with yourself. Pose the question: What is the most disturbing thing I could say about myself? Later you might invite people you trust to inquire into their own shadow. If you are willing, you might share your insights. Remember that when you unveil the shadow, you will be rewarded with a burst of creative energy.

Wishful Thinking

The money shadow is not the only issue we must contend with to know and later grow Conscious Money. One of the most common financial mistakes is the error of wishful thinking (sometimes called magical thinking), which is both pervasive and destructive.

Wishful thinking may have its roots in the shadow, but it possesses an even more exaggerated flavor of denial, which is of course the refusal to recognize or acknowledge something. In combination with shadow elements like greed or fear, denial can be particularly dangerous when it comes to the money shadow. Some financial experts suspect that wishful thinking grows more common during tough economic times. In the story that follows, I have changed the names and all the identifying details about the people involved to protect their privacy. Nevertheless, it happened and it continues to happen often, as victims and law enforcement officials can readily attest.

Marketing manager Sara Smith, age forty-one, and her fifty-year-old husband, Phil, a Silicon Valley software designer, belong to an informal community of professional and creative people who gather on the first Sunday of each month to share fellowship, inspired reading, and a potluck dinner. The group's leader, Tara Wellwood, is a healthcare executive and an ordained minister who has married seven couples, including Sara and Phil, who met each other at one of the group's gatherings.

When Sara's marketing agency was acquired by a large public relations firm, her job was no fun for her anymore. So Sara and Phil dreamed of moving to Northern California to open a bed and breakfast near the Oregon border. A year later, Sara invested half of her IRA, about $200,000, with Prosperity Inc., a business that serves low-income people with short-term, high-interest loans that they otherwise could not obtain. In just ten months, Sara grew her nest egg an amazing 55 percent, enough for a down payment on a ten-room bed and breakfast bungalow near the Pacific Coast. Shortly after, however, the balance on Sara's monthly Prosperity Inc. statement dropped catastrophically, wiping out all of her profits and most of her initial investment.

As an added blow, Prosperity Inc. ignored the couple's concerns and would not return their calls. Finally, time revealed what had happened.

Sara and Phil were victims of a terrible scam and their own wishful thinking. Unfortunately Sara and Phil had not done any due diligence and so they failed to discover that the company was not legitimate. In fact, the people behind it probably put Sara and Phil's money in their own pockets. In any event, their funds disappeared. It certainly appears that Phil and Sara acted out and later sadly faced the consequences of one or more unconscious patterns that they had consigned to their money shadows.

They were also financially naïve. Even if they could not themselves recognize Prosperity Inc. as a dubious operation, they ignored the prudent step of first consulting with a financial professional and other basic principles of personal finance. Any seasoned financial professional would have instantly seen danger. Granted, Sara and Phil might have still proceeded along in the fog of wishful thinking, but there is a chance they might have heeded a warning and preserved their money.

We may think we have rational financial beliefs. But we can become incapacitated when greed or fear are coupled with heady intoxicants like blind enthusiasm, denial, wishful thinking, financial naïveté, or a lack of purpose in money making. Clustered into various combinations, these ingredients represent what I've come to see as a "cultural money virus." A cultural money virus is an energy imbalance that distorts the natural desire for abundance through a collective denial of the real element of risk.

Supposedly sensible money beliefs like "It's smart to seek the highest returns possible" or "You must accept lots of risk to create wealth" tend to prevail during economic boom times, further spreading the cultural money virus. Inoculate yourself against the cultural money virus by observing the first rule of money, the one that wealthy people know by heart: wealth preservation is job one. Consider only legitimate ways to grow your money and consider them only after you've mastered the discipline of saving.

When an "incredible" money opportunity appears, we can willfully choose to go unconscious and refuse to seek advice. ("I won't ask Uncle Fred, the family real estate pro, about that amazing deal. He can be so negative!") That's one reason good people fall for con men, invest in slumlord property, get involved in pyramid schemes, or become seduced by fraudulent advisers.

Euphoria is always a red flag. Look out for it—and then take these steps to avoid such a fate before exposing your money to risk:

- Calm down by taking at least ten slow, deep breaths.
- Temper abundance thinking with common sense, even skepticism.
- Learn the best lesson ever: how to ask good questions.
- Seek the advice of experts (or family members) whose opinion you may not like. Yes, that's right: an opinion you may not like. But this time, open your ears to whatever Uncle Fred has to teach you: "Hey, Uncle Fred, can I run something by you?"
- Take time to sort things out. If you find yourself getting annoyed with the feedback of others, you—and they—just might be on to something, maybe something fraudulent.

Never allow abundance thinking to deteriorate into magical thinking. Find the healthy middle ground between excessive optimism and scornful skepticism. Swindles happen every day, even to highly experienced people. Just ask the "sophisticated" investors, celebrities, and successful business owners scammed in Bernie Madoff's $50 billion pyramid scheme.

The following excellent advice comes from Gary Moore, former senior vice president at Paine Webber and founder of the Financial Seminary, which works with faith-based investors. It appears in his article "Pursuing Ponzi Protection":[1]

1. Remember that con men can look and act impeccably respectable.
2. Never entrust one person or firm with all of your investments.
3. Always separate the management and custody of your money.
4. Never believe a scam won't happen to you.

Please also understand that, even with caution, you will make a few mistakes. That's a part of life and Conscious Money. But if you recognize your blind spots and learn some financial basics, there's a good chance you'll: (1) make sound choices, (2) learn from your mistakes, and (3) avoid major disasters.

Confronting the illusion of wishful thinking powerfully strengthens your ability to grow Conscious Money. But all of us are vulnerable to faulty assumptions and unseen biases concerning money. The journey toward greater money consciousness is definitely one in which we are called to illuminate these pockets of unconsciousness, learn from our mistakes, and hold to our life purpose, as the following story illustrates.

Amy Foster, age forty-three, of Pittsburgh, Pennsylvania, knew that her life purpose was "connecting people to nature, each other, and God." Doing so with businesspeople, she reasoned, would be a powerful catalyst to transform business.[2] An MBA qualified her to achieve her purpose in theory, but as you'll see, she needed to develop self-mastery to live her purpose in a financially sustainable way.

When Amy first centered on her life purpose in her late twenties, she leased an equestrian property and launched a series of off-site retreats in which leaders worked with horses to experience the power of shared leadership. She soon attracted major clients like Alcoa and investors for a new $4.6 million facility. But as Amy focused on the future, her client bookings fell.

In 2005, her dream deal fell through, and she "lost everything." Amy was $300,000 in debt. Nevertheless, her quest for self-mastery took center stage. At a much-needed retreat, she recognized that her extensive financial obligations were blocking her from living her purpose. She owed $7,500 per month in credit card debt and rent and did not earn near enough income to pay it. In 2006, Amy faced the truth and filed for bankruptcy.

"I came to realize that I had been living in magical thinking. I had such clarity about my purpose, but it was not grounded in the reality of this world. I was living on borrowed money," says Amy. From the day she walked out of her lawyer's office, Amy began what she calls a real faith walk. "I knew that I was supposed to build the retreat center, but I shifted my focus to building the business here and now and to becoming a creator, not a victim to life circumstances."[3]

She also released "a sense of entitlement and the feeling that others should help pay for me achieving my dream." Amy recommitted herself to her existing spiritual practice of prayer, journaling, and meditation, vowing it would become more consistent. She stopped living on borrowed money, negotiated delayed payments, paid cash for everything, and saved 10 percent of her earnings.

In 2008, Amy was certified as a Spiritual Intelligence coach. "My work in self-mastery was the turning point," says Amy. Next came a great opportunity. Amy was hired to create a process-related "servant leadership," which provided financial security and also reinforced Amy's vision to bring spirituality to the workplace.

Soon it all came together. In 2010, just a few years after filing for bankruptcy, Amy signed a deal on a 34-acre equestrian property with a farmhouse and meeting facility just twenty minutes from the Pittsburgh Airport. Amy's Triple R Ranch is home to fourteen rescued, rehabilitated horses. With savings and a state-sponsored agritourism loan guarantee, Amy built her 15,000-square-foot facility, Unbridled Performance: The Center for Team and Leadership Breakthroughs, whose first clients were the Cleveland Clinic and the international development division of Land O'Lakes. "Money is flowing," says Amy, and there's plenty of work into next year. "I'm doing the work I love, living on purpose, and making a difference for myself, my family, the horses, my clients, and the planet." Amy's story illustrates the importance of grounding financial wisdom in the quest to live our purpose. It also demonstrates the wealth of satisfaction that is available to us when we grow sufficient mastery to confront and resolve the financial issues that prevent us from living life to the fullest. Amy's website appears in the chapter options.

Cultivating Higher Consciousness

Confronting unconscious patterns and observing our thoughts and emotions dissolves many negative blocks to self-mastery. But at the same time, it is essential to cultivate a strong connection with your higher consciousness, a practice that possesses a very different feel from those we've explored until now.

In this higher state, which is often attained through meditation, yoga, and other contemplative practices, many have enjoyed direct intuitive knowledge, an enhanced problem-solving ability, and a deep sense of peace. They typically feel more awake and alive and are able to simultaneously draw on many levels of intelligence. Such is the power of living in the present moment. Higher awareness can also illuminate unconscious money patterns, thereby preventing or mitigating many of the dangers of wishful thinking and the money shadow. That's why Conscious Money benefits from both expanded consciousness and self-observation.

I invite you to consider four dimensions that are available to a person who is connected to higher consciousness: intuition, creativity, collective (or universal) consciousness, and spirituality. Each dimension is valuable to your Conscious Money practice.

Intuition. First of all, higher consciousness has long been celebrated as the source of intuition. Unlike either mental or emotional awareness, both of which are necessary, intuition is a distinct kind of knowing that transcends and includes both heart and head. You'll mine your intuitive wisdom in every phase of your Conscious Money practice. Chapter 7 discusses the role of intuition in investing, where an intuitive "hit" can enlighten and guide your choices.

Creativity. Tapping into higher consciousness also unlocks your creativity, which, in the context of this book, is a potent force for growing your success and earning power. Summoning higher consciousness is an indispensable element in creative problem solving. In chapter 6, I discuss creativity as the most important job skill you can possess today.

Collective consciousness. Higher consciousness also permits us to see beyond our limited, individual selves. In chapter 8, we discuss the global dimension of Conscious Money and the global consciousness that many experience today. Your unique personal journey toward Conscious Money is part of a larger scheme that is unfolding on our planet today: millions of people the world over seek an expanded awareness and intelligence that transcends the individual mind and everyday reality. Higher consciousness generates a sort of mystical unity—we're all in this together—and shatters the illusion of separation. The financial equivalent of separation is the doctrine of pure, unfettered economic self-interest, the foundation of traditional capitalism. In chapter 4, you will see that free enterprise is today evolving toward a new and more conscious iteration of itself as Conscious Capitalism. Today, growing numbers of people believe humanity shares a common planetary destiny, and that together we are building the new economic infrastructure to support that destiny. With this universal perspective, we can recognize the power we possess as individuals to transform corporate and global finance.

Spirituality. The fourth dimension of human consciousness is spirituality. Spirituality most often refers to our engagement with the Spirit or Higher Self that animates each of us.

In the past decade or so, the newly described capacity of Spiritual Intelligence has attracted growing interest. The late Stephen Covey wrote in his book *The 8th Habit*, "Spiritual intelligence is the central and most fundamental of all the intelligences because it becomes the source of *guidance* of the other three."[4]

I now want you to meet a teacher who has devised a powerful tool that clarifies where you stand in your spiritual journey and can support you as you expand your consciousness to the next level.

The Spiritual Dimension of Consciousness

Cindy Wigglesworth, a dark-eyed, creamy complexioned Texan with a penetrating mind, is a former Exxon human resources executive and founder of Deep Change consultancy. She has taught Spiritual Intelligence (SQ) to thousands of people and led SQ workshops for companies in the energy and healthcare sectors, including clients such as the University of Pittsburgh Medical Center and the Methodist Hospital System.[5] The latter was awarded a place on *Fortune*'s "100 Best Companies to Work For" list, thanks in part to Cindy's work.

Cindy has created something unusual in the field of spirituality: a self-assessment tool to evaluate an individual's level of Spiritual Intelligence. When I interviewed Cindy to find out more about her Spiritual Intelligence assessment, which she calls the SQi for short, I discovered it was connected to questions Cindy asked herself and others early in her SQ work, such as "Who are the spiritual teachers or leaders you admire most?" and "Which character traits do they possess?" By asking questions like these in SQ workshops and collecting the audience's answers, as she designed the SQi, she made a major, practical discovery: people chose the same traits whether they admired Jesus, Mohammed, Mother Teresa, or any other spiritual teacher. Cindy then compiled a list of spiritually intelligent traits and carefully designed questions to measure them.

In addition to Cindy's own corporate SQ work, many mainstream organizations such as Hewlett-Packard, Nokia, Merck Pharmaceuticals, and Starbucks have brought Spiritual Intelligence into their workplaces.[6]

Your Spiritual Skill Set

Cindy's SQ Assessment asks questions related to twenty-one spiritual competencies, which reveal common threads in religion, psychology, philosophy, and spirituality. A person's answers pinpoint his or her level of

Spiritual Intelligence, defined by Cindy as "the ability to act with Wisdom and Compassion while maintaining inner and outer peace, regardless of the circumstances." Furthermore, the SQ assessment's interpretive results, sent to all test takers, recommend the specific growth steps that can support each person to move in a more desired direction.

Here's one question asked in the SQ assessment: "Do you listen to the Higher Self and act in accordance with its guidance?" This question clearly gauges your sense of connection to higher consciousness. You're also invited to rate on a scale from one to five, with five being the highest, the extent to which this statement is true for you: "My Higher Self tells me when I am following the right path and when I am not."

As I reviewed these and others questions, it seemed clear that Spiritual Intelligence, which is certainly a manifestation of higher consciousness, can teach us a lot about good financial sense. If the Higher Self were in charge, even if only for part of the time, for example, we'd be a lot less inclined to act in ways that result in financial folly. The more the Higher Self is in charge, the better our judgment.

There are, of course, degrees of Spiritual Intelligence, and Cindy's assessment tool assigns five of them, with five as the highest theoretical level. But she adds, "I doubt His Holiness the Dalai Lama or the late Mother Teresa would rate themselves at level five," says Cindy. "Because the closer a person gets to it, the less likely they are to claim it. They see the gaps in themselves and grow more humble."

How to Access Higher Consciousness

The way to summon higher consciousness is through a mindful practice such as meditation, yoga, martial arts, journaling, or quiet reflection. Of these, meditation can be simplest, yet for some the most challenging, way to raise consciousness. It is simple in the sense that it needs nothing, except perhaps a place to sit; it is challenging because it requires silence and stillness.

You may already know the blessings of a meditation practice. If you do not have such a practice, you will find a simple one to follow at the end of this chapter.

Mastery on the Mat
Spiritual disciplines like yoga and martial arts may appear to focus on physical mastery. Yet practitioners report that the discipline they acquire "on the mat" readily translates into mental, emotional, and spiritual self-mastery. That is certainly the way matters unfold in the following story of a devoted follower of martial arts who is also a practitioner of Conscious Money.

Thirty years ago Jeff Klein, now fifty-three years old and a successful conscious business leader, was out of work, out of money, and at his wits' end.[7] A voice within him demanded that he develop more focus and discipline. He found what he was looking for while training at a karate dojo in Austin, Texas. When a client called Jeff to New York City, he located a traditional Japanese karate dojo there where he could continue his studies. Martial arts taught Jeff life lessons that developed his personal mastery and gradually opened the doors to future success.

"One day I was invited to spar with a third-degree Japanese black belt," says Jeff, who was a white belt at the time. "I held my own and the teacher commented, 'good work.' The next moment, I was flat on the floor— I didn't even see it happen," says Jeff. From this experience he learned: Be careful of what you think you can do. There may be someone more knowledgeable and skillful right in front of you. Awareness, respect, and humility are essential.

A few years ago, Jeff learned another valuable lesson from his martial arts practice. At the time, he was facing a threatening business situation. One day, as he practiced Thai kickboxing with a twenty-one-year-old instructor, Jeff allowed himself to express all the pent up anger, and frustration he was feeling at the time. "If you lean forward that much and come on that strong in a fight," the teacher told him, "you're going to get clobbered." Jeff then clearly understood that anger and aggression, if unmanaged, will "blind you and lead you into trouble." Conversely, good technique, relaxed awareness, and sensitivity to what is going on between you and your opponent, he says, "are infinitely more important than strength or speed."

Jeff has witnessed the mastery he cultivated in martial arts transfer to work, money, and life. "In martial arts, you feel the movement of your opponent and yourself," he says. When you truly experience the energy of colleagues, clients, or competitors, you can create business situations where service and compensation are well-balanced. He explains: "At times in the past, I undervalued my service, investing untold hours, ideas and energy into projects, for which I was modestly paid." But as Jeff's skill in martial arts deepened, his business relationships became like the "playful dance of a friendly bout." Clients increasingly paid him substantial and consistent fees, acknowledging his value and the power of his presence.

For Jeff, martial arts nurtured the self-mastery that in turn earned him a solid income of Conscious Money doing the work he loved.

Journaling

If you are not a journaler already, let me introduce you to this art form. If you already journal, let me encourage you to continue. I began journaling at age twenty, one summer sitting on a massive rock overlooking the Atlantic Ocean, and continued, sometimes more diligently than at other times, for the next two decades. Then, in midlife, journaling became a near daily practice. Now I can't imagine my life without it. In 2009, I taught my first journaling workshop online to one hundred people from twenty countries.

Journaling is a highly practical tool for bridging our day-to-day thoughts with the higher realms of consciousness. Favored by geniuses like Leonardo da Vinci and Thomas Edison, journaling will promote and enhance your Conscious Money practice—and your life.

Journaling is a date you keep with yourself and an excellent way to capture your reflections. Unlike keeping a diary, which tends to be a record of external events, journaling is a letter to your soul in which you describe the inner journey of your life. It's a snapshot of your consciousness at any one point in time and therefore highly instructive to look back on because it is a treasure trove of personal insights you might otherwise pass over.

Journaling can also be a helpful step in creating a loving relationship with yourself. In your journal, free from social constraints or the fear of rejection, you give yourself permission to speak your truth and to express yourself. Journaling is also a concrete way to help you grow Conscious Wealth. When you quietly and peacefully affirm your financial desires in writing, you energize your intentions, so that, instead of growing discouraged, you gradually manifest what you want.

You can use journaling to incubate important Conscious Money questions, such as, should I buy a new home now? Shall I switch jobs or go back to school for a master's degree? Is this a good time to invest in the stock market? Do not expect immediate answers. But do invite the answers to come from your higher consciousness. Set your intention to receive inner guidance and then return to your question regularly for about one month. Your answer may come slowly over time or in a single lengthy entry that I call a "download," because when I read it, I say, "Where did that come from? It must be a download from the Universe."

Rarely have I failed to get an inspired solution to a personal, creative, or professional problem given enough blank, unlined journal pages (journalers usually have a strong preference for either lined or unlined paper) and Waterman ink cartridges in vivid purple, flaming red, and, my favorite, South Sea Blue.

Before you journal, think about your expectations.

Do not assume you will immediately write down something meaningful. Perhaps you will, but perhaps not. Instead of that mind-set, ease into journaling with kind words to yourself that relieve performance pressure and support you to be more present. Note the time and your location. Slowly tune in to your mood, perhaps by describing the weather or some other innocuous topic. Feel free to record a recent activity or two as part of this warm-up phase. Then gently begin to focus within and take your emotional temperature. How you are feeling in the present moment is always a good place to start. Later, move on to an issue that is important for you right now, or perhaps focus on a creative problem.

The question of how much time to spend journaling makes some people anxious. It needn't. Ten or fifteen minutes is plenty at first. With more practice, thirty to forty-five minutes gives you ample time to check in, record the highlights of your inner life, and write about your current concerns. If you are a prolific dreamer, you may need more time. Dreams often contain messages from your Being that you can capture in your journal. During periods of intense personal growth, I have journaled for several hours each day.

The most common question about journaling is: what if I have nothing to say? At first, it's possible that you will not. Like almost everything else, journaling takes practice. But there's a little trick that will almost always get you started: ask yourself questions. They can be:

1. Open-ended. "Where am I right now in my life?"
2. Focused. "What do I desire, today, this week or this year?"
3. Work-oriented. "What should I do—or not do—about that project?"

There is one question that will almost certainly raise your vibration: "What do I appreciate right now in my life?" Another helpful approach is to generate a list of at least five questions that you will have available to launch a journal entry. They might include a few of the ones listed above, if you wish, or focus on your unique areas of interest, whether personal, creative, or professional. Formulate these questions by asking yourself where you often get "stuck," what issue tends to bother you most, or what areas you tend to resist. If you list your questions on one of the back pages of your journal, you can easily consult them when you sit down to write.

A Commitment Is an Investment in Yourself

So there are many ways to initiate or expand your link to higher consciousness, from meditation to journaling, from Spiritual Intelligence to martial arts. Each of these enjoyable practices will enhance your ability to attract and grow Conscious Money. But none of them will bless or benefit you without one last thing: your personal commitment. Think of this commitment not as another task crowding your to-do list but as an investment in yourself. Focus on the "profits" it will deliver. There are few experiences in life that are as rich as the blessings of greater intuition, spirituality, creativity or a sense of the collective consciousness in which you participate. When you invest in these beneficial practices, you will cultivate an inner garden that overflows with harmony and beauty.

The success of Conscious Money requires the self-observation that can discern and dissolve the old, unconscious patterns that sabotage our best efforts. That may sound like a lot of dedication on your part. But as you liberate and embrace the rejected elements of your shadow, you will find it easier to energize new money habits. As you commit to practices that expand higher consciousness, you will come to know blessings like the integration of head and heart; the wisdom gleaned from experience and good judgment; and a healing of the separation, guilt, or fear that many people feel around money. The rewards of the journey are well worth the effort.

Exercises

Examining a Money Issue

Explore the hidden issues or motives that influence your money consciousness. This may feel a little uncomfortable, so make it easy and gentle. When you know what motivates, worries, or scares you, that is, when it is "conscious," you are better able to clarify and choose which steps to take to save or grow your money.

Choose a money issue or expenditure that concerns you. Take a deep breath and then another. Now look within: How do you feel? Is there something you are avoiding or refuse to face? Is there an underlying thought or emotion that you haven't yet noticed or identified? What is it?

Complete the exercise by asking: "How do I want to feel about this?"

Now revisit your money issue. Is there a hidden motive or perhaps a suppressed emotion? Let it come to light and just allow it to be.

A Simple Meditation

Meditation, yoga, martial arts, and other mindful practices are an essential part of connecting to higher consciousness. If you do not already have such a practice, here is a simple and enjoyable meditation to follow:

1. Sit comfortably and relax the muscles of your body, beginning with your feet and moving up through your legs, pelvis, belly, chest, arms, neck, and head.
2. Invite any tense or uncomfortable spots to dissolve and release.
3. Inhale slowly to the count of three. Exhale to the count of five.
4. As you exhale, think or silently say the word "peace."
5. Continue for five or ten minutes. When thoughts or emotions arise, simply return to your breath: inhale and exhale in peace.

Make a Covenant to Practice Conscious Money

The following five-step contemplation invites you to invoke God, your Higher Self, a Higher Power, or higher consciousness to make a covenant to commit to a Conscious Money practice.

1. Whatever the circumstances of your outer life, you always possess the power of inner choice. In your heart and mind, you have many options. Select the one that represents the truth of who you really are: an abundant and unlimited Being. Perhaps this truth seems hidden right now. Affirm it anyhow.

2. Create a ritual to invoke or celebrate your Conscious Money practice and the abundance it may bring. Connect this choice with the higher realms, perhaps with candles, writing, or reflection. Ask God, your Higher Self, Higher Power, or higher consciousness to witness and support your choice for conscious abundance.

3. Ask the Higher Power you've just called upon to melt any potential resistance. Fully accept your current circumstances. Forgive yourself and others for whatever role you or they might have played in your present financial situation.

4. Use your own words or just say, "I choose Conscious Money."

5. Silently reaffirm your commitment to Conscious Money each day at a time that you are meditating or doing your spiritual work. Or choose a daily reminder to help recall your intention. Each time the phone rings, for example, or before opening an email, silently remind yourself, "I choose Conscious Money."

Options

Reflection

- Ponder this thought: I probably have some unconscious, negative, or self-sabotaging money patterns.
- Look within and ask if you're willing to see and accept these patterns.
- Consider whether you are "infected" with the "cultural money virus."
- Reflect on Cindy Wigglesworth's definition of Spiritual Intelligence: "The ability to act with Wisdom and Compassion while maintaining

inner and outer peace, regardless of the circumstances." On a scale from one to five, with five the highest, how do you rate yourself on this?

- Consider what role you play in humanity's shared destiny and whether you experience the economic dimension of that destiny.

Resources

- Ask friends or family to offer honest feedback about any blind spots you might have concerning money.
- Discipline yourself to listen to the financial ideas of people with whom you very much disagree.
- For more information on Amy Foster, her center, and to see a video showing the horses and executives working together, go to Unbridled Performance.com.
- Create a Conscious Money study group of close friends or family with whom you feel comfortable discussing financial matters. To begin a dialogue, you might each address the question: Where do I stand right now in my Conscious Money practice?
- Read the Robert Johnson classic *Owning Your Own Shadow*.
- There is an informative introduction to the shadow on the website shadowwork.com, which also describes the life and work of Carl Jung.
- Choose a teacher, mentor, or spiritual or creative figure as the inspiration for your self-mastery practice.
- Draw on this quote from Carl Jung to inspire your shadow work: "Everyone carries a Shadow, and the less it is embodied in the individual's conscious life, the blacker and denser it is. At all counts, it forms an unconscious snag, thwarting our most well-meant intentions."[8]
- For the entire text of Gary Moore's article "Pursuing Ponzi Protection" (and for more information), consult the website of the organization he founded, FinancialSeminary.org.

Right Actions

- Cultivate self-mastery through a mindful practice like meditation, yoga, or a martial art like t'ai chi.
- In your journal, record observations of your thoughts and emotions, along with the date, so you can compare and contrast them later.
- Assume you have a money shadow. Take some of the steps recommended in this chapter to reveal and begin healing your shadow.
- Carefully evaluate your propensity toward wishful thinking. If it feels right, you might invite people you trust to offer constructive feedback on this issue.
- Or neutralize the tendency toward wishful thinking by actively seeking the advice of people whose guidance you have resisted in the past, even though you know they are well-informed about money. Notice whether you feel calm, upset, or fearful as they speak.
- If you are an enthusiastic person, appoint a critic or naysayer to your "board of financial advisors," and vice versa.
- Consider working to heal "negative" money thoughts or patterns through Emotional Freedom Technique (EFT), counseling, or therapy.
- Reply to Cindy Wigglesworth's questions in your journal: (1) Who are the spiritual teachers or leaders you admire most? (2) Which character traits do they possess?
- On a scale from one to five, with five being the highest, rate yourself on this SQ statement, "My Higher Self tells me when I am following the right course and when I am not."
- Ask your Higher Self for guidance on a financial issue and record any insights in your journal.
- To take Cindy Wigglesworth's Spiritual Intelligence assessment test, go to DeepChange.com and click on the "Discover Your Skills" tab.
- Strengthen your connection to higher consciousness through prayer, meditation, quiet contemplation, yoga, journaling, or chanting.

- As part of your spiritual practice, notice when you experience unity with others.
- Tune into your personal consciousness around money and embrace the challenge to transform humanity's economic destiny.
- Renew your covenant to practice Conscious Money in an annual ritual.

Conscious Money Affirmation

I recognize that my Conscious Money practice requires that I observe my money shadow and cultivate the higher consciousness of self-mastery.

Part II

The Conscious Marketplace

4

The Trademarks of Conscious Capitalism

Having activated the inner dimension of your Conscious Money practice and clarified your core values in the preceding chapters, we now turn to the practical core of your money practice—calling on your values and consciousness to guide your financial decisions. At this point in your evolving Conscious Money practice, there's a growing appreciation of the true meaning of abundance and a solid respect for the basics of sound finance as you honor these practical principles along with your deepest ideals. The willingness to witness your thoughts and emotions along the path toward self-mastery will stand you in good stead for the monetary choices that lie ahead. So will embracing a contemplative practice to open or expand your connection to higher consciousness. It is important to stay alert to the perils of wishful thinking, the money shadow, and other unconscious patterns that can block the way toward Conscious Money.

While Conscious Money begins within you, it is also a discipline you practice in the marketplace, where goods and services are bought and sold, where people like you discover your purpose, and where you explore a career in which to fulfill it. Having prepared ourselves from the inside out, we are now armed with powerful intuitive techniques and ready to move forward into the world of finance.

Into the Conscious Marketplace

It is time to translate your internal practice into conscious action. At this point, it is important to locate strong allies who will help you navigate the risks and rewards of the marketplace. They should be both knowledgeable and experienced. At the same time, you want to collaborate with partners who honor many of the same values you do, and who, like you, comprehend the inner dimension of money.

You will find such allies in like-minded friends and groups as well as in the growing community of conscious businesses, many of which are not only up and running, but quite successful. More important, progressive companies can also mirror your own consciousness, as you shall see. Doing business with companies as conscious as you are, and avoiding whenever possible those that are not, is one of the key ways that you can translate your consciousness into actions that transform the marketplace.

When I speak of conscious business, I include local shops, restaurants, or service providers in your community, such as your dry cleaner or auto shop.

The idea here is not to become more knowledgeable about business in general, although that can be a useful too, but to learn to recognize those businesses that understand the importance of Conscious Money. This is increasingly important as we move forward. Recognizing conscious companies, be they large or small, serves as a basis for the chapters ahead, where we shall consider in greater detail your roles as a creative earner, discerning consumer, and responsible investor.

The conscious companies you meet in this chapter may very well prove to be among the ones with whom you choose to connect and interact. But my purpose in introducing them lies beyond that premise. When you take a good look at how conscious businesses operate, you'll get a fresh take on where business is headed in the New Economy of Consciousness. Equipped with this understanding, you will be better able to evaluate the businesses large and small, local or national, where you might want to work, shop, or invest. In each of these financial roles, you will want to engage with commercial partners on whose integrity, awareness, and good judgment you can rely.

You will see that I describe many large companies in this chapter. There are several reasons for that. First, I want to demonstrate that it is entirely possible for multibillion-dollar corporations to operate in a conscious manner. Recognizing this truth is an important step in releasing the common business stereotype that "big" must mean "bad." And because these companies are large, they're in a position to touch the lives of millions upon millions of people who work, invest, shop at, or otherwise do business with them. Consider, too, all of the small and midsize firms that are successful because they sell their own products to these corporations. Bear in mind that no conscious business is perfect. Like conscious people, they have flaws or rough edges. But such companies are often willing to address them and change.

Geography is a key factor, too. Small and even midsize firms are generally found in specific localities. A wonderful small business in Maine may hold little interest for a reader in Arizona and vice versa. The larger companies described here are national—and many are retailers, so there is a good chance that one of their stores is located nearby, affording you the option of visiting a conscious company on-site. You might explore becoming a customer or even an employee of such a company.

This chapter marks the pivotal point on the journey toward Conscious Money where you metaphorically leave the comforting confines of the temple and forge ahead. You depart possessing all the temple's teachings, of course, but you will still venture into a new and very different world of cash registers, skyscrapers, and grocery aisles. But you are well-prepared because you've personified the inner or spiritual element of money. And furthermore you will not venture into "business as usual," but will move through the values-friendly territory of conscious enterprise. So let us proceed now—into the conscious marketplace.

Wanted: A Company as Conscious as You Are

To grow Conscious Money, you want to engage with companies that possess positive values. If you value integrity, for example, you will avoid doing business with a firm that repeatedly shortchanges customers on quality. You'll seek instead to shop at, invest in, and earn your salary from a company that's committed to integrity—a company that practices Conscious Capitalism.

When people change, capitalism must evolve to reflect their new values, aspirations, and consciousness. Today, as individuals, we have the power to change free enterprise through the collective impact of our personal financial choices. We are free to buy an organic product and boycott one full of chemicals; to invest in a green corporation rather than a polluter; to put our cash in a community bank or credit union instead of a big national bank; and to commit our talent, energies, and creativity to a life-affirming company.

Conscious Money is expressed in the world of business as Conscious Capitalism, a movement of investors, consumers, leaders, and activists who seek to transform free enterprise. For CEOs and top executives, it also represents a holistic business model about how a company creates and delivers sustainable, economic value.

The Conscious Capitalist companies you'll meet in this chapter practice the principles of Conscious Money. They have an established record of honoring people and values. Such firms also adopt a holistic viewpoint, which is a key indicator of higher consciousness. Both Conscious Capitalism and Conscious Money practice the wisdom of sound finance, which is essential to growing Conscious Wealth, whether personally or in business. Thus Conscious Money and Conscious Capitalism are natural allies.

In this chapter, we explore the trademarks of Conscious Capitalism, so you can use them in choosing where to earn, spend, and invest your Conscious Money.

Positive Examples Boost Your Abundance

I want you to know about Conscious Capitalism for another reason: to enhance your ability to attract abundance. While the media tend to point out scandals and scoundrels—and part of their job is to do so—if you bathe your thoughts in that negative business data, your energetic frequency and abundance potential plummet.

Instead, it's refreshing to open to the truth that there are "good guys" in business. In fact, a large sector of the economy is comprised of millions of creative, conscious people who have devoted their lives to a new vision of business as just, humane, and environmentally aware.

You can deepen your understanding of conscious business by considering the values of the businesses you'll meet in this chapter. Then, as you go about your daily routine, begin to size up the stores, shops, and businesses in your town or region. Notice how you feel as a customer, or ask employees what it's like to work there. As a customer, ask the frontline employees you meet about their company's values. If you feel comfortable doing so, inquire whether they believe their company lives up to its stated values.

Organizations possess consciousness just as individuals do. A business's consciousness is the group awareness residing in its people. It is anchored in the values they share and is expressed in their attitudes and actions.

Capitalism: Traditional versus Conscious

Conscious Capitalism has emerged as an alternative to the shortcomings of traditional capitalism, which largely runs on the belief that "the social responsibility of business is to increase its profits."[1] What this means is that if you're a customer or employee, traditional capitalism has placed your interests after those of the company's investors.

But this traditional mind-set, which states that profit is the "be-all and end-all" of business, distorts the integrity of the marketplace. Because it says, or at least implies, that since profit comes first, then the moral, human, or environmental costs to earn it come second. In the run-up to the subprime mortgage crisis in 2008, traditional capitalist institutions pursued profit so aggressively, and with such little regard for risk or responsibility, that they destroyed trillions of dollars' worth of monetary assets and brought the entire financial system to the brink of collapse. When business gets away with that kind of irresponsibility, you and I must pay with the loss of homes, jobs, savings, or investments. After a decade of enduring such pain, people and businesses alike are ready to entertain a new model of free enterprise.

Conscious Capitalism Beats the Competition

Enter Conscious Capitalism, a proven alternative that is morally—and financially—superior to traditional capitalism. There is clear evidence that the stock market value of Conscious Capitalist companies outperforms that of their less conscious peers—especially in the long term.

Raj Sisodia, marketing professor at Bentley College and a coauthor of *Firms of Endearment* with David Wolfe and Jagdish Sheth, studied twenty-eight companies, including Google, Costco, and Honda, whose management principles fostered positive relationships with employees, customers, and investors.[2] Over a ten-year period, the stock of these Conscious Capitalist companies soared 1,025 percent—versus 122 percent for the S&P 500.[3] Another decade-long study, conducted during tough economic times, showed that the public companies that are "great places to work" outperformed the S&P 500 by a very wide margin.[4]

What these studies demonstrate is that when a business possesses the values, wisdom, and higher consciousness to appreciate that employees, customers, suppliers, and not just investors, contribute to the overall success of the enterprise, that business can achieve profound and sustainable success.

Whole Foods' cofounder and coCEO John Mackey calls this phenomenon "the paradox of profit," which states that by managing the enterprise as a whole, with all parties accorded their proper due— including the investors—a company can earn greater profits.[5] As we decipher this paradox, you'll see it makes a lot of sense.

Let us take the example of Whole Foods itself.

Whole Foods' Whole Strategy

When the 2008 recession descended on the economy, Whole Foods proactively launched more value-packed specials in every department. Two years later, it was clear these initiatives were working, when the company announced a substantial increase in quarterly profits.

Whole Foods investors were very happy. So were Whole Foods team members (the term many conscious companies prefer over "employees"), who earn profit sharing and stock options. And customers enjoyed lower prices, such as a savings of two dollars or more per pound for the highest quality meat and fish. They also liked knowing that the nation's first and only FDA-certified natural retailer was 100 percent wind-powered. Existing patrons kept buying, while new ones appeared. As business thrived, Whole Foods' suppliers got more orders—which benefited communities at home and abroad.

Because Conscious Capitalists like Whole Foods promote the greater good, everyone wins: employees, investors, customers, suppliers, and communities, as well as the environment. That is the "paradox of profit."

The Conscious Appeal of Midsize Corporations

While multibillion dollar companies including Whole Foods may appear to dominate the economic landscape, midsize firms—those employing five hundred or more people and whose annual sales range from $10 million to $1 billion—offer many advantages. In fact, Rand Stagen, managing director of the Stagen management consultancy, and social equity investors Sunny Vanderbeck and Randy Eisenman, founders of Satori Capital, all of whom regularly work with or invest in midsize firms, identify this sector as the "sweet spot for conscious business."[6]

Midsize companies are typically more stable than start-ups or small businesses. So midsize firms can more accurately invest in their businesses and forecast five to seven years out.

If you are seeking a job, midsize businesses are worth investigating. Between 2007 and 2010, in a time of recession, big companies cut 3.7 million jobs (a net figure including new jobs created). But midsize firms added a net of 2.2 million jobs—and 80 percent of those midsize firms expect to grow in the coming years.[7]

If you work for a smaller company, you'll rub elbows with executives and work in a small enough unit to get to know managers and coworkers and build *esprit de corps*. Midsize firms offer the advantage of greater financial stability, increasing your chance of getting hired, keeping your job, and earning a great salary with good benefits.

Consumers can benefit from of midsize firms, too. Because they are well-established, they may be less likely to cut quality or boost prices. Investors favor midsize companies because they've graduated from the financial precariousness of a small business but have not yet reached their full potential. So greater profits are likely to follow.

A strong example of a conscious midsize company is women's clothing retailer and manufacturer Eileen Fisher. With estimated annual sales of $310 million and about one thousand employees, Eileen Fisher is a squarely midsize company. It is consistently named one of the "25 Best Medium-Size Places to Work," ranking 14th on a recent national list.[8] In an industry obsessed with fads, frills, and status, Eileen Fisher exemplifies "beauty, simplicity, and joy," says Eileen Fisher sales associate Lisa Ann Schraffa, who is also a fashion blogger.[9] Eileen Fisher's commitment to the values of well-being, social justice, and sustainability, celebrated in chapter 5, wins my kudos and respect.

While big manufacturers and retailers have been censured for the sweatshop conditions in which their products were produced, Eileen Fisher personally helped develop new social accountability standards and her company was one of the first to officially embrace SA8000, a global accountability accreditation that set more humane standards for child labor, health and safety, worker hours, and wages. Eileen Fisher clothing is made in China, where sweatshop conditions often prevail, but the company takes great pains to guarantee high standards. Leading auditor Global Standards trains and observes the company's Chinese vendors. Social Consciousness Director Amy Hall monitors human rights, green practices, and working conditions. Eileen Fisher is equally dedicated to environmental excellence, and began offering a green clothing line back in 2008.

Bigger is not always better. For a consumer, investor, or employee, reputable midsize companies are great places to do business. And small businesses possess their own distinctive set of advantages.

The Benefits of Small Business: Freedom, Job Creation, and Green Innovation

The unrivaled beauty of small business is that anyone with a vision, a plan, and basic business skills can start one. Whether your dream is to be a floral designer, software guru, or green marketing consultant, you can enjoy the freedom of working for yourself and the adventure of making a difference in the world on your own terms.

There are 27.5 million small businesses in the United States, says the US Small Business Administration (SBA). The vast majority are solo entrepreneurships without employees. Half are home-based. And listen to this: small business (*not* the Fortune 500) typically generates a whopping

65 percent net of new jobs, says the SBA. And many are good jobs: small business hires 43 percent of high-tech workers.[10]

Today's sustainability trend blesses small businesses and entrepreneurs with an unprecedented advantage. Inspired by passion for the environment and enthusiasm to act decisively to manifest their vision, small enterprises created and launched a flurry of green products and innovations before big business even awakened to the prospects.

An example is Rod Sprules and his Java-Log Firelogs. Innovation requires "thinking out of the box," but who'd dream up making fireplace logs out of coffee? Rod did the minute he read that burning coffee grounds generates more energy than burning wood. An engineer and inventor, he collected used grounds from a café, dried them in the oven, stuffed them in an old cigar tube, added wax, and set the whole thing afire.

"It burned really well," he recalls.[11] Rod then married two trends: sustainability and the coffeehouse boom. His Java-Log Firelogs emit up to 78 percent less carbon monoxide than cordwood and keep twelve million pounds of coffee grounds out of landfills yearly.[12] They are sold at chain stores across the United States for about $3.50 each (less if you buy a case), but, as *National Geographic* quipped while reporting on the innovation, there is "no Starbucks smell."[13]

Entrepreneurs like Rod and the companies they found are a hotbed of creativity, especially in green technology, according to the SBA:[14]

- When it comes to patents, small innovative companies are a surprising sixteen times more productive than large innovative companies, especially in the green sector.
- Small firms account for more than 32 percent of the patents in both smart grids and solar energy.
- Top talent is flocking to small business, says the SBA: 80 percent of "prolific" inventors now in small green tech firms had once worked in big business, government, or university labs.

• Green patents from small firms are cited a lot more often in new patents.

Not all green innovation is in high technology, however. Entrepreneurs and small business are also at the forefront of the organic and natural trend. Two examples, both founded in Boulder, Colorado, a hub for small conscious business, are Horizon Organic and WhiteWave Foods, maker of Silk soy milk. Boulder also claims WishGarden Herbs, maker of the aptly named "Kick-Ass Immune Activator," which I can personally report has never failed to keep a nasty cold at bay.

But Boulder is hardly the only place where small, organic companies have captured the ethos of green product innovation and fused it with humanistic workplace practices. Such companies are everywhere across the country. New England and the Midwest, respectively, are home to Seventh Generation and Organic Valley, both highly conscious consumer firms. And the Northwest boasts numerous small to midsize companies devoted to organic and free trade practices.

That said, Boulder is home to one entrepreneurial story that I think will inspire anyone with a green entrepreneurial bent. Joshua Onysko, founder of the Pangea line of organic skin care, calls his business "ecocentric." The ingredients within Pangea's flagship organic soaps biodegrade in forty-eight hours instead of two hundred years. Pangea is a pioneer in green innovation, and especially packaging.[15]

Onysko handcrafted his first bar of soap in his mom's kitchen before setting off to Asia to study sustainable living. Back in the United States, he later launched a microbusiness in organic soaps, which soon rang up $100,000 per year in sales. Onysko then discovered IDEO, the savvy firm that did design work for Apple. Impressed by Onysko's vision, IDEO took on Onysko's sustainable ideas and, on his limited design budget, helped him come up with Pangea's innovative packaging solution, which minimizes the environmental impact of packaging while educating people about sustainable skin care.

When you buy a Pangea product, you don't *recycle* the box it comes in; you plant it. Organic seeds, like sweet basil and amaranth, are folded origami-style into the packaging's 100 percent post-consumer material. Customers soak the box in water for a minute or so, bury it in the earth—and those "packages" blossom into plants. Great packaging helped Pangea win national distribution at Whole Foods and elsewhere.

Today, one business database estimates Pangea's annual sales at $2.5 to $5 million. This robust small business is also committed to fostering a human-friendly workplace. Its products are manufactured in a facility whose carpets and paint are free of deadly chemicals and volatile organic compounds (VOCs). Employees earn a living wage for the Boulder area, full health and dental care, and free statewide public transportation passes. There's an on-site organic garden that provides healthy snacks.

Granted, starting your own business can look like a precarious economic undertaking. Credit tightened considerably during the recession, but later started to flow, says the SBA, which by 2010 counted nearly $700 billion in annual small business loans (of under $1 million per loan) from banks and other sources. Government figures indicate the prospects are not quite as daunting as most of us think: seven out of ten firms with employees survive at least two years, and one third are still in business after ten years.[16]

Moreover some small firms don't survive; they thrive. One example is SoulCycle, a fitness business in New York City. Cofounder Elizabeth Cutler moved to Manhattan to join her new husband after she'd spent many soulful years traveling in India and practicing the healing art of Jin Shin Jyutsu, a precursor of acupuncture. Having also spent time hiking in the Rocky Mountains, Elizabeth was unimpressed with the city's indoor workout options. Elizabeth's new friend Julie Rice was a fan of indoor cycling. "There were certainly enough ways to burn calories," the SoulCycle website reports, yet "nothing that made their hearts sing."[17]

But soon Elizabeth and Julie envisioned SoulCycle: inspiring indoor cycling in a beautiful environment with outstanding customer service. Elizabeth tracked down a studio on West 72nd Street via Craigslist, and Julie handed out "schedule cards up and down" Manhattan's West Side. Soon the riders showed up, too. After expanding to multiple locations, SoulCycle attracted the attention of investors. Elizabeth and Julie later found a partner who helped the business expand and the founders prosper.

Despite their success, I don't expect the still-young entrepreneurial duo to retire any time soon. Creative entrepreneurs like Elizabeth and Julie seldom do so, or at least not for good. Entrepreneurs are notoriously "serial." Having learned the skills of small conscious business, they are often on the lookout for opportunities to start a new one.

Small businesses are a natural platform for Conscious Capitalism because they offer the freedom that comes with minimal infrastructure. Unlike big business, there is a direct line from an entrepreneur's vision to its manifestation. A business start-up might need a bank loan, but it does not require any approvals from a vice president or a board of directors.

What are the other characteristics, then, of conscious companies? When you are familiar with them, you can move into the marketplace and with confidence start identifying the businesses—large and small— that you want to get to know as a potential shopper, a jobholder, or an investor.

Three Characteristics of Conscious Capitalist Companies

Conscious Capitalism is distinguished from traditional capitalism by three main characteristics:

- A Conscious Capitalist company intentionally cultivates constructive and respectful relationships with all the parties that contribute to its success, not just investors.
- It embraces a purpose beyond earning money.

- It is committed to identifying its values and putting them into practice while doing business. This does of course require conscious leadership.

Let's take a look at these traits one by one.

A Great Business Cultivates Great Relationships

Conscious Capitalism views business as a system. For a system to thrive, every element within it must do well. Conscious Capitalists succeed in part because they create positive relationships with all contributors (or "stakeholders") without acquiescing to the interests of any one of them. Stakeholders are the parties with a "stake" in the success or failure of an entity, and every organization, private, public, co-op, or nonprofit, has them; they constitute the system in which a firm does business.

Who are they?

Customers. Customers align their Conscious Money with business, buying products that reflect their needs, values, and priorities and avoiding those that do not.

Employees. Many conscious leaders believe that if their companies take care of their employees, those employees will take care of the customers. Several Conscious Capitalists described in this chapter, Whole Foods, The Container Store, REI, and W. L. Gore & Associates—as well as Nordstrom, Google, and Starbucks—often appear on *Fortune's* "100 Best Companies to Work For" list, which meticulously surveys employees to identify which workplaces employees themselves rate as outstanding.

Investors. People who invest their capital in companies' operations are repaid when the companies are successful. Repayment takes the form of a rising stock price, regular payments called dividends, or both.

There are other stakeholders, such as the suppliers who provide goods and services, the communities in which companies operate, and society at large. The green movement advocates for the biggest stakeholder of all: the Earth. Taking into account all of these relationships is the first trademark of Conscious Capitalism. Not favoring one party over another helps to balance and stabilize conscious business.

When a company honors its stakeholders, it makes decisions in a way that differs greatly from traditional companies. And those policies are often highly beneficial to employees, as this story, for which I thank my researcher Joy Molony, illustrates.

Callie Micek, now age thirty-four, started working at The Container Store (TCS) in Houston in 2000, after graduating from Texas A&M University. Like all new hires, she received 260 hours of training—thirty times the industry average. "I just knew it was not just a job, but a career," says Callie.[18]

The Container Store's leadership profile offers good reason for Callie's optimism. Unlike many retailers, twelve out of fourteen vice presidents there are women. After just six months, Callie moved to the White Plains, New York, store as an inventory coordinator. "I'm from a small West Texas town, so it felt very glamorous." By 2006, she was building a new team at the midtown Manhattan store.

Callie was thriving financially—and personally. Full-time TCS salespeople average $46,000 per year, a far cry from the industry average of $25,000. She met her husband, a fellow TCS employee, in New York.

The couple returned to Texas to start a family. Many employers would be unable to accommodate such personal goals. The Container Store is not one of them. The company soon found her a position in Texas. When she later became pregnant, she received eight weeks of paid maternity leave and took two added weeks of paid vacation to spend with her baby. Later, TCS helped her find a position at corporate headquarters.

When the Great Recession hit, Callie was in the North Park Dallas store. Naturally, salespeople at many retailers worried about getting laid off. But TCS leadership made a decisive commitment: no layoffs.[19] The company temporarily suspended 401K matches to manage the balance sheet, a tradeoff that employees understood and accepted. When sales picked up, 401K matching benefits were back on.

"This is my calling," she says. "TCS has shaped my management style. It's how I became who I am."

Costco, a national discount retailer with more than 425 locations in most US states, is another great example of a company that earns success by honoring its many stakeholders. Costco takes good care of its employees. In 2012, the Simply Hired website estimated the average annual Costco salary at $61,0000 and compared with $30,000 for Costco rival Sam's Club. Costco also offers generous health insurance and 401K retirement plans and pays close attention to customer satisfaction too. It refuses to raise prices over a certain level. "This is not altruistic," says Costco CEO Jim Sinegal. "This is just good business."[20]

But Wall Street is not so happy. One investment analyst called Sinegal "too benevolent." "At Costco," complained another, "it's better to be a customer or an employee than a shareholder." Not so now, if it once was. As any stock chart can tell you, Costco has generally outperformed Wal-Mart of late. In one recent year, for example, Costco stock rose 20 percent while Wal-Mart stock remained flat.[21]

I'd rather work at Costco—and own their stock, too.

A Higher Purpose than Profit

While Conscious Capitalists earn sizable profits and market credibility even as they honor relationships, conscious business requires something more: a purpose beyond making money. That's the second trademark of conscious business.

The purpose of business is not to make money. It never was and can never be. Not because there is anything immoral about profit. On the contrary, profit rewards investors, fuels generous employee compensation, and funds the research and development that delights customers with new products. But profit is a business *result*, not a purpose.

Nikos Mourkogiannis, the author of *Purpose: The Starting Point of Great Companies* and a Greek who loves to quote Plato and evoke the ideals of ancient Greece, describes purpose as "a dialogue about the Good . . . that requires moral ideas."[22] While capitalism celebrates profit, it is purpose that infuses the quest for profit with consciousness. Purpose is therefore the soul of Conscious Capitalism. A conscious enterprise intends and seeks to earn money. But it exists to fulfill a larger objective, such as to "serve a customer," "make a difference," or "contribute to life."

Purpose Is Where You're Going

At one Conscious Capitalism gathering, I co-led a session with Roy Spence, chairman and cofounder of GSD&M Idea City, an Austin, Texas, marketing and branding firm that helps high-profile companies discover the power of their purpose. Roy is an engaging Texas character whose clients include Southwest Airlines founder Herb Kelleher, one of business's most enduring icons.

Roy talked about Kelleher's business plan, plotted on a cocktail napkin one night in San Antonio in 1971. The plan was to fly from Dallas to Houston to San Antonio and back to Houston—in that era a daring proposition. Airlines had yet to be deregulated, and only 15 percent of the American population had ever flown. Southwest was about to change all that. Today, 85 percent of Americans fly, thanks in part to Southwest's pursuit of its purpose: freedom—in this case, the freedom to travel.

After our session on the topic of purpose, I had the opportunity to ask Roy: "But what about the word that is most associated with Southwest, 'love'?"

"Love is Southwest's top value," says Roy.

"And the difference is?" I persisted.

"Purpose is where you're going. Values are how you get there."[23]

The Purpose of The Container Store

I am the type of person whose motto is "a place for everything and every-thing in its place," so The Container Store (TCS) is one of my favorite retailers. As I thought about how TCS shoe racks and desk organizers have improved my life, it occurred to me that the way the store has helped resolve my organization issues must be part of its purpose.

As we saw before in Callie Micek's story, TCS is founded on some powerful principles such as anticipating customer needs with fantastic employee training. As one of those happy customers, I could not help but speculate that perhaps TCS's purpose might not be just storage or order, but something grander, such as supporting customers who wish to get rid of clutter and create clear sacred space and better energetic flow.

It is a tenet of feng shui that messy environments prevent fresh energy from circulating. Clearing your clutter opens the door to new energy and the blessings it brings, including money. One common anecdote is that when people load trash bags full of old, unused belongings and haul them to Goodwill, they then receive unexpected financial rewards. What a great ritual for tough times.

It's good feng shui to own only the possessions you need, love, and use. The Container Store's storage products help people to house these items in an orderly, dedicated way.

The Business of Values

Values are central to business and personal success. While many people are tossed about by external forces, the individual or company with strong values possesses an inner compass that directs the course, providing focus and inspiration through the inevitable challenges we all confront.

The third trademark of a conscious business is knowing and honoring values. When individuals invoke their values as they make choices, they can transcend ordinary experience to express their greatest potential. The same is true for a company. When a business genuinely embraces values, it sets a higher standard for people to live up to. Such standards may also exceed those of its competitors. This commitment creates a unique platform for a company's success, and distinguishes it from its peers.

Some people scoff at the very idea of values being relevant to business, and maybe they have reason to do so. Perhaps the company they work for has lauded a value, like excellence—but used it to justify overworking people to achieve its monetary goals. Such a distortion understandably causes skepticism, even cynicism.

In fact, one of the first things you or I notice upon entering a place of business is its values. Walk into any shop or store. Within minutes, you can get a very good read on the values espoused there—or the lack thereof. The failure of values spawns a poor work environment that breeds boredom, gossip, and inattention to customers. On the other hand, when values are honored, they're visible and palpable, whether in people's behavior or in corporate policy.

At Whole Foods Market, for example, signs that display and express company values, such as "satisfying and delighting our customers," are posted on the store walls. These values are put into practice on the spot. Whole Foods encourages customers to try new products and to return items they do not like. I've taken them up on this offer more than once. When I returned an item, the team members were always gracious. I was "delighted." So I bought more.

In the profit-oriented world of business, values reside in people. It is generally believed that a leader's job is to determine which values a company stands for. But leaders cannot touch people where they live—unless those leaders themselves personify values that their people cherish. So in fact, values are ultimately a sort of collaboration between the leaders and the people they lead. The world's most conscious CEOs, managers, and executives place values at the core of their leadership practice.

Living by Their Values

Consider these examples of corporations that have clear values and live by them:

Interface, Inc., one of the world's greatest corporate environmentalists, launched its green vision long before most businesses and people focused on sustainability. Initially sales and profits slumped, but the late CEO Ray Anderson demonstrated the courage and conviction to stay the course. As he continued to do so, his commitment to the environment later inspired the winning strategy of making and selling recyclable carpet tiles, thereby keeping vast amounts of used carpeting out of dump sites. By the time the rest of the business world grew to embrace environmentalism, Interface's star had ascended and its example taught other companies how to go green.

The internet sales company eBay is built on the value of trust. Early on, founder Pierre Omidyar posted this statement on the website: "We believe people are basically good."[24] Trust became the core of eBay's commercial policies. eBay technology reinforced that trust, so that considerably less than 1 percent of eBay transactions resulted in fraud.[25]

Agilent, the world's leading maker of measurement equipment with annual sales of $6.6 billion, was once compelled to lay off thousands of its people. But Agilent did so with heart, exemplifying the values of truthfulness and trust in its commitment to openness and transparency in word and deed. The company informed employees about the layoffs before the media or anyone else could. Agilent specially trained its managers to relate honestly, compassionately, and respectfully with those who were losing their jobs. Even ex-employees later sang the firm's praises.[26]

The stated principles of Conscious Capitalist Green Mountain Coffee Roasters, available on its website, include sustainability and a vibrant workplace. But observe the Vermont-based company's actions and you will also find a commitment to the values of social justice, personal growth, and spirituality. In 2010, Green Mountain was named to "The 100 Best Corporate Citizens" list and is a leader in the free trade movement, described in chapter 5.[27] In 2008, the International Center for Spirit at Work presented its annual award to Green Mountain for fostering an environment where employees practice spirituality, meditation, yoga, and appreciative inquiry, the art of asking questions to bring out constructive potential instead of negative diagnosis or criticism.

Green Mountain, cited in the past as a "Best Medium Company to Work for in America,"[28] grew so rapidly between 2009 and 2011—from a $700 million to a $2.6 billion company—that it can no longer be considered for that honor. But expansion hasn't dimmed its values.

Green Mountain's commitment to meditation and other conscious tools enhances the lives of its employees. Green Mountain senior graphic designer Ryan Dreimiller, who is thirty-nine years old, enrolled in the company's mindful meditation course and reaped solid benefits. "I'm less distracted and less reactive to situations around me. I get more done, and I'm easier to live with."[29]

Employees have a good chance of securing coveted benefits such as leadership coaching. Josh Martin, age thirty-three, a service process improvement coordinator for Green Mountain, puts it this way: "I've never been told no . . . My requests are always met with 'Go for it.'"[30]

Corporate Culture 101

When a business's leaders consistently affirm values like trust, truth, and courage, they forge those ideals into the foundation of a corporate culture. In addition to observing a company's atmosphere, you can collect great clues about its culture when connecting with a company on the phone or reading its advertisements. But corporate culture runs even deeper than that: a culture's values determine which behaviors a company rewards. Thus corporate culture is fundamental to the choices we make as individuals about whether to work at, invest in, or patronize a company.

Advising companies on how to develop "humane, collaborative, and economically vibrant" business environments is the goal of Gerry McDonough, CEO of LeadFirst Learning Systems, based in Charlotte, North Carolina. McDonough, a man who is part wise professor and part no-nonsense consultant, has measured, quantified, and sometimes transformed more than nine thousand corporate cultures in his twenty-five-year career. He classifies corporate cultures as either aggressive, passive-aggressive (defensive), or competent.[31]

The nature of a corporate culture has profound effects on the individuals who work there, in particular. As I see it, a passive-aggressive, or defensive, culture fails to ignite the genius of consciousness, while an aggressive culture beats human consciousness into submission. A balanced, competent culture, on the other hand, powerfully nurtures the genius of consciousness—none more so that Conscious Capitalist W. L. Gore & Associates.

W. L. Gore & Associates CEO Terri Kelly is as elegant a female executive as you'll ever meet. A twenty-five-year Gore engineering veteran, she took charge of the now $3 billion firm in 2005. Terri considers herself fortunate to be free to execute global strategies rather than to focus on instilling strong values.[32] That is because the company's values were firmly established back in 1958, when Bill Gore and his wife, Vieve, manifested their vision: to re-create the *esprit de corps* Bill had loved while working on a small task force at chemical giant Dupont. Why can't an entire company run like this? he asked.[33]

Though Gore is best known for the ubiquitous outdoor fabric Gore-Tex, the company also manufactures medical devices, guitar strings, filters, cellular telephone parts, and fuel cell technologies. "Polymers unite Gore's diverse product line," says Terri.

But it's the "glue" of Gore's values and culture that fascinates business analysts and global industry leaders who visit Gore's Delaware headquarters to try to crack its innovation code. I met the Gores in 1985, shortly before

Bill passed away. I still recall him speaking about his management philosophy: "It is commitment, not authority, that creates results." Commitment and freedom are arguably two of Gore's top values, and both foster innovation and success at W. L. Gore & Associates.

The company breaks tradition with its emphasis not on leadership but "followership," which is clearly another core value. As Terri explains, "You are only a leader when someone follows you."[34] How does it work in practice? If you're a Gore associate with an idea for a new product, you call a meeting. If people sign on to your project, you're a leader.

The home page of the Gore website, consulted in spring 2012, puts forth several intriguing questions that successively flash across your computer screen. The one that caught my eye asked: "Can a company known for fairness, trust, and integrity consistently produce innovation?" The answer is yes, and the reasons why are its values and culture.

As a Conscious Money practitioner, it is very likely that you will want to do business with companies that possess a balanced, stimulating culture and that reward competence while avoiding active or passive aggression. Gerry McDonough's findings make it clear that authentic values are the best and most sustainable way to engage and motivate employees. As you will see in later chapters, consumers and investors are equally motivated by positive values.

Researching Conscious Businesses

You now know about many of the practices and values of specific Conscious Capitalist companies. While feeding your mental faculties with the information in this chapter, you may also have gained an instinctive sense of the business environments and practices that attract you. It's time to turn inward, tap into your intuitive potential, and "get a feel" for companies where you might want to do business.

Intuitive Contemplation

1. *Creating a sacred space.* Pick a time and place where you won't be disturbed for about fifteen minutes.
2. *Collecting questions.* Think of a company you might want to work for or otherwise do business with, perhaps as a supplier or customer. Identify any issues or questions you have about the firm. (You can jot these down in your journal.) Later you will research these questions. But since research might prejudice you one way or the other, take the next intuitive step first.
3. *Connecting to a "felt sense."* Take five deep, slow breaths to relax. Spend the next five minutes attempting to "feel into" the business. Notice any place in your body that enters your awareness. If you feel constriction, for example, inquire as to what that feeling might be telling you. If your heart feels open, invite it to speak its message.
4. *Harvesting the fruits of intuition.* Afterward, write down any thoughts and feelings that arose for you. When you access intuition, you enter an altered state of consciousness. Like a dream remembered on waking, the fruits of intuition can sometimes fade as you go about your day. That's why it's good to take some notes.

Research On- and Offline

Turn back to the issues you had noted in the second point listed above. This time, instead of the intuitive approach, you'll draw on your mental facilities to research and gather useful data.

You can check out a wealth of information about local and national businesses on the web. But don't limit yourself to company websites. Seek out sites where customers or employees rate firms, such as Glassdoor.com, which lists free reviews of more than ten thousand companies. Turn to your social and professional network to see what insiders know of the company or companies that particularly interest you.

Visiting a Place of Business

Perhaps you have read glowing reports about a company, restaurant, or local boutique on its website, yet read harsh criticism of the same place elsewhere. How do you know which is true? Or perhaps you simply want to experience the business yourself for any reason. It's possible to plan a visit in order to gather valuable, in-person "intelligence."

Set up a brief meeting with a manager, executive, or perhaps the owner of a small store. If none are available, ask to speak with someone else who works there. (Avoid combining this visit with a job interview, which has a very different purpose.)

Prepare in advance for your visit. Spend some time developing a short list of your best questions. You may want to do a meditation on seeking truth. To be fully present and to observe your surroundings once onsite, you can review the following points before your visit:

- Consider the physical space. Old or new, the energy should feel fresh. Look for a positive vibrant atmosphere.
- Study the employees and how they relate to each other and present themselves.
- Observe any interactions between managers and employees in order to try to get a feel for the company's management style.
- Notice the noise level. Listen for an agreeable, productive hum.

After your visit to the company, take some time in a quiet place and debrief by collecting your impressions in your journal. How did your initial sense of the company measure against the findings of your personal visit? What is your intuition telling you about the place? How would you describe the environment? Is this a company with which you would feel good doing business—whether as a shopper, employee, supplier, or investor?

Getting to Know Some Conscious Money Companies

What follows is a list of companies that embody some and, in a few cases, many of the trademarks of Conscious Money and Conscious Capitalism. But this list is not intended as a statement about which firms are conscious and which, by their absence, are not. Its purpose is rather to offer examples to help you get a handle on conscious business. There are today many exciting new companies appearing on the scene, as the megatrend of Conscious Capitalism accelerates. Two that immediately come to mind are in the shoe business: Zappos and TOMS, both of which certainly look to be highly conscious. In this list, however, I've limited myself to companies that I have been observing or experiencing for a decade or more.

As you review the list, remember that a company's strategy, policies, and culture can swiftly change with new leadership. Troubling information can also come to light and quickly change the public perception about a company or its brand. In describing these companies I sometimes cite details to help you get a feel for the company, and not always as a marker for a company's level of consciousness.

There are undoubtedly hundreds of Conscious Capitalists that I have not encountered, most probably thousands. This list describes mostly large companies because these, rather than smaller local firms, offer most readers the chance for in-person study.

To enhance your knowledge about conscious business, select two or three of these corporations to follow in the media. As you learn more about them, consider whether you might want to do business with them—and why. Identify which companies listed here sound like interesting places to work and decide if you want to pursue a position there.

As a consumer, you might sample one or more of the products these firms offer. If you are a conscious entrepreneur or small business person, these corporations might represent attractive markets for your products or services.

This is a general list for consumers, potential employees, suppliers, and other partners. In some cases, you may want to evaluate the companies on this list as possible investments. But do so in conjunction with an investment advisor. Several of these companies are private, so their stock is not available on the public market. Although this list may inspire investment ideas for some, it is not designed or intended as an investment "buy" list.

Google: At Google, a top global innovator, engineers invest 20 percent of their time on pet projects. Outstanding benefits keep the consciousness of more than thirty thousand employees in top creative form. Google is so green that it won a place on SustainableBusiness.com's short list of the top twenty firms.

Nordstrom: This department store would be my favorite even if it were not one of *Fortune's* "100 Best Companies to Work For." But that distinction certainly explains a lot about my experience as a customer. When I walk inside, I instantly inhale what feels to me like a rush of consciousness, positive energy, and an alertness in the salespeople that sets the gold standard for customer service, leaving competitors in the dust.

REI: Must a Conscious Capitalist be a corporation? Not necessarily. Outdoor outfitter REI (Recreation Equipment Inc.) is a customer-owned co-op. CEO Sally Jewell, a fit, fresh-faced woman and a great model for REI active wear, explains one way REI fulfills its purpose: by supporting organizations that take inactive urban kids—who watch too much television—on outdoor adventures, thereby cultivating a relationship with local communities. Beloved by customer/owners, who get a nice annual rebate on their purchases, and by employees, who consistently rate it a "Great Place to Work," this co-op is as financially stable as many corporations.

Novo Nordisk: The Danish pharmaceutical firm, and the world's largest insulin maker, has a powerful purpose: to cure diabetes and put itself out of business. The company invited animal rights activists into its laboratories to bear witness to its conducting of compassionate animal research, thereby demonstrating a strong commitment to the value of transparency.

3M: Former CEO George Buckley, who retired in 2012, restored 3M's famous creative culture after a past CEO had clamped down on innovation. The company makes consumers happy with Post-it Notes and Thinsulate. Engineers at 3M now spend 15 percent of their time on favorite projects. Because of that initiative, new products released over a five-year period can account for 25 to 33 percent of sales.

Intel: The global computer chip maker is widely admired as an exemplary environmentalist, in particular for corporate initiatives to reduce greenhouse gases. Intel often wins awards as an employer and corporate citizen. The corporation also disperses a 3 percent dividend.

Genentech: Employees arrive at work greeted by posters of people healed by the company's medicines. Says CEO Arthur Levinson, "Hire innovative people, listen to them tell you what they want, and do it." Genentech nationally is rated as having one of the top ten best employee retirement plans.

Starbucks: Even part-timers are eligible for health insurance, and the company's planetary contribution to the Fair Trade movement is extraordinary.

Medtronic: This medical technology firm invented the pacemaker and features an in-house meditation center. Retired CEO Bill George, who now teaches at Harvard Business School, stood up to Wall Street: "We are not in business to create shareholder value, but to heal patients." Medtronic's "Medallion Ceremony" initiates new employees into the firm's culture and values.

Costco: Customers, employees, and investors are pleased with low prices, exemplary labor standards, and strong shareholder value, respectively. Thus Costco exemplifies the Conscious Capitalism principle of honoring relationships with all stakeholders.

Herman Miller: Founded on spiritual and humane principles, this famous environmentalist design company created the iconic Aeron chair. It is known for collaborating with gifted artists such as Charles and Ray Eames and also supports young, yet-to-be-recognized talent.

Whole Foods: The company's commitment to Conscious Capitalism is everywhere. Its values are broadcasted on huge posters on store walls. Employees, called team members, make virtually all decisions locally. Stores are 100 percent wind-powered. During the recession, Whole Foods delighted customers with lower prices. And the company thrives financially. During one recent quarter, profit surged nearly 80 percent.[35] What about investors? Consult any online financial site, enter the company's stock symbol, WFM, and you will soon see Whole Foods shareholders are a very happy lot.

Ford: This business icon made my Conscious Company list even before it refused a government bailout and returned to profitability. Ford was the first American automobile manufacturer to offer a hybrid vehicle. Ford's employee faith-based initiatives also helped heal community tensions in Arab-American Detroit after September 11, 2001.

Green Mountain Coffee Roasters: An impressive 86 percent of Green Mountain employees agree they have "special and unique" benefits. Since 1992, Green Mountain has sponsored employee trips to coffee plantations, where they meet farmers face to face, and handpick the coffee crop. Thirteen percent of full-time employees have participated. Having seen the hard work of growing coffee, one employee (according to company lore) carefully swept up a single coffee bean.[36]

Eileen Fisher: This company's devotion to social awareness engages and inspires employees, while the benefits at this high-quality fashion retailer are beyond generous, including two $1,000 annual stipends, one for education and one for wellness, as well as great healthcare, bonuses, and liberal employee discounts.

W. L. Gore & Associates: The company has been awarded a place on the "100 Best Places to Work" every year since 1984.

The Container Store: This is a company known for supporting its people to deliver inspired customer service. Management refused to lay off associates during the Great Recession. It would probably delight investors, too, except that it is privately held.

Joie de Vivre: Founder Chip Conley articulates the Conscious Capitalist philosophy of Joie de Vivre, a stylish, innovative collection of forty boutique hotels, restaurants and spas, in his book *Peak: How Great Companies Get Their Mojo from Maslow.* Conley argues that key stakeholders—employees, customers and investors—are motivated by peak experiences. Companies that address the near universal desire for peak experience, which is rarely acknowledged in business, can flourish. This approach helped Joie de Vivre, which employs three thousand people and was named the second best place to work in San Francisco, to triple revenues from 2001 to 2008.

The Deeper Meaning of Conscious Business

Conscious Capitalism is a new economic operating system that represents the sort of upgrade we only witness once every two or three hundred years. In this emerging economic order, commercial success is fueled not by greed but by purpose, values, and positive relationships.

Today "nice guys" finish first. They may indeed be nice. But, as we have seen, they also earn profits that are more sustainable. A "kinder, gentler" capitalism earns more money not just because it is kind or gentle; it is also productive and efficient. Conscious Capitalism, which honors a higher purpose, succeeds where its secular cousin fails, because spiritual values can be profoundly practical.

Conscious Capitalism will continue to flourish because it considers the whole of the business ecosystem. It is wise to be responsible for the environment in which you live and work. It is also a better way to do business: when you understand that larger environment, you are better prepared to mitigate risk and maximize opportunity.

R. Edward Freeman, a professor at the University of Virginia's Darden School of Business, captures the spirit of this change in business when he states: "Conscious Capitalism is the new story of business."[37]

In 2010, I spoke at a Conscious Capitalism gathering at Lake Arrowhead, California, where spiritual teacher Marianne Williamson addressed the group as well. Marianne expressed a truth I've vaguely sensed yet never dared to attempt to articulate. Somehow I did not think it would "work" with businesspeople. Yet as she spoke, I felt something powerful coming forward:

"You think Conscious Capitalism will succeed because it earns more money," she stated fearlessly. In fact I had often made this very argument. "That is incorrect," she continued. Silently, I wondered where she was going next.

"We will succeed because Conscious Capitalism contributes to life."[38]

Exercises

Identify a Business's Values

A business's values can often be found on its website or another business platform. But this exercise is about your direct experience of those values, which may or may not match the company's view. This exercise may also help you get a handle on a company's purpose. Earlier you researched and explored your felt sense about a company. Now with this checklist expand your take on the company by focusing in on its values:

- What is the firm's reputation? How is it portrayed in the media?
- How well, or poorly, does it treat you as a customer?
- Does its brand reflect positive, uplifting values?
- What is the quality of its products?

- Are people eager to work there? Would you work there?
- Does the company give back to communities?
- How do employees characterize the company's values?

Conscious Capitalism Trademarks Checklist

Look for these characteristics as you consider doing business with a company as conscious as you are:

Positive Stakeholder Relationships
Treats its people fairly and well
Satisfies and delights customers
Expects employees to go out of their way to deliver customer service
Produces sustainable shareholder value
Commits to the enterprise as a whole

Purpose
Has a purpose beyond moneymaking
Embodies and lives up to that purpose
Expresses its purpose in policies, marketing, and actions

Healthy Values and Culture
Endorses, advocates, and lives transcendent values
Promotes healthy, positive productivity, not aggressive competition
Seeks the satisfaction of all stakeholders

Options

Reflect

- Tune in to the consciousness of the businesses around you.

- Keep the trademarks of conscious business, (relationships, purpose, and values), in your wallet, mobile device, or on a sticky note at your desk.
- Evaluate your local bank, grocery, drugstore, dry cleaner, and discount and department stores in terms of these trademarks.
- Clearly articulate the purpose of your own financial life and the values that inspire your monetary choices. How do these shape your choices as you do business with companies?
- Become comfortable explaining the hallmarks of Conscious Capitalism to your friends and family.

Resources

- Each January, review *Fortune's* annual list of the "100 Best Companies to Work For" or find the archived list online.
- Find great small and midsize workplaces in *Entrepreneur* magazine.
- Deepen your knowledge of Conscious Capitalism by reading *Megatrends 2010: The Rise of Conscious Capitalism* and *Firms of Endearment*.
- Visit the comprehensive website ConsciousCapitalism.org for conferences and numerous additional resources.
- Check out Lisa Ann Schraffa's conscious fashion blog at style64.blogspot.com

Right Action

- Work for, shop at, and invest in businesses that honor the trademarks of Conscious Capitalism.
- Set out to discover three local conscious stores with whom you want to do business.
- Be particularly supportive of local companies famed for treating their employees especially well.

- Identify the values and purposes of the companies you frequent.
- Like the businesses that cultivate stakeholder relationships, nurture your relationships with people who have a stake in your financial success.
- Start a conscious business reading or study group.
- Visit two or three conscious businesses.
- Invite the conscious businesspeople you meet to address your group.

Conscious Money Affirmation

I do business with companies that cultivate positive relationships with all stakeholders, embrace a higher purpose than profit, and honor transcendent values.

5

The Joy of Mindful Spending

Now that we have discussed the inner principles of Conscious Money along with the characteristics of Conscious Capitalist companies, it's time to put these tools and this wisdom to work as you make financial choices in the shops, stores, and markets you visit. In an economy where the primary basis of exchange is money, everyone spends. As people become more conscious about their financial choices, however, they will naturally want to spend their money with greater intention and awareness.

Individuals often think that the overwhelming power of big corporations dominates the economy. So many doubt that their actions, however well intended, can really make a difference in the marketplace. But that is not the case. Nearly 70 percent of the United States' gross national product is directly comprised of the spending of consumers like you and me. If we ignore our economic power, we endorse and validate unconscious capitalism. By embracing the strength of our commercial influence, on the other hand, we actively assume responsibility for determining which products succeed or fail, instead of blaming Madison Avenue or Wall Street.

If you want to change the world, you possess the power to do so when your wallet mirrors your values. For personal fulfillment and to transform the marketplace of humanity, choose to shop mindfully.

The inner dimension of mindful spending is the personal and spiritual fulfillment you experience when your purchases reflect your values and your integrity. On a more external level, however, mindful spending also requires a good deal of conscious decision making. Carefully consider each potential purchase. Inquire as to whether there's a more sustainable way to acquire it, for example, with a vintage purchase or by borrowing from, or bartering with, a friend or through a website such as Freecycle.org, which lists various communities where people can post items they want to give away, barter, or trade.

It is also important to determine, through an honest personal appraisal, whether a prospective purchase is genuinely useful and meaningful for you or an empty gesture, whose only purpose is to fill your need for something that is unsatisfying right now in your life, such as love, companionship, self-esteem, well-being, free time, or the bolstering of a fragile sense of identity. Compulsive spending requires professional counseling, of course, but people who occasionally shop for emotional reasons can more successfully resolve such issues with inner work, which also enhances self-mastery, rather than by the kind of "shopping therapy" that will send them into debt.

When you shop with your values, you chose your purchases from the inside out, based on the values you hold most dear. Such a stance rejects the credo of a consumerist society, which sanctions the purchase of more and more goods. People who overconsume allow the media and its marketing messages to determine their financial choices. When you shop with your values, by contrast, it is your inner self that shapes your spending decisions. Shopping with your values feels good because it fosters a natural harmony between your ideals and the actions you take in the marketplace. But to shop with your values, you must be very clear about what those values are.

Identify Your Top Consumer Values

Earlier you chose your top personal values, including transcendent values like Compassion or Truth, as well as some practical values. From that list, note the values that influence you as a consumer. You will probably "take" those values with you when shopping. But it's also possible that there are additional values, or priorities, that come into play when you go to the store. These consumer values might include durability or frugality. Please review the list below, which includes both transcendent and practical consumer values. Feel free to add to or focus on any additional values that inspire your own mindful spending. This list is intended to suggest possible values but not replace the values you hold most dear.

Affordability	Durability	Integrity	Safety	Sustainability
Authenticity	Ecology	Joy	Self-reliance	Transparency
Beauty	Elegance	Love	Sensuality	
Comfort	Frugality	Modesty	Simplicity	
Compassion	Health	Quality	Social justice	

Write down in your Conscious Money journal the top five values that shape you as a consumer. Briefly describe why these values matter to you. As you did earlier, you might also accept the challenge of isolating a single top consumer value, one that you know will always engage you because you feel so strongly about it. It could be either a "practical" or more transcendent value, so long as it embodies you as a consumer.

The next time you go shopping, take your top consumer value or values along with you—literally. Write them out on a piece of paper or enter them in your favorite digital device. Then if you wonder whether or not to buy an item, review your values list to clarify your choice.

You practice mindful spending when you follow these steps:

1. Tune out mindless marketing messages. Refuse to be manipulated. Ask yourself: Do I really need this, or even want it? Make your shopping list a free will zone.
2. Look within for your consumer values and align those values with your desires. For example, if you are inspired by *social justice* from the list of values just provided, allow that value to shape you as a shopper.
3. Then scan the marketplace for items that reflect your conscientiousness about social justice or another chosen value. Boycott brands that violate your values.

Conscious Spending Is Here to Stay

Some skeptics wonder if the green movement is nothing but a Madison Avenue marketing scheme to help corporations sell products that appear to satisfy people's desire to make a planetary difference or take advantage of their idealism. My professional opinion is that this is not the case and that sustainability is a grassroots, transformative trend that's anchored in conscious consumers. The virtue of sustainability was born of humanity's love of nature, forged by the fire of human values, and tempered in tough economic times. This enduring value has already proven to be authentic. Many pundits predicted that the willingness of shoppers to buy green products would wither away in the face of an economic downturn. It did not. (Of course, spending is hardly the only or best way to be sustainable. When we recycle plastics, paper, and clothing, it usually doesn't cost a dime.) Green spending, however, is a useful indicator since it can be carefully measured.

During the Great Recession, 10 percent of shoppers did in fact spend less on green products, but 35 percent of consumers spent more, and 65 percent of shoppers spent more money on products that "benefit a good cause," reports Edward Kerschner, chief strategist for Citigroup's Global Wealth Management unit, as noted in a *Fortune* magazine story.[1]

Furthermore, underlying and animating the meaning of sustainability are transcendent values like Love and Truth: truth as in, "We are poisoning our planet and our bodies, and I will stop it now by rethinking my Conscious Money choices every day," and love as in, "I commit to loving the planet, and the community of living beings dwelling on it."

At the same time, discerning consumers are on the lookout for what some call "greenwashing," that is, superficial corporate policies that appear "environmentalist" in order to promote a marketing strategy:

- In the United States, 39 percent of shoppers say companies' assertions about the environment are "not accurate."[2]
- Most people, 81 percent, care more about what companies *do* than what they say.[3]
- Of conscious consumers polled, 80 percent want trusted, independent sources to verify the authenticity of corporate claims.[4]
- More than 40 percent of all shoppers want to buy products with a seal or certification.[5]

Furthermore, at a time when activists and watchdogs can instantly debunk fraudulent product claims, legitimate brands cannot survive, let alone succeed, by willingly misleading customers. The value of trust today is priceless.

"We're seeing a shift from conspicuous consumption to conscious consumption," concluded Citigroup's Kerschner.[6]

A Note on Sustainability

The virtue of sustainability propelled the green movement into public awareness. The verb "sustain," says Merriam-Webster.com, means using a resource so that it is "not depleted or permanently damaged." That definition invokes ideals like stewardship, responsibility, and a longer-term time horizon. So today mindful consumers contemplate a host of new green options, from Energy Star appliances to geothermal energy, from CFL or LED lighting to e-waste recycling, from VOC-free paints to green building. These choices—and many more I have not listed here—are fully worthy of your consideration. But because sustainability is such a large and growing area, I will focus on a few major sectors that impact most people, including transportation, personal care, and household products, which embody the values of well-being, sustainability, or both. We'll also explore the consumer sector that exemplifies the value of social justice.

The Energy of Mindful Spending

Mindful spending is vital to your money life. Your spending habits are as important to your Conscious Money practice as the money you earn or how wisely you invest it. When spending is thoughtless or unconscious, you are probably overspending, a habit that undermines Conscious Wealth creation.

But a person's spending is also a question of energy. Money is a current, as the word "currency," a synonym for money, suggests. Picture the lively currents animating a bubbly spring stream. Like these currents, money is in constant motion. Even when money appears safely deposited into your savings account, it is subject to the forces of inflation and deflation, the economic equivalent of the universal principles of expansion and contraction.

Saving is vital to Conscious Money. But if we try to confine money too much or for too long, its energy stagnates. That's why spending and giving are essential aspects of Conscious Money. It is true that overspending won't help you grow Conscious Money. But if we go too far in the opposite direction and hoard our resources, we miss the mark and begrudge ourselves and others of pleasure and fulfillment.

Mindful spending, by contrast, evokes a balanced flow of money that is essential to Conscious Money, because money is energy and the energy of Conscious Money is in its essence a clear, coherent, and positive vibration. When you spend (or give) money with discernment and intention, it is an act of choice, self-expression, and joy.

But mindless spending creates a very different scenario. Have you ever overspent and later experienced remorse? Many years ago, this would happen to me when I would buy a lot of expensive clothing. Even though I could afford the clothes financially, I could not spiritually "afford" owning things I did not really need or enjoy. I felt remorse as an unpleasant sensation low in my stomach which seemed to say, "Not only did you spend too much, what you bought is not even what you really want." I later looked within about my clothing expenditures and discovered to my surprise that what I really wanted was more quality time with my loved ones.

Over time, I learned that what I genuinely enjoyed was purchasing only the clothing I both wanted and needed and returning anything that did not seem like a good idea when I brought it home.

Many years later, I spent a goodly sum furnishing a new home—and it felt wonderful. First, I could afford the purchase, because I had the funds in the proceeds from of my previous home, which was sold partly furnished. So I needed and had budgeted for the new furniture. Second, the quality of the pieces I chose were in good proportion to their cost: it felt like an excellent value. Finally, each detail of my new furniture—its style, size, fabric, color, and wood—deeply pleased me and suited my new home. Looking back, I realize that the values I was honoring were balance, value, and quality. That experience began to define mindful spending for me. If you spend in a way that's meaningful and satisfying, aligned with your values, and appropriate to your overall financial situation, you are probably spending mindfully.

Mindful Spending and Fair Trade

When you and I honor values like justice, well-being, or compassion in the marketplace, we may do it for ourselves and for the environment. But today, there is also a growing movement to consider and respect the people who produce the items we buy. This new and expanding consumer trend challenges one of the most basic assumptions in free enterprise: that buyers always seek the lowest price, which some call the free trade price. To which mindful shoppers reply, "No, thanks. We choose to pay a fair price and to be sure the producer receives a living wage." This is the philosophy behind the growing phenomenon of Fair Trade.

"The roots of Fair Trade are in coffee, but the model can be applied to many more categories, and in recent years the list of certified products has expanded dramatically," said Paul Rice, President and CEO of Fair Trade USA. "Fair Trade empowers consumers to make a difference. With every cup of coffee, every bar of chocolate and every banana we can actually lift people out of poverty and help preserve the land."[7]

Fair Trade (FT for short) products must be certified to meet social and economic standards. The two largest certifiers are Fairtrade International and Fair Trade USA, although there are other certifying outfits. The standards that each endorses, while similar, do vary somewhat.

FT shoppers refuse to support a system where farmers with no bargaining power cannot receive the prices they need to survive and invest in their business or community. Fair Trade advocates might also consider that farmers faced with such an untenable system may turn to growing drug crops for needed revenue, thus destabilizing communities from the poppy fields in Asia to cities in Latin America to the streets of Amsterdam.

Carolyn Long, age sixty-eight, of Chevy Chase, Maryland, starts her day with a ritual of mindful reflection, global responsibility, and the aromatic scent of FT-sourced Ethiopian light-roast coffee. "It means a lot to know my choice is making a difference in the lives of farmers," says Carolyn, who also enjoys Chocolove organic FT chocolate bars.[8]

Carolyn would buy more FT products if she knew where to find them. A recent survey revealed that 62 percent of consumers feel the same way. Today, Fair Trade USA's "Fair Trade Finder" mobile applications for iPhone and Android deliver a national directory of FT-certified products. Fair Trade fans can now tag their favorite products and share their locations with other users. Find out how to download the free app in this chapter's options.[9]

The Conscious Money of millions of FT advocates fosters empowerment instead of exploitation and promotes the self-sufficiency of 1.2 million farmers and workers in seventy countries throughout Asia, Latin America, Oceania, the Caribbean, and Africa. Fair Trade shoppers have translated the spiritual value of compassion into a $4.5 billion global movement, which grew 15 percent in 2009, despite the global recession.[10]

Fair Trade sales were flat in 2010, but rose dramatically the following year, according to Paul Rice of Fair Trade USA, which estimates 2011 US Fair Trade sales alone at $1.2 billion.[11]

The efforts of FT shoppers are transforming the marketplace through social justice: more than sixty thousand locations in the United States sell ten thousand FT products, such as tea, sugar, fruit, chocolate, and soccer balls.[12] New FT products regularly appear on the shelves. Today, South Africa exports FT wine and the Palestinian West Bank exports FT olive oil. You can find FT vodka and even FT-mined gold.

Your Conscious Money Fair Trade Options

Look for the FT label whenever you shop. Lobby your favorite stores to expand their FT offerings and be sure to thank them when they do. Here are several popular items and stores where you can find them:[13]

- Buy FT bananas, rice, and body care at Whole Foods.
- Find FT flowers at the local Giant supermarket.
- Pick up Ben & Jerry's diverse array of FT ice-cream flavors anywhere.
- Dagoba chocolate, made with FT-certified cacao, is widely available.
- Get your Kirkland Signature FT coffee at Costco.
- Buy FT wine at Sam's Club, Target, or Whole Foods.

- You'll also find FT products at Wal-Mart, Wegman's, Trader Joe's, and Kroger.

Coffee

The most ubiquitous FT product is still coffee. In 2010, Fair Trade USA certified more than 100 million pounds of FT coffee. More than half of FT coffee is also organic.[14] Green Mountain Coffee Roasters is committed to purchasing at least 30 percent FT beans.[15] If you start your day at Starbucks, know that Starbucks began buying Fair Trade coffee in 2000. Its role was critical in building the FT coffee market in the United States. Starbucks offers FT-certified French Roast coffee.[16]

"In the hyper-caffeinated world of coffee marketing, it is very difficult to tell the truth from a load of beans," says Dean Cycon of Dean's Beans.[17] His company sells five hundred thousand pounds of FT organic coffee each year. "The choices we make at the supermarket and café impact millions of people around the world. Fair Trade works."

Dunkin' Donuts was the first national brand to sell espresso drinks made exclusively of FT beans.[18] The criteria of specialty outfits such as Portland, Oregon's, Stumptown Coffee and Sustainable Harvest can rival or exceed FT standards in order to guarantee sound ecological practices and delicious coffee.[19] Peet's Coffee, Allegro, and Crop to Cup are also respected for their high standards for social and environmental responsibility and direct relationships with coffee growers. Fair Trade coffee has gained more and more fans over the years.

United States FT fans can take inspiration from the United Kingdom. The beans of Ireland's Insomnia Coffee Company are 100 percent Fair Trade. British national retailer Marks & Spencer's coffee sells only FT coffee and tea.[20] Virgin Airlines serves an estimated twelve million cups of coffee and tea per day: all of it Fair Trade. The airline recently added green tea to its FT offerings.[21]

Handicrafts and Justice

"Social change consumers" spend $45 billion a year, says eBay's Robert Chatwani, who helped build the website of Good World Solutions (GWS), formerly known as World of Good.[22] Founded by Priya Haji, and featured on PBS's *NewsHour with Jim Lehrer*, GWS works with thirty thousand artisans and workers globally. The GWS Fair Wage Guide is an open-source web-based platform that calculates the wages workers and craftspeople need to support themselves and their communities. "Our technology gives workers a voice," says GWS director Heather Franzese. Today it is used by 900 companies in eighty-one countries. Good World Solutions' latest tool, Labor Link, surveys artisans directly via cellphone.[23]

The organization Ten Thousand Villages supports tens of thousands of artisans; its 256 stores sell "eclectic village wares" from more than thirty countries. The Ethisphere Institute named Ten Thousand Villages one of the "World's Most Ethical Companies."[24]

Fair Trade handicrafts illuminate awareness by focusing on the people who make each handcrafted item, reminding us that every FT purchase is a values statement. It is a joy to know that each object is filled with the craftsperson's soul and character.

As Buckminster Fuller, the great American engineer, inventor, and futurist, said: "You never change things by fighting the existing reality. . . [instead] build a new model that makes the existing model obsolete."[25] That's exactly what the entire Fair Trade movement—from crafts to coffee, and from farmers and certifiers to consumers—is well along the way toward achieving.

The Value of Well-Being: Our Bodies, Our Selves

Conscious shoppers have transformed the produce section by celebrating the organic and local food trends. But today they've expanded their vigilance to drugstores and the cosmetic aisle. That's because of the many toxic chemicals that show up in the products we apply on our bodies or use at home.

As we grow more concerned about the impact of these toxins on well-being, we also ask: But what about their residues? Aren't they harming the environment, too? This welcome trend is radically changing three product categories: personal care, household cleaning products—and of course food, for both people and pets.

Discovering that products we use every day might contain dangerous ingredients can feel like an assault to our sense of wellness. We can take a step to restore our balance with a reflection on well-being exercise at the end of the chapter.

Personal Care Products

Today, personal care products—the substances we apply to our bodies— are coming under growing scrutiny for a simple reason: skin is permeable and chemicals can be toxic. Such products include a variety of items such as cosmetics, skin care, deodorant, shaving lotion, shampoo, soap and gels, conditioners, sunscreen, hand lotion, and similar products. Skin is the body's largest organ, covering nearly 100 percent of us. Some people think chemicals in cosmetics, for example, can't be that bad since we aren't eating them. But in fact, daubing toxins on your body may be even more hazardous than ingesting them.

"Toxic ingredients applied to the skin bypass liver enzymes," says Dr. Samuel Epstein, professor emeritus of environmental medicine at the University of Chicago.[26] Put simply, the digestive system actually does a pretty good job of dealing with toxins when they are eaten. However when they are applied topically, these toxins can go straight into the bloodstream.

Let the Buyer Beware

Despite concerns about personal care products, many people assume these products are safe. Agencies like the Federal Drug Administration (FDA) keep an eye on public safety, we tell ourselves. They have to approve products before they go to market, don't they?

Sadly, that's not the case for personal care. The vast majority of personal care ingredients are not reviewed by the FDA, or any other watchdog agency, before we buy them.[27] The US personal care industry polices itself, and critics charge it is doing a poor job.[28]

Nearly 80 percent of the 10,500 ingredients in personal care products have not been evaluated for safety by the Cosmetic Ingredient Review, the research arm of the cosmetic and personal care industry, says the Environmental Working Group (EWG).[29] And the FDA has banned only eleven ingredients, reports The Campaign for Safe Cosmetics, described below.[30]

At the same time, more than 500 cosmetic products sold in the United States contained ingredients banned in Japan, Canada, and the European Union. To sell their products abroad, US firms were required to remove the questionable substances for those markets.[31]

United States consumers and activists were outraged that the products they bought and applied contained chemicals prohibited elsewhere. This state of affairs galvanized an independent coalition called The Campaign for Safe Cosmetics, comprised of 170 health, environmental, and consumer organizations, as well as other nonprofits, to protect consumers, expand public awareness, and advocate corporate and governmental reform to remove harmful ingredients. The group includes respected outfits like the EWG, Friends of the Earth, the National Council of Churches, and the Breast Cancer Fund, among many others.[32]

The Campaign and its cofounder EWG carefully analyzed cosmetics and personal care product ingredients against definitive government, industry, and academic databases of hazardous chemicals. Their findings are chilling indeed:

- More than one in five personal care products contains chemicals linked to cancer.
- Of the products tested, 80 percent contain ingredients that commonly include hazardous impurities.[33]
- And 22 percent of personal care products, including children's products, may contain the organic compound 1,4-dioxane, which is linked to cancer.[34]

When I first encountered this information, I was skeptical. Granted, I'd rather avoid chemicals, whenever possible. But what kind of harm could small amounts really cause a person? But the issue is that women are repeatedly exposed to numerous chemicals in the many cosmetics and personal care product that most use every day.

So are teens and even babies. Bowing to years of activist pressure, Johnson & Johnson, famous for its "No more tears" tagline, agreed in 2011 to gradually phase out the controversial chemical 1,4-dioxane from its baby shampoo.[35] When EWG tested twenty teens, they found phthalates, parabens, and other chemicals in each young woman. Studies link these chemicals to cancer and hormone disruption, says EWG.[36]

Your Dangerous Beauty Checklist

Scan the ingredient labels of personal care products you own for the following substances. Please note that the short list below is limited to the ingredients that several reputable sources recommend avoiding. There are many additional ingredients that are "suspect" or dangerous:

- Parabens (methylparaben, propylparaben, or ethylparaben)

- Petrochemicals in mineral oils and petrolatum
- Phthalates
- Sodium lauryl sulfate and sodium laureth sulfate
- Mercury
- Synthetic fragrance

Lead, which has been banned for use in paint since 1977, largely due to the harmful and even fatal effects of lead on children who ate paint chips peeling from walls, also appeared in twenty of the thirty lipstick brands tested by The Campaign for Safe Cosmetics in 2007.[37] Five years later, the FDA determined that 400 lipsticks contained lead. The highest levels appeared in well-known brands such as Maybelline, L'Oréal, Cover Girl, and NARS.[38] The Campaign's Stacey Malkan, author of *Not Just a Pretty Face*, calls lead "a proven neurotoxin . . . linked to miscarriage and infertility."[39] Couple that with new market research showing that 63 percent of girls seven to ten years old wear lipstick, and you can draw but one conclusion: It defies reason that regulatory officials could allow lead in lipstick, even in relatively small quantities. It endangers women's health and outrageously puts young girls at risk too.[40]

Given these concerns, natural beauty products are in big demand. One quarter of American shoppers purchased an organic or natural personal care product in the past six months.[41] But beware: some products are not as natural or organic as they are advertised to be, as the following example illustrates.

In 2008, Dr. Bronner's Magic Soaps, a sixty-year-old natural care firm, sued Avalon Organics, Kiss My Face, and Jason Natural, as well as certifier Ecocert and the OASIS standard for "misleading organic branding." A product is not organic unless it is 100 percent organic, the lawsuit charged. "We have been deeply disappointed and frustrated by . . . products that were not natural in the first place, let alone organic," said David Bronner.[42]

Around the same time, Exova, formerly known as Bodycote, an independent third-party laboratory, examined several body care products and
determined these brands to be authentically organic: Dr. Bronnor's, Sensi-
bility Soaps, Dr. Haushka, Aubrey Organics, Intelligent Nutrients, and
Terressentials.[43]

Since these studies appeared, some companies have reformulated their
products, others have not. Dr. Bronner's Magic Soaps is settling its suits
against some companies, says David Bronner.[44] To be certain of what you
are buying, check the product evaluations on EWG's Deep Skin website,
described below, and the Organic Consumer Association Safety Guide,
cited in this book's chapter options.

Mindful shoppers want a lot more information about what's natural
or organic and what is not. Until government watchdogs require greater
disclosure or the industry voluntarily embraces more transparency, body
care consumers had best rely on ethical, independent, third-party ratings
and seals of approval, such as the following:

The Natural Products Association Seal of Approval is awarded to
products that are free of ingredients like phthalates, petroleum, parabens,
sodium laureth sulfates, and other harmful substances.[45]

The Whole Foods "Premium Body Care" seal vetoes more than 400
synthetic ingredients, including those cited above. There is a link to the
full list in this chapter's endnotes.[46]

The EWG Skin Deep Cosmetics Database offers a list of sixty-nine
thousand products rated for their degree of hazard. It can be found at
EWG.org/SkinDeep.

The desire for authentic, organic, and toxic-free beauty is prompting
the creation of new cosmetic lines and promoting the visibility of reliable
distributors and retailers that adhere to the highest safety standards. Ann
Garrity is one example. As a thirty-eight-year-old Minneapolis marketing
consultant, she had just recovered from surgeries for endometriosis and

fibroids when her doctor advised: "Get rid of every lotion, every soap, every cosmetic you put on your body."[47]

Ann had previously lived by the belief that, "If it promised to make me more beautiful, I'd use it." After her surgeries, though, she began a three-year journey to learn everything about toxic beauty ingredients. She also felt a sense of duty to share her newfound information with friends and family. But they replied, "I don't have time to read product ingredients. Just tell me what to use."

That reaction inspired Ann to begin her online beauty collection, Organic Diva. Her business offers only the highest quality, safest cosmetics made by companies who've signed the Compact for Safe Cosmetics' pledge to shun cancer-causing or hormone-disrupting ingredients. Ann knows that her customers face breast cancer, fertility issues, and melanoma, and that there is research suggesting a link between these health concerns and the use of body care products that contain certain chemicals.

Through Organic Diva, she has grown to be a strong advocate for all-natural ingredients in cosmetics and other body care products. Organic Diva sells two of my favorite lines: Suki and Jane Iredale (described below). Both masterfully fuse beauty and well-being.

More Conscious Personal Care Options

Consider the following brands if you want to be sure your personal care products are toxin-free:

- Horst Rechelbacher sold his natural beauty line Aveda and created the 100 percent food-certified organic Intelligent Nutrients, available in salons and Whole Foods.[48]
- In 1985, German biochemist and naturopath Dr. Jurgen Klein and his horticulturalist wife Ulrike founded Jurlique in Australia. The

brand's organic ingredients are grown on a 153-acre biodynamic farm in Australia.[49]

- Jane Iredale mineral makeup soothes inflamed skin, resists bacteria, protects skin from UVA and UVB rays without chemicals, and forms a protective barrier that lets the skin breathe. It is so safe that it's recommend by plastic surgeons.[50]
- Suki's 100 percent synthetic-free and organic ingredients are carefully distilled and triple filtered to preserve their essential properties. The line is sold in 800 stores.[51]
- Inara is a 100 percent organic-certified body care line that features *babassu* oil, a rich emollient from southeastern Brazil where Inara works with indigenous co-ops.[52]
- Dr. Hauschka, the forty-five-year-old German beauty products firm, makes holistic skin care treatments from biodynamic and socially responsible sources.[53]

Meanwhile, the good efforts of The Campaign for Safe Cosmetics are bringing forth remarkable results. Thus far the Campaign has identified 321 cosmetic companies as "Champions" for having met all of the Campaign's safety goals. Another 111 companies, its "Innovators," have made significant progress. For information on these companies, consult this chapter's options list.[54]

The Sustainable Food Trend

The quest for safe, organic cosmetics is the logical extension of the organic food trend. Organic food is grown without toxic pesticides, harmful chemicals, or irradiation. Lauded since the 1930s by naturalists like fitness expert Jack LaLanne, organic food grew in popularity in the iconoclastic 1970s, which birthed a multitude of small, local health food stores.

Despite the lingering effects of recession, the US organic food and drink market grew nearly 8 percent in 2010, becoming a $29 billion market.[55] Global organic sales reached $59 billion in 2010.[56] In the United States, 78 percent of families said they purchased organic food in 2011, reports the Organic Trade Association.[57]

But today's top food trend can be defined in one word: local.

Wander the aisles of the Alewife Whole Foods store in Cambridge, Massachusetts, as I did one day in August 2011, and you will find banners identifying local farmers' produce and signs boasting: "Local: 89" (as in 89 kinds of local produce) and "Organic: 263" (as in 263 varieties of organic produce). Local produce is usually less expensive and always fresher than produce shipped in. Local food that is also organic will almost surely delight mindful shoppers.

Shedding Light on the Food Chain

Beneath the positive and upbeat organic and local food trends, however, there are profound and disturbing questions about what some call corporate agriculture. In an era of fast food, "junk" food, highly processed supermarket offerings, and shrink-wrapped meats, too many of us, critics assert, are unconscious about where our food comes from and the dangerous, distasteful conditions under which it was grown or raised.

These criticisms, voiced in the film *Food, Inc.*, and by people like Michael Pollen, author of *The Omnivore's Dilemma* and *In Defense of Food*, charge that today's industrial food system puts small farms out of business, depletes soil nutrients, threatens public health with harmful pesticides, and serves up tasteless, unhealthy foodstuffs.

Enter the sustainable food movement.

Just as Fair Trade educates people by proposing viable new solutions to a deeply troubling issue, sustainable food advocates offer "foodies" and food activists alike a wealth of ways to achieve their goals, be they taste or transformation. Sustainable food initiatives promote local, often organic, farm-to-table food from farmers' markets, consumer co-ops, and community-supported agriculture (CSA) to revitalize the family farm, the land, and safe, delicious food. Local Harvest, a comprehensive sustainable food website, counts more than 800 existing consumer food co-ops and grocers, accessible by your local zip code.[58]

Community-Supported Agriculture

The great taste of local food and a passion to support family farms merge deliciously in the innovative, twenty-year-old agricultural model known as community-supported agriculture. CSA members purchase a share in a local farmer's harvest. Each week during the growing season, members receive their shares, which typically consist of vegetables but can also include eggs, cheese, fruit, or other farm products. The system benefits farmers, who receive much needed cash early in the season. Customers get great fresh food, of course, and invitations to visit the farm, while farmers and customers develop a great bond. Some parents discover that even finicky kids devour food grown by a farmer with whom they feel a special connection.

Local Harvest lists nearly 5,000 CSA farms.[59] Its online database, the nation's largest, connects local food lovers with nearby farmers. In spring 2012, when I entered my zip code on the North Shore of Massachusetts, where winters are harsh and the lovely summers are far too short, I expected to find perhaps a few nearby farms offering CSA shares. Instead, I located forty-three farmers' markets and forty-four CSA farms!

Changing the Face of Agriculture

There are more than 2.2 million farms in the United States, 98 percent of them family-owned.[60] Farmers' markets, which date back to ancient times and thrived a century ago, are enjoying a great revival, which tracks the growing desire for local food. Together, these trends are transforming the agricultural-economic landscape. During the period between 2002 and 2007, there were seventy-six thousand *more* American farms than in the previous five years.[61] These family farms are the prime providers of local food. However, the criteria that define "local" can vary greatly, from distance, such as one hundred or four hundred miles away, to geography, such as "within a state's borders," explains a US Department of Agriculture publication.[62]

As family farms increase, so do farmers' markets. In 2011, there were 7,175 markets, up 17 percent since 2010, says the US Department of Agriculture.[63] "I would probably purchase a local nonorganic tomato before . . . an organic one . . . from California," Whole Foods' co-founder John Mackey—an organic foods pioneer—told *Time* magazine. "The local tomato . . . will just taste better."[64]

Well-Being Comes Home: Household Cleaning Products

"You are what you eat," said the early food activists of the 1960s. "We're also what we apply on our bodies," mindful cosmetic shoppers chimed in circa 2005. Today's values-driven consumers expand the discussion into the home, asking: "What about toxic emissions we breathe indoors every day?" With that question come fresh concerns about common household products that harm personal and planetary well-being.

Most of us all worry about air pollution, but to a large extent we assume that pollution is something that only happens outdoors. In reality, our exposure to pollutants inside a house often runs two to five times higher, and sometimes much higher, than those outside, says a US government report.[65] Chemical residues linger indoors, causing some people to sniffle and sneeze. A four-year study at the University of California, Berkeley, determined that many household cleaners and air fresheners discharge toxins that can lead to health risks.[66]

There are many sources of indoor air pollution, such as insulation, particleboard, or fumes from carpets and upholstery. But one of the worst culprits is toxic cleaning products. Labels on traditional household products openly warn of their toxicity. Household cleaning products are the third leading substance that generates calls to poison control centers, and half of those calls involve children age six and under.[67] Bleach, which contains corrosive chlorine, is the most common cleaning product accidentally swallowed by children.[68]

When the University of Washington analyzed twenty-five widely used consumer products, such as laundry detergents and household cleaners, researchers determined these products emitted 133 different volatile organic compounds (VOCs), nearly one-fourth of which were classified as toxic or hazardous under federal laws. Some VOCs found were deemed "probable carcinogens with no safe exposure level," by the US Environmental Protection Agency.[69]

Furthermore, women and children are at greater risk than others. The United States employs about 1.4 million maids and household cleaning people; nearly 90 percent of them are women. And women often do the cleaning in their own homes.[70]

Children are the most vulnerable to chemical risks. Because their bodies are smaller, the toxins have a larger impact. Besides, children crawl on the floor and then put their tiny fingers into their mouths. Lawyer Sam Katz, who was then the father of a one-year-old, fastened locks on household cabinets to keep his baby away from these dangerous chemicals. Then he realized that he sprayed the same cleaners on his child's bathtub, routinely exposing his child to toxins.[71]

Scientific and medical studies have connected household products with childhood wheezing and asthma.[72] Indoor chemicals damage children's well-being and interfere with education. Asthma accounts for nearly thirteen million missed school days per year.[73] Besides, according to the Environmental Protection Agency (EPA), fifty-five million people (including teachers, school employees, and students) spend their day in a secondary or elementary school. Half of those schools, EPA adds, have air quality problems.[74]

New York State has responded in part with policies that require schools to use cleaners free of "carcinogens, reproductive toxins, or scents that could aggravate asthma."[75] By 2011, Illinois, Connecticut, Maryland, Hawaii, Nevada, and Iowa had also passed legislation requiring green cleaning products in schools.[76]

Toxic indoor cleaning chemicals affect the environment outside the home as well:

- The average US household generates more than twenty pounds of household hazardous waste per year.[77]
- Each day Americans pour thirty-two million pounds of household cleaners down the drain, which can pollute ground water and septic systems.[78]
- In North America, 69 percent of streams contain detergent residue.[79]

So conscious shoppers reject conventional cleaning products in favor of the newly created green household products sector. Green cleaning embodies the values of both well-being and sustainability, because there is growing awareness that the same chemicals that harm people are also despoiling the Earth's air and water.

A Question of Cost

Yet, some people continue to use toxic chemicals inside their homes, because they complain that green cleaning products are more expensive than traditional options. I disagree with that reasoning. First, chemicals are toxic; it is worth it, I would argue, to spend a little more to protect yourself, your family, and the Earth.

Second, the belief that green cleaning is expensive is only partly right. You can reduce the cost of green cleaners by buying in bulk or waiting for special deals. Target is known for a good selection and low prices on green cleaning products, according to Yahoo Finance.

My third, and perhaps most compelling, reason is this: with a little ingenuity, green cleaning can be downright frugal. Old-fashioned non-toxic cleaning agents such as vinegar and baking soda, which are enjoying a recent revival, cost substantially less than commercial products. If you buy these inexpensive options, and then supplement them with green cleaners on sale, you will create a much greener, cleaner home—and actually save more Conscious Money.

Clean, Green, and Gaining Traction

The *New York Times* reported that in as early as 2007, three hundred Stop & Shop supermarket locations stocked green cleaning brands like Seventh Generation, Method, and Imus Greening the Cleaning.[80] By 2010, 42 percent of consumers had used "natural, organic, or ecologically friendly" cleaning or laundry products.[81] Half of eighteen- to twenty-nine-year-olds say they'd spend more on green products.[82] Market researcher Mintel International forecasts that green products will account for 30 percent of the overall household cleaning market by 2013.[83]

The merits of green cleaning were dramatically brought home one day to Gabrielle Lennon of Idyllwild, California. While unloading the dishwasher, she did not notice that it had malfunctioned and was still full of unused detergent. In a moment of distraction, Gabrielle looked down to see that her daughter, a curious toddler, had scooped up the dishwashing powder and stuck a handful into her mouth. Frantic, Gabrielle dialed Poison Control and was immediately asked what brand it was.

"Seventh Generation," she replied. Then she heard the words that let her breathe again: "Oh, it's fine. Just wash it off her hands, and give her a glass of water."

In a letter to Seventh Generation, she wrote: "My heart has been overflowing . . . Thank you, thank you, thank you!"[84]

Seventh Generation's name comes from The Great Law of the Iroquois Confederacy, which declared, "In our every deliberation, we must consider the impact on the next seven generations," which is quoted on Seventh Generation packaging. All of the company's products are 100 percent nontoxic, from detergents to diapers. Seventh Generation bathroom cleaner, for example, reveals all of its ingredients and their purposes: hydrogen peroxide (the active stain remover); biodegradable surfactants (for soil removal); citrus oil (for grease); food-grade, nontoxic oxygen stabilizers (to preserve the peroxide); and water. The label also states what the product does not contain. There is no "chlorine, petroleum-based solvents, glycol ethers, phosphates, acids, caustics, dyes, and perfumes."[85]

Method, a private nontoxic-cleaning firm, was founded by childhood friends Eric Ryan and Adam Lowry during the 2001 recession. By 2009, Method was selling 130 products in eight thousand stores globally. Known for its savvy design and 100 percent recycled plastic bottles, Method quickly grew into a $100 million business.[86] Both Method and Seventh Generation registered double-digit sales growth in 2010, reports the *New York Times*.[87]

Monica Nassif, a former marketing executive, decided to launch a line of nontoxic cleaning products that smell good. One line of products became two. Caldrea, named after Nassif's daughters, Calla and Aundrea, and Mrs. Meyer's, named after her mother, Thelma Meyer, are sold at The Container Store, Target, and Whole Foods.[88]

Clorox was one of the first big brands to go green with its Green Works line, which is biodegradable and made from at least 95 percent natural ingredients.[89] Green Works was the first product ever endorsed by the Sierra Club in the club's 116-year history.[90] Some Sierra Club chapters have criticized the arrangement. Clorox was once listed among the most dangerous household products by consumer advocate Public Interest Research Group. A spokesperson for the Sierra Club said the goal was to make green cleaners as popular at Wal-Mart as they are at organic co-ops.[91]

Like Clorox, other industrial giants have explored or launched green product lines but the majority of mainstream cleaning products still contain toxins—that most manufacturers proclaim as safe. A spokesperson for SC Johnson, maker of brands like Windex and Pledge, proclaims such traditional products "safe and effective." A representative of Proctor & Gamble, maker of brands like Tide and Cheer, insists the company hires "PhD toxicologists . . . to make sure our products are safe."[92]

But here is the problem. Mindful shoppers want to choose products that are completely toxin-free, not just ones that have been declared safe by the companies that produce them. But as the *New York Times* reports, "Federal law doesn't require full disclosure of all the chemical ingredients." So some companies resist taking responsibility by arguing that "listing three hundred to four hundred raw ingredients . . . could be confusing to customers and might reveal trade secrets."[93] That response is unacceptable; it only invites a good dose of consumer activism to force them toward a new direction. If their trade secrets are poisonous, you and I have the right to know that!

Today Clorox posts all its household product ingredients on its website.[94] So does S C Johnson at whatsinsidescjohnson.com. But Proctor & Gamble, Colgate-Palmolive, and others still do not disclose chemical ingredients, says nonprofit law firm Earthjustice. Of course, disclosing toxins does *not* remove them. So, today, the best way to guard your home, well-being, and the planet is with clean green products. But some of them have been around for a very long time.

Back to Baking Soda and Vinegar?

Once favored by our great-grandmothers as all-purpose cleaners, vinegar and baking soda are making a big comeback—and for good reason. They're natural, inexpensive, safe, and effective.

Vinegar melts grease on counter tops and appliances, disinfects toilet bowls dissolving even mineral stains from well water, and makes mirrors sparkle. The recommended formula is one part water to one part vinegar, but at our house we buy it by the gallon, pour it in a spray bottle, and apply it full strength. The vinegar smell disappears in two or three minutes. There are a few exceptions to be aware of, such as don't ever use vinegar on marble.

Baking soda is a safe, gentle abrasive that dissolves dirt, grime, and stubborn stains like tea and rust. Use it on the bathtub, carpets, garbage can, or cat litter box. Baking soda and vinegar used together, that is, in sequence, is an old-fashioned, but effective, way to clear drains and a safe one that plumbers recommend. Check out a link for this tried-and-true remedy in this chapter's options list.

Conscious, earth-friendly, inexpensive baking soda and vinegar will not meet every cleaning challenge; so green nontoxic cleaners will always have a place in your cabinet. When you need a safe, tough cleanser, try an all-natural abrasive cleaning product named Bon Ami.

Green Cars and Other Sustainable Transportation Options

Transportation is one of the most expensive items in your Conscious Money budget. Furthermore, the personally owned car is a well-known environmental hazard. So, mindful consumers who are naturally concerned about conservation and clean air, also want to make conscious automotive choices.

In the United States alone, there are 254 million registered vehicles, the vast majority of which rely on petroleum and are responsible for up to

50 percent of air pollution.[95] Transportation accounts for 29 percent of US greenhouse gas emissions.[96] Add those facts to what we all know: that oil is an expensive, polluting, limited resource that is known to provoke wars.

Today, however, is a new day for conscious drivers. We can now choose from a range of eco-friendly options like electric vehicles (EVs), hybrids, plug-in hybrids, and clean biodiesel models—all of which are worthy transportation choices on which to spend your Conscious Money.

Green Car? No, Thanks!

But perhaps you do not want to own a car—green, blue or otherwise. Maybe you're in the market for new transportation choices that save you money, from the tried and true, like mass transit, to the radically new, like car sharing.

The greenest, least costly, most mindful proposition is to not own a car at all, a step that many drivers cannot even imagine. The first motivating move toward exploring a car-free lifestyle is calculating how much it actually costs to keep a car on the road.

There's the car payment or rental fee of perhaps $200 to $500 per month ($2,400 to $6,000 per year). Gas might cost anywhere from $30 to $100 per week ($1,560 to $5,200 per year). Insurance could cost you $1,000 per year or a lot more. Registration might run from a low $100 to much more. Let's estimate maintenance at $300 to $500 per year. Parking varies a lot, so suppose we round it off to $1,000. With expenses like these, you see how owning a car can easily range from a low of $6,000 to well over $12,000 per year. Choosing to not own a car can save you a lot of Conscious Money.

The Joy of Car Sharing

But most of us sometimes need a car. Suppose you could:

- Reserve a car online and pick it up at anytime.
- Drive the car only when you need it.
- Pay an hourly or daily rate including gas, insurance, and parking.
- Reduce your transportation budget from 19 to 6 percent of your income, saving around $500 per month, which amounts to an impressive $6,000 per year.
- Drive a cool, trendy Mini Cooper, Prius, Ford hybrid, or BMW.

These enjoyable, practical Conscious Money–saving benefits explain why the greenest car around is not an EV or a plug-in hybrid. It is a car that is shared. Boston-based Zipcar, the industry leader in car sharing, counts more than 650,000 values-driven customers (called Zipsters) in 16 major urban areas and on more than 250 college and university campuses.[97] Reserve your car and pick it up at a nearby commercial lot. Costs start as low as $8.50 per hour and $66 per day including gas, parking, insurance, and up to 180 driving miles per day. Each shared car replaces at least fifteen cars on the road, states the Zipcar website, citing the research of global consultant Frost & Sullivan.

Zipcar is now getting competition from Hertz and Enterprise. There are more than 200 car share programs in 600 US cities.[98] Many are non-profit, like City CarShare in San Francisco. This is great news for frugal, conscious drivers. "In this economy," says Zipcar CEO Scott Griffith, "people want to be more sustainable."[99]

But Zipcar's success raises the question: why stop at cars? Suppose neighbors, families and friends were to share big-ticket items like tools and baby carriages too? They already do, reports the *Washington Post*, sharing or swapping, "tools, books, handbags, time and talent."[100] When Tom Burdett of Annapolis, Maryland, wanted to cut some tiles, a friend offered his tools. When that friend needed to install a satellite dish, Burdett in turn stepped in to help out. A weak economy can only accelerate this positive trend.

The Planet's Greenest Transportation Options

The overall issue, though, is not just about more green cars, or even alternative transportation like car sharing, it's also about driving less.

In 1970, nearly 9 percent of Americans took public transit to work, according to the Census Bureau.[101] Since 1990, however, the figure has averaged only about 5 percent.[102] But in 2007, when gas prices surged, Americans took 10.3 billion rides on trolleys, streetcars, subways, and buses—the most since 1957.[103] In 2008, with prices still very high, gas consumption dropped again, leading Americans to drive twenty billion fewer miles than in 2007, reports the US Department of Transportation.[104]

Consider this fresh perspective: bicycling is a way of life in Asia and Europe, while Americans generally cycle only for exercise or pleasure. But when gas prices peaked around four dollars a gallon in the summer of 2008, bike commuting rose 15 percent nationwide, according to US Census data. "We're starting to see the same thing in 2011," said Andy Clarke, president of the League of American Bicyclists. In early 2011, sales of road bikes, often used by commuters, jumped 29 percent, says Scott Jaeger, senior retail analyst at Leisure Trends Group.[105] Such examples indicate that when the price hurts enough, people become more motivated to change.

There is one more factor I invite you to consider: where you live. Some people live a long way from where they work and play in order to save money, or so they think. Seriously explore whether this is a false economy. What sense does it make to save a lot on rent, and then spend much of your savings on a car payment? And that is not all a car can "cost." The more time a person spends commuting, the more he or she is exposed to the dangers of driving: road rage and accidents—even fatal ones. Besides, consider that every mile you bike, walk, carpool, or ride mass transit (instead of driving) cuts pollution, shrinks demand for oil, heals the environment, and saves, as well as better allocates, your Conscious Money.

The Age of the Electric Car

Automotive alternatives like car sharing can prove ideal for young drivers, while rental cars can work well for older drivers. But many will still choose to own a car. Mindful drivers have patiently awaited the arrival of electric vehicles (EVs), which run on batteries and release zero emissions. Meanwhile the number of charging stations to power these vehicles is expanding daily. In May 2012, there were more than 3,000 EV charging systems around the nation, most in California, reported CarStations.com, which encourages drivers to identify and report new EV charging stations.[106] In fact, new charging stations appear so rapidly that it's difficult to calculate how many there are—or will be in six months, says CEO of CarStations.com, David Raboy.[107] New EVs can also be recharged at home.

One consumer issue with EVs is dubbed "range anxiety," which asks: How far will the car go before it stops dead until you recharge it? Bearing in mind that the national average for a round-trip commute is thirty-two miles a day, most of us could manage with a one-hundred-mile-per-day range for work and errands.[108] Families might own a second car, perhaps a hybrid—or rent a car for longer trips. Such strategies would drastically cut gas consumption.

General Motors, Nissan, and two German luxury brands are pioneering the Age of the Electric Car. Pike Research forecasts that the United States will become the world's second largest EV market, after China.[109] If owning an electric car sounds good to you, review the following options to determine the best value for your Conscious Money:

Nissan's Leaf, the first mass-produced all-electric car, has a one-hundred-mile range, and starts at $35,200 before a federal tax credit of up to $7,500. Another $2,200 buys you a home charging station. There's no engine or transmission—and the Leaf is super quiet.

The GM Chevy Volt has a forty-mile range on a single battery charge. You can then fire up a small gas engine, and you're good to go for another

300 miles. The Volt recharges overnight for about $1.50. The price tag reads $41,000, but incentives drop it to about $34,000. In 2012, the US government proclaimed the Volt "safe" after probing the potential for fire hazards in EVs.

Conscious car lovers might catch sight of BMW's all-electric Mini Cooper, which is being tested in the Los Angeles and New York City areas. The tiny electric version of the Smart ForTwo, dubbed the Smart ED, (which stands for electric drive) is an urban parking dream. It debuts in 2013 and boasts a seventy-to-eighty-mile range and a top speed of sixty miles an hour.[110]

Conscious Hybrid Options

Electric vehicles, however, are not the only new car in town. Conscious drivers launched and are still enthusiastic about hybrid cars, which remain a highly sustainable option. And the promise of plug-in hybrids is finally coming to fruition.

Hybrids, first mass-produced in 2000, revolutionized the green transportation space. With this innovation, mindful consumers could select environmentally sustainable—and, when gas prices soared, far thriftier—automotive options. By 2011, Toyota alone had sold one million Prius hybrids in the United States and three million Toyota hybrids globally.[111]

When Toyota, Honda, and Ford pioneered the hybrid, it was not clear that other carmakers would follow. Industry experts and manufacturers pooh-poohed hybrids as a fad. Consumers would soon reject the $3,000 or $4,000 hybrid "premium," they argued, and opt for conventional cars that were fuel efficient or diesel. But hybrid sales soared.

Later, some thought electric cars would spell the demise of hybrids. For example, the *Washington Post's* Warren Brown said, "Hybrids are merely a way-station until we get proper electric cars and infrastructure." Not so, replied HybridCars.com, which proclaims: "It's all about options."[112]

Reviewers and automotive experts believe those options are still improving and that newer, and less expensive, hybrids are cutting into Toyota's market dominance:

- The Ford Fusion hybrid "drives better" than the Prius, says a review in *USA Today*.[113]
- Hyundai's hybrid Sonata represents "solid value," reports car site Autoblog.com.[114]
- *Popular Mechanics* dubbed the 2012 Honda Civic hybrid "Honda's Prius" and preferred the Civic over the Prius.[115]

When Google's RechargeIT program converted its Prius fleet into plug-in (PHEV) hybrids, the program's average mileage per gallon surged from forty-eight to ninety-three.[116] Research your plug-in hybrid options (or consider a conversion kit) from Plug-In America, Plug-In Partners, CalCars, and similar outfits.

The Pros and Cons of Biofuel

In the face of growing concerns about oil prices, energy independence, and greenhouse gas emissions, biofuel has attracted more and more attention from both consumers and policymakers. The two most common biofuels are ethanol and biodiesel. These fuels differ in their sources and regional acceptance.

Ethanol fuel is an alcohol that is derived from corn, sugar cane, and other foodstuffs. The United States and Brazil generate 90 percent of global ethanol.[117] In the United States, ethanol is made from corn. Blended with standard gasoline, ethanol generally reduces tailpipe emissions.[118]

In Brazil, where ethanol is derived from sugar cane, some cars run on pure ethanol. But ethanol fuel raises key issues. "Growing the crops, making fertilizers and pesticides, and processing the plants into fuel consumes a lot of energy," states *National Geographic*, "so . . . there is debate about whether ethanol from corn actually provides more energy than is required to grow and process it."[119]

Another serious downside of corn-based ethanol is that it has caused already high food costs to soar (including products made with corn syrup for example), especially harming people in the developing world. But the next generation of ethanol, called cellulosic ethanol, is made from nonfood agricultural waste like cornstalks or crops like switchgrass, which would mitigate the widespread criticism of the fuel.[120]

For this and other reasons, more Americans are investigating another biofuel.

Brave New Biodiesel

Biodiesel is widely available in the European Union, which produced 53 percent of the world's biodiesel in 2010.[121] Biodiesel is made from renewable, biodegradable, nontoxic sources like plant oils, as well as from nonfood sources. Biodiesel "essentially eliminates" sulfur oxides and sulfates, the major components of acid rain, says the US-based National Biodiesel Board, and is "the only alternative fuel to have fully completed the health effects testing requirements of the Clean Air Act."[122]

Biodiesel is often blended with regular diesel; "B20," for example, consists of 20 percent biodiesel and 80 percent standard petroleum diesel—and it substantially cuts harmful emissions. Biodiesel reduces greenhouse gases by 57–86 percent compared with petroleum-based biodiesel, says the Biodiesel Board, citing the EPA as its source.[123] For tips on where to buy biodiesel, consult the "Guide to Buying Biodiesel" on the website Biodeisel.org

Avid do-it-yourselfers make their own biodiesel, often with used cooking oil gathered from willing restaurants. In this chapter's options list, you'll find resources to help you explore the possibility of doing so.

Biofuels can potentially meet more than one quarter of world transportation energy demands by 2050, says the International Energy Agency.[124] In fact, in 2012 airlines won the right to combine traditional fuel with biofuels made from algae and wood waste.[125] The prospect of engineering biofuels from these nonfood sources is an exciting and inspired vision of our energy future.

• • •

The practice of mindful spending activates the power of discernment, one of the highest octaves of conscious choice. Discernment directs the wisdom of higher consciousness into the decisions you make as a conscious consumer every day. Yet mindful spending holds even greater possibilities. Whether you are brewing a cup of Fair Trade coffee, checking the train schedule, or eyeing the ingredients on a shampoo label, do not limit your experience to a mental exercise. Allow the power of conscious choice to rouse your heart. Enjoy the harmony that conscious spending bestows on your body and its energy. Allow yourself to feel the joy of mindful spending.

Exercises

Reflection on Well-Being

To calm and harmonize your emotions, invoke your higher intelligence to align with the quiet but powerful energy of well-being:

1. Choose a time when you won't be disturbed for ten to fifteen minutes.
2. Settle into a comfortable chair and take several deep breaths.
3. When you are ready, meditate on the phrase: "I deserve well-being."

4. Be aware of the thoughts that arise and complete your reflection.
5. In your Conscious Money journal note any "yes but" reactions ("I'll think about well-being when I get a new job"), mental objections ("It costs too much"), or insights ("I'm not sure I've ever experienced well-being").

As you try this exercise, you may experience a sense of well-being that is so understated that you are tempted to dismiss is. Welcome it, instead. Well-being, even if it appears subtle, represents a positive emotional state that is the foundation for higher states like love, joy, and excitement.

Get an Automotive Tune-up

Cars symbolize freedom. As a mindful shopper, it is time to ponder the cost of that freedom. With your green values growing stronger, the habit of owning a car may now be an outdated burden for you. By changing one or more of your transportation habits, you could help free yourself from an external—and expensive—sense of identity:

1. Choose a time when you will not be disturbed for at least fifteen minutes.
2. Reflect on the value of freedom.
3. Honestly ponder whether you use your car to express your identity. Ask yourself whether there are more authentic, less costly ways to be yourself.
4. Consider new transportation habits that better express your values. Which new routines might you be willing to try? Are there any old patterns you might be willing to give up?
5. Open your Conscious Money journal and review your consumer values. Examine whether your current lifestyle truly reflects those values.

6. List the steps you would need to take to better align your values with your transportation choices.

7. Write down related notes in your journal.

Options

Reflections

- Clearly identify the human values that inspire you when shopping.
- Regularly review and update your personal and consumer values.
- When new values emerge for you, consider which changes to make in your spending habits. If you aspire to be a greener shopper, for example, examine your cleaning products for toxic chemicals.
- List five to ten products or services you "can't do without." Note any that are in conflict with your values.

Resources

- Join a grassroots outfit like Green America.
- Review Green America's "National Green Pages," a directory of socially responsible, green businesses at their website GreenAmerica.org. It's free when you join the organization, or you can buy it at Barnes & Noble or Amazon.
- Create a values reminder: place a short list of your values in your wallet or mobile device. When considering a purchase, review your list.
- The organization Freecycle sets up lists in different communities on which people can post things that they want to give away. Check them out at Freecycle.org.
- Follow @FairTradeUSA on Twitter and Facebook: Facebook.com/FairTradeCertified.

- Spread the word and inspire more Fair Trade shoppers; ask shops to stock more FT-certified goods, and thank them when they do.
- Download Fair Trade USA's "Fair Trade Finder" mobile apps from the Android and iTunes app stores, or locate the app on Fair Trade USA's Facebook page.
- Green America's beautifully illustrated *Guide to Fair Trade* is a free PDF download at GreenAmerica.org.
- Explore safe cosmetics on the website OrganicDivas.com.
- Get inspired to give up your car by reading the *Carfree USA Blog* or the *Carfree Family* blog, both on BlogSpot.com.
- Check out a professional plumber's green advice for unclogging drains at HowStuffWorks.com/home-improvement/plumbing/how-to-unclog -a-drain.htm.
- Bookmark your local public transit options for quick, easy reference.
- Check out YouTube videos on how to make DIY biodiesel. A simple backyard technique combining lye, methanol, and vegetable oil is illustrated in the video "DIY Biodiesel: 5 Minute Microbatches."
- For a more complex setup requiring multiple tanks, gauges, and heating elements, watch "How to Make Biodiesel Using Used Cooking Oil." It's also on YouTube.
- In the *Do It Yourself Guide to Biodiesel*, author Guy Purcella supplies basic information about biodiesel, as well as directions on making it.

Right Action

- Conduct a values audit on your credit card statements. Write the pertinent value beside each charge. Then, ask how to honor that value by spending less, or through barter, recycling, sharing, or renting the item.
- Jumpstart new habits by highlighting one value each season. In autumn, make it *social justice*, in winter, *sustainability*, and so forth.

Buy a Fair Trade item in the fall. In winter, try baking soda or a green cleaner on sale.

- Favor products certified by independent parties like the USDA, Marine Stewardship Council, and Green Good Housekeeping, or buy brands that partner with NGOs like Greenpeace or the World Wildlife Fund.

- To research hundreds of cosmetic companies deemed "Champions" and "Innovators" by The Campaign for Safe Cosmetics, consult the article "Market Shift: The Story of the Compact for Safe Cosmetics and the Growth in Demand for Safe Cosmetics" at SafeCosmetics.org.

- Choose a conscious consumer issue to become an activist for (or against), such as recycling, CFL light bulbs, Fair Trade, or toxic cosmetics.

- Review the Organic Consumer Association's (OCA) list of recommended household cleaning products, which appears at the end of the OCA article "How Toxic Are Your Household Cleaning Supplies?" at OrganicConsumers.org. Enter the article title in OCA's easy, efficient search feature powered by Google.

- OCA's outstanding "Shoppers Safety Guide," which evaluates numerous personal care and cleaning products, rating them "Safe, Caution, or Avoid," is easily accessible on the site as well.

- Make three to five "sustainability commitments," such as scheduling a home energy audit, washing clothes in cold water, observing one car-free day per week, or cutting back on the heat and A/C.

Conscious Money Affirmation

When I shop, I consider whether the products I may purchase embody my values—or not.

6

The Wealth of Creativity

As conscious individuals, we appreciate the importance of values-driven businesses that honor a higher purpose beyond making money. Similarly, in the marketplace where we spend our Conscious Money, we carefully select products that mirror our personal and practical values. To become a conscious earner, we must embrace a similar practice.

Most people earn their income from a job, occupation, or profession, which is therefore the primary source of their Conscious Money. Naturally, people want to affiliate with employers whose values match their own. But there is another consideration to bear in mind as well and that is the value of creativity. To be genuinely creative, you must nurture and readily access your personal connection to higher consciousness.

In the New Economy of Consciousness, creativity is the single most important way that an individual can add value to any economic activity or enterprise. That means your earning power today is largely dependent on your ability to be creative, which is also an excellent investment in job security. In a competitive global economy, where jobs head overseas every day, there's one function that cannot be outsourced—creativity. Apple computers, iPhones, iPods, and iPads are manufactured to Apple specifications in

China. But they are designed through the power of human ingenuity at Apple headquarters in Cupertino, California.

Your creativity is essential to your success, whether you're self-employed, run a small business, work at a Fortune 500 company, or serve in a government agency or nonprofit. Because your occupation also determines how you spend most of your time, it has an enormous influence on your feelings and well-being. So it is well worth your while to develop the ability to access higher consciousness and translate it into creativity at work.

Fortunately, this is exactly what most people already want to do: 96 percent of Generation Y wants a job that "requires creativity."[1] Besides, when you use your creative gifts and talents, you experience greater meaning and fulfillment. Early in the twenty-first century, more than one third of Americans made a living through work requiring creativity, estimates creativity expert Richard Florida, author of *The Rise of the Creative Class*.[2] I'd wager it is now 40 percent or more.

The Economy of Consciousness

Today we have entered a new economic era in which creativity and the genius of human consciousness are increasingly recognized as the primary factors that generate success and wealth creation. It is the New Economy of Consciousness. Whenever we undergo such a massive and dramatic shift, it can leave people feeling unsettled. In the 1982 book *Megatrends*, John Naisbitt and I declared the Industrial period was over and that the Information Age had begun. It was a very controversial idea at the time. "How can you make any money on information?" cried skeptics. "It is not land; you can't grow food on it. It's not steel; you can't make a car out of it."

When I relate those responses now to audiences in their 20s or 30s, it generally gets a pretty good laugh. But as many young people today have realized now, the Information Age is in its twilight.

In the New Economy of Consciousness, creativity and human consciousness are a "raw material," which is both precious and limitless. Today, conscious creativity is more valuable than financial capital, oil, or the latest technology. From this remarkable "commodity," we shall forge solutions from business and technology to social and environmental issues. That's why in workplaces in both the private and public sectors, the capacity to creatively resolve challenging problems is prized above all other abilities, as I will illustrate.

Creative problem solving impacts your role as a conscious earner, no matter where or how you work—and the reason is simple. We are abandoning the obsolete economic framework of traditional capitalism and adopting the superior model of Conscious Capitalism. Nevertheless, many people cannot as yet perceive or understand this new operating system. As a result, instability is rampant and problems abound. But so do opportunities—for creative people who can accept ambiguity, embrace the unknown, and appreciate exciting new solutions. Such visionaries are positioned to earn a great deal of Conscious Money in this transition time.

What Is Creativity?

Creativity requires imaginative thinking and fresh approaches. In short, creativity is insight followed by action. But the definition of creativity often varies depending on the arena involved. Nevertheless, from psychology to art to technology and beyond, it is universally agreed that creativity is a highly valuable attribute.

The distinguishing trait of creativity is that it requires us to reach beyond the scope of the rational mind, toward the realm of intuition, in order to invoke higher consciousness and spark divine inspiration.

We all possess the ability to be creative. And creativity serves you whether you sell real estate, repair home appliances, cater local weddings, or write software programs.

But many of us do not exercise that creativity very much. In fact, in traditional business settings, creativity is a somewhat foreign concept. Michael Gelb, a creativity expert and the author of *How to Think Like Leonardo da Vinci*, offers this insight: "Corporate executives today tend to be overly linear, logical, analytical."[3]

Of course, that might apply to people outside of business as well. But we can all learn from the experience I had a few years ago when I made a presentation to a group of smart, personable, and spirited executives. We'd just finished a discussion on leadership during which they'd revealed great wisdom. I then shifted to a new conversation and asked, "Where do you get your most creative ideas?"

Their once lively faces went blank. Ideas? Apparently creative ideas were about the last thing that concerned these high achievers. We then began an exercise about creativity. "I heard that you should just daydream," said one executive. "I mean, literally stare out the window. But I never do."

Logic and analysis were important tools in the Age of Information. But an era based on consciousness demands new techniques. Today it is only when you regularly access creativity and direct it toward your work that you attain greater success and grow more Conscious Money.

The *sine qua non* of creativity is the capacity to be present, or to "be here now," as one guru put it in the 1960s. The best way to develop presence is through practices typically associated with personal growth or spirituality. In fact, millions of people have cultivated consciousness or presence, not at work, but in their personal lives, through meditation, yoga, and martial arts, journaling, and other contemplative pursuits.

Meditation in particular is the gateway to presence because it teaches us to release mental distractions and emotional baggage. Yet this same presence and spaciousness invoked in a work setting can similarly free the mind to focus on a business or creative challenge. The conscious skill of presence delivers a strategic advantage in today's marketplace and tomorrow's.

Creativity Applied in the World of Work

The power of individuals to leverage their creative talent and earn Conscious Money has dramatically accelerated in the last twenty years, due in large part to advancements in personal computers. Putting the right tools in the hands of people, all sorts of people, not just experts, has powerfully catalyzed greater creative genius and more Conscious Wealth.

Remember, in the Economy of Consciousness, the most valuable resource is not land, industry, information or even technology itself. It is instead the power of human consciousness. The economic power of artists, writers, and high-tech geniuses can now rival that of business icons and heads of state, to say nothing of royalty.

Several years ago, *Forbes* estimated that J. K. Rowling, renowned author of the *Harry Potter* books, had in a few short years accrued a net worth of $1 billion.[4] Prior to her success, she was a single welfare mother living in Edinburgh, Scotland, who wrote stories in local cafés as her infant daughter slept. She then endured numerous literary rejections before finally landing a publisher. Ms. Rowling's swift ascent epitomizes the financial power of creativity and higher consciousness. So does this amazing fact, reported by London's *Sunday Times* in 2003: J. K. Rowling is now wealthier than the queen of England.[5]

Creativity can appear gradually over the course of many years, as it did for J. K. Rowling, or it can come in the classic fashion as a bolt "out of the blue." Either way, creativity can potentially earn you a goodly sum of Conscious Money, as artist Lynne Sausele discovered.[6] Lynne felt "life as she knew it" was over. She and her beau of ten years had split up for good, around the time that her youngest son would leave the house for college, exacerbating her heartbreaking empty nest feelings.

Lynne says her challenge is to remember to ask for guidance. "I can get so caught up that I forget the most obvious solution, just ask!" Fortunately in this case, she remembered. "What now?" she prayed. The surprising answer came in a flash: "Lamps!"

For two decades Lynne had painted in oil and acrylics, showed in museums, sold to private and corporate collections, and created a striking one-of-a-kind jewelry collection. But now, seeking a change of pace, she had vaguely thought about creating a line of table lamps. Creativity and her higher consciousness clearly confirmed the idea. "That single word from the cosmos came to me like a soothing balm of love, inspiration, and energy."

In the weeks that followed, she hand-painted fifty-seven lamp bases with simple designs befitting modern or traditional décor, assembled their inner workings like an electrical pro, and marketed the lamps at shows and fairs. When an interior designer saw the colorful creations, Lynne won a commission to design the light fixtures for a fashionable new restaurant. All told, Lynne's brilliant inspiration earned her more than $50,000 in income in a single assignment.

Lynne's one-word solution illuminated her journey to a new life, demonstrated that she was far more capable than she'd imagined, and expanded her role from an artist to that of a micro-manufacturer. "It greatly helped heal the love lost and set a brand-new course for meeting new people, travel, great abundance, and eventually my new love."

"Know that the answers are there for all of us," Lynne advises. "Be ready and waiting. The answer may surprise you."

Creative Problem Solving

To maximize opportunity, find fulfillment at work, and grow your Conscious Money at a career you love, it is wise to be open to inspiration, just as Lynne was, and to embrace the art of creative problem solving.

Imagine you are faced with a situation in which you do not know how to move forward. Perhaps you feel "stuck." Such circumstances often involve some kind of problem or conflicting priorities. Suppose you are self-employed as a consultant and your client wants a project finished by Friday. To make that client happy, a project for another client will have to be delivered late. As a manager or small business owner, you face conflicts like this almost every day. Problems and situations that appear to involve conflict are an open invitation to creativity, because tough intractable issues are rarely settled with a simple mental fix. They are resolved only through ingenuity and fresh thinking.

Successful creative people continuously invoke higher consciousness to solve problems, without even realizing they're doing so. But many of us may require a more structured approach. Here is a nine-step system to creative problem solving that you might try:

1. *Choose a work or business issue.* Describe it in your journal. Spare no detail or complaint. Write until you feel complete.

2. *Appreciate it.* When you have what feels like an intractable problem, do not focus on the "stuck" aspect. That will only block access to the intuitive consciousness where your solution lies. As the poet Rainer Maria Rilke said, "Try to love the questions themselves." Frame your issue like a beautiful painting. Notice its multilayered texture or how the background contrasts with the central theme. Appreciate any positive feelings you have about the issue, even if they do not seem to bring you closer to resolution.

3. *Clarify the scope of your creative problem.* Having set the stage with the first two creative steps, you can now benefit from a more logical tactic. Perhaps you phrase your issue like a question, such as: "How do I get Bill and Kathy to share information on the Stone Ridge project?" or, "Are there funding sources we haven't even considered yet?" You might also summarize the core issue in a few words.

4. *Invoke higher consciousness.* Affirm that there *is* a solution, even though you do not know what it is just now. As Einstein said, "No

problem can be solved from the same level of consciousness that created it." Do not attempt to resolve your issue. Rather, give the problem to your intuition. But do allow yourself to feel as if the issue was decided.

5. *Incubate the issue.* Return to daily consciousness and allow your issue to "just be." Do not focus on it, but do incubate, or nurture, it. Invite your subconscious to contemplate the problem while you quietly go about your business, anticipating a positive outcome. When I get stuck writing one chapter of a book, I follow these steps and start on another chapter. While happily working on something else, a fresh solution for the chapter I've set aside often occurs to me.

6. *Play.* Get away from your desk. Take a walk. Exercise. When Thomas Edison had done everything possible to move a project forward, he'd go fishing.[7]

7. *Talk it through.* It is natural to seek the advice of others when we're stuck. Yet sometimes that illusive but key insight comes the moment you describe your predicament to another—while speaking out loud.

8. *Harvest.* When inspiration strikes, it's a good bet you'll be in an altered state of consciousness. You may think that you'll recall the details, but you might not. So bridge the gap between different levels of consciousness with foresight and preparation. Pack your digital device or a notebook and pen. Take time to capture insights, images, and key words. Establish a regular journaling practice.

9. *Resolve and refine.* Review your insights, downloads, and good ideas. Put the pieces, key words, and images together in a working hypothesis for a possible solution. Share this resolution with colleagues or advisors. Refine it. When you are ready, put your proposal before the person or people who can accept it. Receive their response. Integrate their needs. Polish your resolution and resubmit it. Repeat these steps as needed.

Manager, Consultant, or Entrepreneur:
Creative Problem Solving Is Your Top Skill

Today's economy—and the organizations that comprise it—rewards a new brand of problem solver. But not surprisingly, the best of the breed are found in the ranks of the self-employed. Gail McMeekin, coach, consultant, and author of *The 12 Secrets of Highly Creative Women* and *The 12 Secrets of Highly Successful Women*, is blessed with a steady flow of ideas.[8] Sorting and organizing them is her real challenge. "My issue is staying focused and not getting overwhelmed by these ideas." So Gail has devised an elegant solution. "I just write them on Post-it notes and throw them in a basket."

Gail is a master at collecting ideas on the spot, and then later sorting through them and putting them to work. This is a skill we all can learn to develop. Gail's system takes into account that creativity is comprised of several steps. It is not necessary or even desirable to complete an entire creation all at once. By recognizing the phases of creativity, Gail is freer to be systematically focused, as she was recently when she wrote two books within one year while also running a coaching and consulting business.

"When it comes to marketing my business, there are thousands of options. I must force myself to pick and choose among the possibilities." When Gail gets "stuck," she describes the situation in her journal, asks her inner guidance specific questions, and then waits for the answers.

Gail's creativity practice is enhanced by art and music. "I get attached to a piece of music and play it over and over as I create. The repetition seems to lull me into a state of mind with heightened intuition." Or she often paints a watercolor depicting the dilemma she faces. "The imagery illuminates what I need to know," she says. She also gathers insights from inspirational cards and divination tools, like Viking runes. "Once when I was recovering from a long illness, I picked the Standstill rune, which means—as the name implies—to stand still, again and again, for almost a year." It comforted Gail as a sign that it was just fine to simply "stand still," that is, heal and recover if not literally then metaphorically.

Gail and her photographer husband created a deck of Creativity Courage Cards, which pair powerful affirmations with metaphorical photos to help people leverage their creative ideas into heartfelt projects or businesses.

Creativity in Business

Creative problem solving is critical not only for solo entrepreneurs like Gail but also for heads of the largest corporations. IBM asked 1,500 global chief executives which trait they most seek in managers and executives.[9] Was it financial mastery? Networking expertise? Marketing savvy? No. The surprising attribute atop their list was creativity.

These findings should excite and inspire you, whether you're a creative job seeker or already working, because they confirm that your talents and abilities are in growing demand in a changing world.

CEOs need creativity for the same reason you and I do: the world has grown so complicated that mental skills alone are no longer enough. As retired CEO Samuel Palmisano, who left IBM in 2011, said, "Events, threats, and opportunities aren't just coming at us faster . . . they are converging and influencing each other to create entirely unique situations."[10]

For this reason, he further commented, creativity is "a more important leadership quality than . . . management discipline, rigor, or operational acumen." Creativity is imperative, not just for executives, but also for managers or the team leader of a four- or five-person group.

IBM learned about creativity the hard way. Big Blue, as IBM is often dubbed, had ruled the mainframe computer world until "two kids in a garage," Steve Wozniak and Steve Jobs, as the illustrative business fable goes, invented the Apple personal computer and launched the revolution that sent the power of high tech into your hands and mine.

Many mainframe computer firms soon failed, but IBM recovered and thrived. Now it sponsors global research that is helping us understand that to sort through today's challenges and find sustainable solutions, we must access our higher levels of consciousness and tap not just mental, but intuitive, emotional, and spiritual resources as well. Thanks to IBM research, creative people are now recognized as having the skills companies need to:[11]

- Confront challenges from climate change to natural disasters, yet still see opportunity in the midst of crisis
- Break with the status quo in order to discover "fresh thinking" and new solutions
- Think through "continuous, rapid-fire shifts and adjustments"

The IBM study's most inspiring recommendation is a new emphasis on the importance of human values. It acknowledges the need for people who rely on their "deeply held values, vision, and convictions" to guide them through the unknown.

Many corporations sponsor creativity-enhancing workshops and seminars for their employees. Companies like Google, pharmaceutical giant AstraZeneca, and management consultant McKinsey, along with thousands of businesses and nonprofits, have discovered the practical value of presence, and, as a result, host meditation classes for their personnel.[12]

When Bad Things Happen to Good, Creative Companies— and People

Business depends on creativity, and people long to be more creative at work. Specifically, corporations must launch new products to grow sales and profit. This task is known as innovation, but it's impossible without the genius of human consciousness, which abides in creative people. Meanwhile, you and I yearn to create for pleasure, fulfillment and to grow

Conscious Money. It's a perfect match, or should be. But old business models (and habits) die hard. Many firms are still operating in the Age of Information. In fact, some are run by Industrial Era thinkers who have no idea how to go about engaging or nurturing human consciousness.

When 3M, one of the world's greenest, most inventive industrialists, hired a new CEO in 2001, he systematized research and development and pressured the company's engineers to deliver fast. There was "no way anything like the Post-it Note would ever emerge from this new system," said one 3M veteran. (The Post-it Note famously came into being through unstructured, free-flowing experimentation.) 3M's brands faltered, its innovation suffered, and the firm dropped from number two to seven on a global list of top innovators. The positive work environment was restored when that CEO left and 3M hired insider George Buckley, who restored the creative culture—and ran the company until retiring in 2012.[13]

The business media sometimes fosters this unfortunate dismissal of creativity. For example, the respected international weekly *The Economist* reported: "One reason why bosses might not want to be too obsessive about creativity is that generating ideas is the easy part. Exploiting them has always been harder." But generating just any idea is not the point. Creative people are the ones who come up with great, actionable ideas. *The Economist* goes on to suggest that managers might take a "hard-nosed approach . . . to fragile creative types."[14]

Fragile creative types? Not a chance. Creativity in business requires resilience and hardiness, as one famous and creative firm illustrates. This company, in fact, sets the watermark in creativity against which every global corporation must be measured.

Apple: Premier Company of the New Economy of Consciousness

In 2000, when I first suspected we were shifting into the New Economy of Consciousness, I thought then that the company to watch was Apple Computer. Long venerated for its single-minded devotion to creativity; sleek, user-friendly designs; and matchless reliability, Apple was widely admired as an innovator since debuting its first computer. I was also intrigued to learn then that Steve Jobs had studied meditation and Buddhism.

So I consulted a few business magazines to research my theory that Apple was poised to become the premier company of the New Economy of Consciousness. But the media were in full disagreement with my hypothesis. Apple, they concurred, was going nowhere, because of its tiny market share, expensive though pretty product line, and loyal but geeky following. The brand to watch instead, they wrote, was Microsoft: ubiquitous, cash rich, and dominant.

One year later, in 2001, Apple launched the iPod. (As they say in metaphysical circles, "Don't give up ten minutes before the miracle.") Today, Apple's iPod, iPhone, and iPad continue to break sales records. In 2010, it was widely reported that Apple eclipsed Microsoft in market capitalization. Apple later topped Microsoft in profit.[15] Then in August 2011, Apple had surpassed Exxon Mobil to become the world's largest corporation in terms of total stock market value.[16]

Apple succeeds because its people love the thrill of imagination and create products that also engage the creative powers of Apple's customers. Compile your favorite inspiring songs on an iTunes playlist; arrange family pictures in an iPhoto album; edit home videos in iMovie: Apple continuously shows us that creativity is fulfilling and fun.

With the example of Apple before them, global business leaders are compelled to recognize the robust profits the market delivers when creativity drives product development.

How to "Hire" a Creative Employer

Consider how much time you spend at work. Many successful people regularly work a ten-hour day or longer. That means your choice of work powerfully influences the feeling state that you most often inhabit. And that frequency or vibration determines your ability to attract abundance.

Have you ever heard the expression: "Do what you love and the money will follow"? I've lived by those words since reading Marsha Sinetar's book by the same title decades ago. But until now I've never thought about the phrase's deep link to prosperity. Aside from the income you earn in your career, performing work you love raises your frequency and boosts your power to manifest money.

The issue for you as an individual—whether seeking a job or fully employed—is whether business leaders are putting creativity-affirming policies in place. You want to invest your consciousness in a firm that respects and rewards the role of creativity. In such a workplace, you'll enjoy the satisfaction of being creative, boost your Conscious Money, and earn a good return on your investment of consciousness; that is to say, you'll grow both personally and professionally. Similarly, if you are a business owner, you want to know how to boost the creativity of your people if you expect to succeed. Employer or employee, the key is to understand the business policies that promote creation and innovation. When you do, you'll find companies that appreciate creative people. The policies I'll now describe will help you identify them.

Hire Creative People

When people are surrounded by imaginative, excited colleagues who inspire them to do their best, work is a lot more fun. The Human Resource department calls it "employee engagement" and researchers have now proven that "engaged employees" are a primary reason for corporate success—and profit. According to a study conducted by global consultant Towers Watson, highly engaged people grew profits by 19.2 percent while apathetic employees reduced profits by 32.7 percent.[17] That is an enormous differential. Yet it is not at all surprising. And it certainly illustrates the unmistakable link between creativity and money making. A *Gallup*

Management Journal survey of US workers found that 59 percent of engaged employees "strongly agreed" that their job brought out their "most creative ideas."[18]

More than one employee-engagement study has concluded that disengaged employees demoralized productive people. There is no question that working in an uninspired place that rewards mediocrity will block the growth of your Conscious Money.

Listen to the advice of Arthur Levinson, chairman and CEO of biotech leader Genentech: "Hire innovative people, listen to them tell you what they want, and do it."[19] This kind of leadership inspires you to excel and fosters the growth of Conscious Money.

Invest in Creativity

Work for (or run) a company that puts its money where the creativity is. The true source of business innovation is people. Back in 2006, an earlier IBM international study of 765 CEOs revealed that 40 percent of the executives agreed with this assessment.[20] Today, it is clearly a lot higher.

So find (or become) a firm that recognizes and invests in the true source of innovation: human creativity. That is the successful strategy followed by Conscious Money companies like 3M, Google, and W. L. Gore & Associates.

Promote a Culture that Values Creativity

Larry Page and Sergey Brin, who founded Google while students at Stanford's computer science department, deliberately nurture a collegial culture at their company. It is a place where engineers are encouraged to devote 20 percent of their time to projects of their own choosing, a policy that has proven to be highly cost-effective. About half of Google's new products emerge from these engineers' pet projects, says Google executive

Marissa Mayer, age thirty-six.[21] Google's "20 percent policy" honors an abiding wisdom: "Follow your bliss."

Similarly, *Businessweek* reported that the fifty most innovative companies in the world "nurture cultures that value creative people in good times and bad."[22]

Sponsor or Encourage Mindful Practices

Apple, Yahoo, and other high tech leaders host in-house meditation or mindfulness sessions.[23] Marc Benioff, CEO of Salesforce.com, is an outspoken advocate of meditation.[24] Some companies suggest the reason they promote meditation is for stress management. This is probably true, at least in part. But it is also well-established that meditation elevates the alpha, delta, and theta brain waves that spark creativity and enhance the profound state of presence required for scientific and technological discovery.

At Google, Chade-Meng "Meng" Tan, a Buddhist, launched Google's Search Inside Yourself (SIY) initiative, which promotes meditation to achieve "peace and happiness." But SIY is "more than a corporate meditation program," says the Buddhist magazine *Shambala Sun*. An introductory SIY course devotes a full day to mindfulness and examines journaling, mindful listening, walking meditation—and even mindful emailing. Said one participant: "This course changed my life."[25]

If you find a great company that promotes creativity but does *not* sponsor a mindful practice, that can be fine, so long as employees are free to organize their own groups.

The Conscious Money Creative Company Checklist

I'll now summarize a few key points to help you determine whether your company or would-be employer affirms creativity. Ask yourself or a company representative these questions:

1. *Policy.* Does the company put great ideas on the fast track? Is there a special fund to finance new projects? Are there formal and informal ways to collect employee input and insights?
2. *Priority.* Is the company committed to creative skill building? For example, does it sponsor workshops or coaching designed to enhance creativity?
3. *Resources.* Does the firm fund creative people and programs?
4. *Culture.* Does the company reward curiosity and appreciate natural ambiguity? Or is the firm more likely to impose rigid guidelines?
5. *Walk the talk.* Does the firm send mixed messages, such as vocally advocating novel approaches but then failing to follow through on them?

Charting the Economics of Creativity

In 2011, the United Nations released the *Creative Economy Report 2010*, a long-awaited update of an earlier and landmark UN study chartering the dimensions of one critical subset of the New Economy of Consciousness: the creative sector. The creative economy, the report states, is comprised of four categories:[26]

- *Cultural Heritage:* from museums to festivals
- *Arts:* including painting, photography, and performing arts
- *Media:* such as publishing, film, and broadcasting
- *Functional:* categories of design; digital media; research and development; and creative services, from advertising to architecture

The United Nations discovered that creative commerce contributes a great deal to the world economy. From 2002 to 2008, the value of the global creative economy doubled to nearly $600 billion. In the recession year of 2008, the global creative economy sector surged 14 percent, even as global business plunged 12 percent overall.[27] The developing world is a major player in the creative economy, exporting $176 billion in creative trade in 2008.[28] Nigeria's $2.75 billion film industry is the third largest in the world, after the United States and India.[29]

Personal Creativity R&D

Success today challenges you to tap into your creativity. Whether you work in a small business, state agency, or at your kitchen table, the ability to imagine fresh inventive solutions and then act on them pays you the reward of Conscious Money. To earn it, however, you must first nurture your personal creativity and then apply it in your work.

Today, most people have multiple careers. Whereas your parents or grandparents probably had one job with the same firm for thirty years, you will likely have several distinctly different careers during your life. Not jobs, but careers. That of course is because occupations change rapidly in a fast-paced, tech-fueled economy. In a sense, therefore, we are all self-employed, since we must ultimately rely solely on ourselves (and not an employer) to come up with the next ideal work situation in which to grow our talents, skills, and Conscious Money. When you take responsibility for your creativity, however, your inner wealth compounds regularly—and it's mobile, like an IRA or 401K account that you bring with you from one career or profession to your next calling.

Furthermore, in an economy based on consciousness, it is up to you to keep your greatest assets—consciousness, presence, and creativity—nourished, fine-tuned, and ready at hand. In other words, you must personally invest in your creativity.

How, you might ask, does a person do that?

Let me draw an analogy from business. Corporations budget time and money for the function known as "research and development" (R&D), that is, the systematic, in-house pursuit of knowledge that is then applied to new product development. As individuals living in a conscious economy, we need to adopt a similar strategy for investing in our creative power. Doing so entails little money, but it does require quiet time, personal reflection, and a method for collecting the insights we have received. I call this personal pursuit "Creative R&D."

Cracking the Code of Creativity

To stay "fit" for conscious creativity, take time for contemplation and renewal. Dancers and athletes stretch. Singers perform their scales. Musicians practice their instrument. Today, we are all creators. If you accept that premise, you understand why creativity requires its own regular practices. With an open heart, follow these guidelines to enrich your creativity:

- Openness
- Sacred space
- Mindful activity
- Quiet transition time
- A way to harvest your insights

Whether you're a marketing diva, software engineer, real estate broker, entrepreneur, or team leader, the personal practice of "Creative R&D" will support you to naturally discover practical, fresh solutions.

Cultivate Openness

The greatest creative breakthroughs come not from knowing, but from *not knowing*. You foster openness with an open mind, which is the essence of a wise, old, and still-famous book title, *Zen Mind, Beginner's Mind*, by Shunryu Suzuki.

"I don't know" can be a humble yet powerful prayer that links you to higher consciousness and calls forth answers you cannot possibly anticipate.

As a beginner, you possess a distinct advantage over people who consider themselves "advanced." These so-called advanced people, however, must often spend years, even decades, unlearning erroneous or antiquated views.

When Steve Jobs was ousted from Apple in 1984, he was "devastated." But in retrospect, as he told graduates of Stanford University in his famous commencement speech in 2005, it was "the best thing that could ever have happened to me ... The heaviness of being successful was replaced by the lightness of being a beginner again, less sure about everything," he says. "It freed me to enter one of the most creative periods of my life."[30]

Do not be afraid to say "I don't know." It is not a statement of ignorance but an open invitation to creativity.

Create Sacred Space

Sacred space is not meditation or yoga, but like a spiritual practice, it does require you to dedicate time to be spent in reflection or contemplation. Many people go through life buffeted about by external circumstances. Taking regular time for sacred space anchors you in the inner world of your values and consciousness. You can practice sacred space for as little as ten or fifteen minutes each day, whether sitting quietly with your morning coffee, walking in nature, taking time to light a candle after returning home, or silently practicing breathing. Sacred space strengthens the link between higher consciousness, the source of creativity, and the realm of everyday thought.

Practice a Mindful Activity

Some scientists grumble that in today's overly commercial world, there's too much emphasis on applied science and not enough devotion to pure science. That is probably because our society wants quick results. But it is often impossible to generate sustainable results right on schedule, because such findings often rest on the insights of pure science, that is, the pursuit of knowledge for its own sake. For example, it is only in the speculative curiosity of the question "Why does a cell behave the way it does?" that humanity will finally discover the cure for cancer.

Similarly, creativity requires the "pure science" of being present to your Self, through spiritual practices like meditation, yoga, t'ai chi, or perhaps "meditative" walking. This pure presence is the precursor to genuine creativity because it connects us to higher states of consciousness. In meditation we confront the ambiguity and discomfort of the unknown. But as we apply ourselves to the discipline of observing and releasing our thoughts, we gradually develop the capacity for presence. As we spend more time in the sacred space of "Now," while experiencing a mindful practice, the unknown grows more habitable—and even joyful. Living in the moment renews your spirit, lifts your heart, and nurtures creativity. Your "Now" time, whether spent walking in nature or sitting in silence, is its own self-validating reward—pure science for the soul.

Transition Time: The Quiet Zone

You can also extend the afterglow of your "Now" time by gently emerging from an altered state of higher consciousness into a quiet zone that is not yet day-to-day awareness. This is a rich and fertile space in which to capture the insights you received in silence or to gently voice your desires. Prayer from this clear, peaceful place is very powerful. You might also simply take some extra time to appreciate the joy or peace you have just experienced.

You might discover, as I have, that this transition zone is essential to your creative practice. Meditation offers a long list of wonderful benefits, but it poses one curious problem for me: practitioners are *not* encouraged to take notes.

When I'm in a meditative state, I find myself experiencing creative breakthroughs and fantastic ideas, but recalling those gems afterward is difficult at best. One thing I've learned over decades is that the ideas that appear in an altered state of consciousness can vanish in an instant. So I help myself bridge this gap by pausing to carefully collect and appreciate those precious insights.

Harvest Your Creative Insights

The method I use is to follow my meditation with journaling. With pen in hand, I sit in silence, reflect, look out the window, brainstorm—and journal. Journaling is a commitment I keep with my higher consciousness, as in "I'll be there every morning, pen in hand, just in case there's anything you want to tell me."

Journaling enhances your creative practice by supporting you to gather and apply your reflections. Your journaling practice is the best way to discover and nurture your unique inner voice. From the notes in your journal, you might draft your first book, compile a brilliant marketing plan, or sketch a technological breakthrough.

While journaling, you follow in the footsteps of humanity's most creative geniuses. As I mentioned before, Leonardo da Vinci and Thomas Edison were great aficionados of journaling. Da Vinci filled seven thousand pages with jokes, reflections, sketches for works of art, inventions, and even financial records, says Michael Gelb, who has written books about both da Vinci and Edison. Edison jotted down "words, pictures, and diagrams" filling some 2,500 notebooks in his lifetime, says Gelb, and the inventor instructed his teams to take extensive notes on their experiments.[31]

Creativity with Sneakers On

Lawler Kang, age forty-four, founded Ingage, an employee engagement consultancy, with business partner Karen Davis. He has a different take on how to do his Creative R&D.[32] Although Lawler studied meditation as a student in Japan, he prefers "meditating in full motion," by engaging in sports, shoveling snow, or other activities where time stands still.

"The key to unlocking creativity is shutting down the rational brain and giving the creative brain permission to take over," says Lawler. That is exactly what motion achieves. "When I need to get creative, I tend to put on my sneakers," he adds.

In fact, Lawler was raking a pile of leaves and taking a break from writing his book *Passion at Work* when one particular creative brainstorm occurred. Without it he would not have won business clients such as Cisco Systems and Pfizer or earned the Conscious Money their contracts generated, because at the time his book and other tools were addressed to individuals. Then his breakthrough hit: the work of individuals is first assimilated into small teams and then into the organization as a whole. "My work could have a major impact on organizations," he realized. With that insight, Lawler went on to win corporate clients and a nice inflow of Conscious Money.

Practicing Creative R&D lifts you above day-to-day responsibilities, restores your energy, and sharpens your creative skills so that you're poised to engage a challenging problem. Creativity unravels complexity, provides a platform to experience Spirit in your profession, and helps you achieve difficult tasks with grace. Creative R&D optimizes your talent at a time when the world yearns for fresh approaches that can only come from inventive individuals who access their creative power.

In the past, humanity gave permission to cultural shamans like artists and scientists to access higher dimensions or journey into the Great Unknown. In the New Economy of Consciousness, we reclaim our creative power and give ourselves permission to do so too.

Humanity Steps into Its Power

During each economic era, the raw materials required by that economy were external to the human being. In the agriculture economy, it was land. During the industrial period, it was the factory or the engine. Even during the information era, the data aggregated by computers existed outside the person who reviewed it. Today, you might say that the raw material itself is us.

The true revolution of the New Economy of Consciousness is that the critical resource needed to create jobs, generate new wealth, and fuel the economy exists within humanity. Today the power of human consciousness is ushering in a whole new era as consciousness permeates and transforms the jobs generated in the agricultural, industrial, or information-based past.

Consider the farmer who, through the power of consciousness, discovers new methods of organic agriculture; the factory worker whose handheld computer taps into the consciousness of a colleague half a world away; or the administrator who thinks up a better way to store digital medical images and transforms the department's protocol. The New Economy of Consciousness reinvents all previous economies through the power of creative genius.

Farmer, laborer, clerk. And now creator. What a perfect metaphor for human beings decisively stepping into their power.

Exercises

Conduct a Creativity Audit

To enrich your creative powers, determine how you feel about your personal creativity. Rate these three statements on a scale of one to ten, with ten being the highest rating. Note your scores in your Conscious Money journal:

- I have the ability to be creative.
- I regularly engage in being creative to support my daily tasks.
- I invest time and energy in being creative.

Rate yourself "excellent" if you scored twenty-five or higher, and "good" if twenty or higher. If you scored below ten, take heart. You can learn to be more creative. Now open your journal and your creative imagination. Answer this question in a paragraph: How would I design a personal creativity program in terms of times, places, activities, or companions?

Honoring the Place of Creativity

Where or when do you get your best ideas? For some, inspiration occurs while:

Cleaning the house	Hiking	Showering	Vacationing
Dreaming	Listening to music	Staying up late	Waking up
Driving	Meditating	Thinking out loud	Working out

Please list in your journal the times and places that most inspire you. Of equal importance is how you collect, develop, and act on your ideas.

Options

Reflections

- Affirm Creativity as a divinely orchestrated gift. You are creative.
- Begin today: invoke Creativity to resolve daily challenges at work.
- Welcome creative challenges as opportunities to appreciate complexity and grow creative mastery.
- State creative problems appreciatively. See them as paintings or poems.
- Affirm the existence of your ideal solution.
- Be alert to creative rhythms. Are you a morning person? Night owl?
- Protect your creative hours. Be creative when you *feel* most creative. Save mundane tasks for your least creative times.

- Ask your inner guidance to send images or words that help you resolve a creative problem.
- Affirm Creativity and higher consciousness and call upon them to grow or save Conscious Money.

Resources

- Befriend creative people and find a source of constant inspiration.
- Ask questions in your journal that are positive and open-ended: "What does my creativity say about that deadline on Thursday?"
- Master the art of incubation: voice your "issue," give it to your higher consciousness, turn to another task, and happily await your answer.
- Practice incubating small creative issues first. Later on, incubate larger issues like "Should I quit my job?"
- When you get new insights, jot down how it happened. Did you describe the issue in your journal before bedtime and wake with an answer?
- Hire a creativity coach, perhaps through the Creativity Coaching Association, whose members serve writers, executives, artists, and entrepreneurs.
- Enhance your ability to describe images by recording your dreams. An unusual dream symbol may hold the answer to a problem that you've been incubating.

Right Actions

- Embrace a practice like meditation, yoga, or martial arts. When you regularly experience the altered state each induces, your brain "remembers" that there are different levels of consciousness, priming the pump for creativity.
- Honor the fruitful time or place in which you get your best ideas; weave the magic of time and place into your creative practice.

- Expand your spiritual practice to include extra time to capture insights that may unravel practical problems.
- Work for a company that values your creativity as much as you do.
- Summon the courage to find a new creative job and quit an unimaginative one.
- Consider self-employment.
- Ask potential employers to describe their policies on creativity and innovation.
- Start a mindfulness or meditation circle at work.
- Take a friend on a journaling "date" to your favorite café. After thirty minutes of quiet writing while enjoying your favorite beverage, share your insights.
- Capture creative insights, perhaps with two of my favorite brands of pens. The Uni-ball "Vision" line is particularly fluid and there's an eight-pack of vivid multicolored roller-ball-type pens sold at Staples or online. Inexpensive color fountain pens are difficult to find, but Pilot's Varsity line comes in shades of pink, purple, and aqua. Plus, these fountain pens rarely, if ever, leak. You'll find them through various online sources.

Conscious Money Affirmation

When I face a "challenging" work issue, I invite higher consciousness to step in and come up with a great solution that I might not discover.

7

The Rewards of Conscious Investing

One of the best ways to grow Conscious Wealth is by owning stock in corporations that are both financially strong and highly responsible. Recalling what we learned about conscious business in chapter 4, you will want to consider companies that embrace positive values, an appreciation of all the people involved, and sound financial principles. But even armed with these sensible guidelines, you might find that the very idea of investing brings troubling images of greedy speculators, frenetic traders, and grave financial loss.

Such feelings are understandable, but look at it this way: to weather a complex, contradictory market, you need *inner* strength, clear conviction, and a good deal of self-mastery. This is exactly what you will possess when your choices are guided by higher consciousness and your values. And it is especially prudent during volatile economic times. Most conventional investment advisors, however, do not believe values should play any role in your investment strategy. That is why conscious investors generally work with like-minded, values-driven financial counselors.

As you come to understand the nuts and bolts of conscious investing, you'll discover that investing can be both a conscious and rewarding practice. Conscious investors seek to thrive financially without damaging others, themselves, or the Earth. Instead they:

- Rely on human values to guide investment choices
- Invest in initiatives that further human and planetary evolution
- Tap into intuition to balance and complement rational, objective financial data

Conscious investing fulfills your heart and soul while earning returns that often match and sometimes exceed the results of mainstream investing.

Insights and Guidelines? Yes. Investing Advice? No.

Before you engage the practice of conscious investing, however, please be aware that this book does not offer specific investment advice. That is the work of a reputable investment professional, a qualification that I do not possess.

But what I *will* do, however, might be equally beneficial: I'll introduce you to some of the wisest and most experienced conscious investors and help you think about topics ranging from green mutual funds to managing the emotion most associated with investing—fear. I will share my own experiences and report to you on several conscious investment strategies. This information will give you the background you need to consider your investment options. I'll also offer a few questions to ask a potential advisor.

Getting Started as a Values-Driven Investor

The first step in conscious investing is to start becoming aware of companies whose conscious policies you admire. I describe several in chapter 4.

But do not limit yourself to my choices. Start collecting information about the firms with which you do business or those you learn about in the newspaper, magazines, or online. Ask your trusted friends and advisors to suggest a few more.

Knowing the basic ways to invest (or investment vehicles) gives you a framework for evaluating your investment options, such as stocks, for example. Stocks are the assets that allow you to own shares in individual companies. Owning stock is like buying an interest in a company. Suppose you are a fan of a company described in chapter 4, such as Costco, you might elect to purchase shares in the company.

Purchasing stocks requires having an account with a brokerage or individual financial advisor. Some discount brokerages require a minimum investment of, say, $1,000, at least for a retirement account. So that would be an issue to consider. Individual investment advisors, as opposed to brokerages, often require larger investment minimums, which might be $50,000 or well over $100,000. In deciding whether or not to open an account with a broker or advisor, you'd consider factors like your level of investment experience and whether you enjoy investing on your own or prefer the advice of a financial advisor.

The most popular investment asset is arguably mutual funds, a professionally managed, legally regulated investment vehicle that purchases various stocks (bonds or other investments) by pooling the monies of its investors. Suppose you have $2,000 to invest. Instead of owning 100 shares of one company (whose stock sells for $20), you could purchase $2,000 worth of mutual fund shares and own smaller interest in perhaps thirty firms, or several hundred depending on the fund.

Mutual funds offer great diversity. It is often said, somewhat tongue-in-cheek, that the number one rule of investing is "Don't lose money." If so, "Diversify" is a close second. It also helps you honor the first rule. During the last two market downdrafts, diversity was the saving grace for many investors.

Your investments are diversified when they:

- Include many different sectors, such as technology, real estate, health-care, or finance
- Involve different types of assets, including stocks and "fixed income" investments such as bonds
- Encompass both domestic and global assets
- Feature a good mix of small, medium, and large public companies

Later, as a more sophisticated investor, diversity might entail owning more complex assets such as commodities, currencies, or precious metals.

But even if you limit your investments to mutual funds, you should still form opinions about which companies you consider conscious and worthy of owning. That is important for a few reasons. First, you can then compare the stocks that a mutual fund owns against those you admire. Mutual funds typically list the stocks that make up their ten top holdings on their website. If you like Apple, for example, you might not want to own a mutual fund whose largest holding is Microsoft, or vice versa. Second, in addition to your mutual funds, you might purchase single stocks in companies you particularly respect to round out your portfolio.

Other popular investment vehicles are exchange traded funds (ETFs), which are described later in this chapter, and money market funds, which own short-term, cash equivalent securities issued by governments, corporations, or banks. Bonds are longer-term securities, with fixed rates of return, usually issued by governments and corporations.

Are There Times When Not Investigating Is a Good Idea?

Conscious investing tempers risk with awareness, balance, and positive values, but it can never entirely eliminate risk. That's why even as a passionate advocate of conscious investing, I believe there are times in life when people simply do not have much risk tolerance, even for conscious risks. Because I know that some financial spokespeople would dispute that viewpoint, I want to take time to explain why it sometimes makes sense for some people.

Consider this story about a dear friend, who I will call Sara Abbington to protect her privacy. Sara emerged from a divorce at age forty-seven with responsibility for her own retirement account. In the past, Sara, her ex-husband, and their financial advisor had managed these decisions. But Sara, who has great intuition about money, had also made a few wise investments on her own. Now she looked forward to taking charge of her money, in addition to her busy personal and professional life.

As weeks became months and then a year, however, she found herself paralyzed when faced with investment choices and harshly judged herself for her state of mind. When we chatted, I pointed out the upside: she had avoided the subprime crisis and preserved her holdings in a down market. "You should be celebrating," I said.

Over time, Sara interviewed several investment advisors but did not find one she deeply trusted. Meanwhile, after stocks hit rock bottom during the worst of the recession, they soared nearly 100 percent. Now Sara criticized herself for missing out on the bull market. Again I disagreed. Of course, it would have been great had she benefited from the boom. But in fact Sara was in the midst of a tumultuous transition, a time when people tend to feel vulnerable and uncertain. She needed time to heal, choose where to make a home, explore new relationships, and envision her professional options.

In actual dollars, it's hard to calculate whether Sara's retirement fund would have grown, shrunk, or stayed about the same had it been invested since her divorce. But there are times in life when peace of mind and the freedom to focus on personal priorities without worrying about investments can be a good thing for your Conscious Wealth. This is especially true during uncertain financial times. Asset preservation is still the most important rule in growing Conscious Wealth.

Midlife transitions are not the only time when it may be wise to limit risk. As any financial planner will tell you, it is not a good idea for young people to invest in the stock market until they have amassed sizable savings. People in their 20s or 30s, who may be paying off education loans or credit card debt, have rarely saved even a three- to six-month emergency fund which, most financial advisors agree, should be a first priority.

Another time to consider limiting your investing is when you are older, when asset preservation is often a better course of action than putting too much money at risk. Many baby boomers whose retirement accounts plummeted during the subprime crisis can sadly attest to this. On the other hand, even after retirement, you will still want your money to grow, even if you are more conservative. A long-standing guideline is to invest the same percentage as your age in less risky assets. For example if you are forty years old, 40 percent of your portfolio should be in more stable assets and 60 percent should be allocated to riskier ones, such as stocks. If you are seventy, you'll want a lot more conservative and a lot fewer risky investments.

Finding the Middle Path

But investing need not be an either/or decision. You can find a middle path; that is, you can protect most or much of your money yet expose some of it to risk.

You can also move into investing gradually by taking a series of small, deliberate actions. This strategy gives you a chance to test yourself (and your appetite for risk) with some manageable steps that may also boost your investment confidence. Whether you are young, taking personal time to heal, or savoring that senior discount, research these simple, conscious investment strategies:

1. *Start small.* Consider exposing a limited percentage of your money to risk, perhaps between 5 and 10 percent of your savings, while safeguarding the rest. If, for example, you have saved $10,000, you might invest $1,000 of it in a responsible mutual fund.

2. *Take one small step.* Or you might open an account with a discount broker like Charles Schwab, Fidelity, or TD Ameritrade. You needn't take any further step until you are ready (do not allow a representative to pressure you to act). Brokers like these offer customer service almost anytime by phone and online. You might take advantage of this service to ask representatives which investments they'd recommend for someone of your age and circumstances. Customer representatives should answer questions graciously. If not, hang up, call back, and find a helpful person.

3. *Place a conservative bet.* Research the possibility of cashing in a small bank certificate of deposit (CD) that earns a low rate of return and investing the funds in a relatively safe top-rated AAA corporate bond (remember, however, that while the money in your CD may be guaranteed by the government-funded FDIC, your investments will not be) or a government bond. Ask your broker's customer service rep to suggest a few possibilities. Attempt to find one with a greater yield than your CD. Remember, too, that bonds are not as safe as a CD. As of 2012, some observers are steering investors away from bonds because they expect their value to decline. That is something to consider as well. Unfortunately the time to get good rates on safe assets is when interest rates are high, which creates other financial problems.

4. *Grow financial self-confidence.* Consider purchasing shares in a stock that is considered steady and also pays a dividend. In May 2011, three sample stocks that fit this description were Verizon, Pfizer, and Kraft Food. As you do your own research, experts suggest picking stocks that have consistently increased their dividend over the years.

This is seen as a marker of success and stability—though it's important to understand that dividend-paying stocks can lose value like any other stock.

5. *Re-evaluate your investments quarterly.* The market mood can shift dramatically when unforeseen events shake investor confidence. While you would probably not want to make big changes in your portfolio just because market sentiment has changed, it is essential that you consciously evaluate the factors behind any change. Don't emulate the investors, so often described in the media, who refuse to open their brokerage statements for months on end after a time when the market is down. Being a conscious investor means gritting your teeth and facing the uncomfortable truth. There is of course a silver lining to a down market: it is a very good time to buy.

The Passion, Values, and Priorities of Investing

When you invest consciously, you consider factors that traditional investors overlook. The typical investing mind-set is strictly analytical—and certainly you want to draw on your intellectual faculties to make sensible investment decisions. Yet as a conscious investor, you can also call upon your passions, that is, the interests that most attract your attention, as well as your values. Your investing priorities also come into play. We will look at each of these three and then see how they can work together.

Identifying Your Investing Passion

Conscious investors translate their passion into investment strategies. Passion is where your heart leads and your mind follows. Combining head and heart can be the basis for making good investment choices. Some people associate the term "passion" with life purpose or work. Let's expand the definition to embrace our avocational interests as well.

When you deeply care about something, you're drawn to the people and information related to it. Whether you enjoy high fashion or high technology, your passion immerses you in a learning zone where your natural fascination for the topic lets you effortlessly integrate facts, figures, and anecdotes. That wisdom and expertise may later help you make sound investments. Of course, you must balance what you know about that passion with reliable financial data and solid investing advice.

Below are some widely enjoyed passions that may help you in affirming or discovering your own. Note your passion (or passions) in your Conscious Money journal.

Animals	Education	Home	Technology
Art	Environment	Music	Wine
Cars	Fashion	Natural healing	
Creativity	Food	Nature	

Choosing Your Investing Values

Values also play a decisive role in your conscious investment choices, because it is essential to align your Conscious Money with companies that reflect your values. If you care deeply about social justice, you would experience a terrible imbalance were you to invest in a company that exploits sweatshop labor. Yet some investors willingly own tobacco companies despite the unequivocal health risks of smoking because their stocks pay a lucrative dividend. Although some people think this is a perfectly okay way to earn money, it is, in my opinion, the very definition of unconscious investing.

As in chapter 5, "The Joy of Mindful Spending," here too I invite you to identify any values that for you pertain specifically to investing. Your transcendent values of course are still operative in making investing choices. The question is: Does investing bring up any additional particular values for you?

The following list offers some suggestions:

Beauty	Excellence	Health	Long term
Compassion	Freedom	Innovation	Love
Courage	Frugality	Integrity	Sustainability
Education	Global	Justice	Transparency

Now that you've established your values, write them down in your Conscious Money journal and connect to the energy within them. Ask yourself what sort of investments they might inspire. Add any insights, ideas, or company names that exemplify your ideals.

Investing Priorities

Priorities qualitatively differ from both values and passions in the sense that they represent the more grounding financial aspects of your Conscious Money strategy. It is possible that your priorities will change over time, and that may be entirely appropriate, whereas your values may not change very much.

In investing, your priorities say a lot about the point of view you bring to the table. Being clear about your priorities is essential, whether you invest on your own or work with an advisor. After identifying your values, the next priority you should address is whether your style as an investor is conservative, aggressive, or somewhere in between. Read and consider each of the statements below and decide which apply to you. Or write one or more new declarations that better describe you.

"I'm investing to earn income I plan to spend in the near future."
"I want to grow wealth and am willing to take a good bit of risk to do so."
"My goal is to avoid risk and slowly grow my money."

"I want to earn income but grow my portfolio, too."

Describe your investment priorities in your Conscious Money journal. Statements like the four listed above help you or your advisor determine which kind of investments to research or purchase.

How do values, passions, and priorities work together? Suppose you selected sustainability as your top value, land as your passion, and growth as a priority. You might want to invest in a company like the market leader in organic food, Whole Foods, which pays a 0.70 percent dividend.

If healing is your passion; compassion, your top value; and income, your priority, you may want to investigate the medical device sector. Medtronic, which invented pacemakers in 1957, initiates new employees into its healing-oriented business culture with a moving medallion ceremony. Medtronic pays a 2.6 percent dividend. Please note that the dividend a stock pays varies somewhat according to the value of the stock, which obviously changes often. (The dividend rates cited here are for late spring 2012.)

If you chose innovation, technology, and value, you might consider Intel, which might be dubbed a mature innovator. Intel offers what income-loving investors crave: a 3.2 percent dividend.

Suppose animals are your passion, and their beauty or health is among your top values. Suppose also that you seek a stock that delivers both income and growth. In such a case, you might consider investing in retailer PetSmart, whose stock soared in 2011 and into 2012, while delivering income by way of a 1 percent dividend.

As you follow the business news, make notations about which companies exemplify your particular trio of passion, values, and priorities. For example, note which firms are known for paying people fairly (social justice), opening their financial books (transparency), or embracing exemplary environmental policies (sustainability). When you read or hear a news item about a company, consider what the deeper meaning of that information tells you about the firm.

If you are just starting out in investing and are unfamiliar with very many companies, you can get some interesting ideas by researching which stocks are held by funds that specialize in Socially Responsible Investing (SRI), which I'll soon describe—because choosing to research and invest in responsible values-driven companies is the prime investment criterion for a sound investment strategy.

Growth versus Value Investments

Whether you invest alone or work with a professional advisor, it is important to know where you stand in terms of another investing basic: whether you prefer to invest in growth stocks or value stocks. (This is true even if you invest only in mutual funds because such funds are often characterized as a growth or value fund.) An advisor will probably ask which approach you favor, so prepare for this discussion with some basic definitions. Typically value stocks are considered more conservative investments. A value stock "tends to trade at a lower price relative to its fundamentals (that is, dividends, earnings, sales, and so forth) and thus is considered undervalued," explains Investopedia.com, the online investing site.[1] But value stocks are generally not expected to grow dramatically.

Growth stocks are shares in companies "whose earnings are expected to grow at an above-average rate relative to the market," says *Investopedia*.[2] But growth stocks may be deemed "expensive" compared to the company's earnings and profits, and they are usually considered more risky. Some advisors suggest that young people should own growth stocks since their time horizon is longer than that of their parents' generation. It is not unusual for people to want investments that deliver both value and growth.

Take some notes in your journal about where you stand on value versus growth stocks or whether you seek a balanced approach.

Creating or Joining an Investment Club

As you can already see, investing requires a good deal of thinking, research, and decision making, and you might find this preparation a lot more enjoyable if you engage in it with a group of investors who share your interest in the topic.

Pooling resources with your peers can also be an excellent way to get started. You can create a like-minded community in which to investigate companies that may fit your passions, values, and priorities. Rather than having to do all the legwork on your own, each member of a club can do the research on a different possible investment. Then as a group, you can debate the possible pros and cons of investing in certain companies and the most effective ways of leveraging your values and passions in the marketplace.

Members can also help each other learn about investing, how it works, different strategies to pursue, the basics of business, and so on, within a supportive community. If this approach interests you, start your research with Better Investing, formerly known as the National Association of Investors Corporation, a member-driven, educational, nonprofit organization that provides online resources, financial software, and a list of local chapters. For more information, consult this chapter's option list.

Karen Gross, sixty-two, a dental hygienist, joined a ten-woman investment club in 1998.[3] Like many women, Karen possessed strong investing instincts, but when a male advisor or spouse would boldly express his opinions, she sometimes felt reluctant to defend her view. Female stock groups create an intellectually stimulating but supportive atmosphere in which women are free, as Karen puts it, "to educate ourselves in our own way."

Karen's club, which calls itself the Fortune Cookies, invests in companies with "the potential for sustained growth," but also, as Karen notes, "strives to be conscious" in all of its investment decisions. The club refuses to own oil stocks, for example, and vetoes firms whose leaders earn excessive compensation. The Fortune Cookies bought shares in Wall Street banker Goldman Sachs in part because of its outstanding green policies. But when the firm's dealings in credit derivatives, the risky financial instruments that triggered the subprime crisis, were revealed, Karen says the group "did not want anything to do with the stock" and sold its shares at a sizable loss.

The Fortune Cookies consider health issues too. In the late 1990s, doughnut retailer Krispy Kreme was a hot stock. But the club wouldn't even give serious consideration to investing in it. "First," says Karen, "it's a fad. Second, it's an unhealthy fad." The stock soared, then crashed, and the Fortune Cookies remained true to their values while also avoiding the entire drama.

Today their thirty-stock portfolio is a diversified list of solid companies such as Apple, Whole Foods, Ford, Caterpillar, IBM, and Costco. Every month the women debate buying, selling, or holding their stocks. They fund their portfolio with a minimum investment of $25 monthly per member. Each woman owns "units" comprised of her investment and its appreciation. Should anyone leave the club, they take their earnings with them. By 2012, the Fortune Cookies counted more than $28,000 in profit on an account now valued at about $91,000. But the women have earned a lot more than money.

Karen now confidently asserts herself in discussions with her husband or broker. "They're looking at whether the market is up or down. I examine the whole picture." Karen says that belonging to an investment club has widened her horizons. "I find myself wondering how developments in China or India will influence our stocks."

The Fortune Cookies' interest in conscious investing reflects one of the biggest trends in modern money markets—and illustrates a great way for beginners to get started. But you need not follow the example of the Fortune Cookies and research individual stocks to capitalize on this trend. There is a simple and well-established way to honor your values while investing: all you need to do is educate yourself about Socially Responsible Investing (SRI).

What Is Socially Responsible Investing?

Socially responsible investors seek financial gain by investing in firms with high ethical standards and corporate values that reflect their own. Socially responsible investors refuse to take positions in firms they or the funds and advisors they trust deem immoral, irresponsible, or dubious. Therefore, most refuse to invest in tobacco, alcohol, gaming, and weaponry stocks. Many also veto companies engaged in oil or coal industries, businesses that pollute, and firms that employ sweatshop labor or violate human rights.

During tough economic times, investor trust in SRI reached an all-time high. In a three-year period during the height of the Great Recession, the total monies invested in United States SRI assets surged 13 percent, while mainstream assets essentially remained flat. Today, SRI in the United States alone is a $3.07 trillion industry, representing 12.2 percent of total assets under professional management.[4]

In the past, the investment establishment failed to recognize the value and importance of Socially Responsible Investing. Conventional investment wisdom, declares The Motley Fool, a respected investing website, "loves to argue that any form of Socially Responsible Investing will inevitably endanger your portfolio returns."[5] The Motley Fool refutes that groupthink. But today this antiquated point of view is definitely changing. "On average," concludes one prestigious report, SRI "portfolios perform comparably to conventional ones."[6] And sometimes SRI funds enjoy astounding success. In one year during the Great Recession, nearly 70 percent of SRI funds beat their benchmarks, which are the indices against which those SRI funds are measured.[7]

In recent years, as investors have come to embrace the value of sustainability, the acronym SRI is also evolving to stand for the newly coined concept "Sustainable Responsible Impact Investing." Impact investing bankrolls socially valuable community projects and social entrepreneurship. Its aims are to "do good" first and earn money secondarily.

SRI funds own well-managed comapnies, but there is another reason why they fare well. Companies that fail to meet their societal responsibilities can deliver unhappy surprises that hurt the bottom line: British Petroleum stock plummeted in the wake of the Deepwater Horizon oil spill in the Gulf of Mexico. So did the stock of Goldman Sachs after the US government launched a conflict of interest investigation.

British Petroleum and other companies that activists deem irresponsible, however, are conspicuously absent from the popular SRI fund I shall now describe.

Amy Domini: Conscious Evolutionary

One of the world's greatest SRI pioneers is Amy Domini, the petite, honey-haired stock portfolio manager who in 1990 developed the Domini 400 Social Index and later a mutual fund based on it. (The Domini 400 Social Index is now known as the MSCI KLD 400 Social Index.) These innovations revolutionized index mutual funds, the investment vehicles designed to deliver investors a broad spectrum of companies and industries.

Typically offered by big brokerage houses like Vanguard or Fidelity, many index funds are based on the S&P 500 index of the largest companies traded on US exchanges (though they can also be based on other indices). But such funds present real problems for conscious investors because they require that you own stock in all the companies listed on the index in question, the good, bad, and the mediocre companies. An environmentalist, for example, considering an S&P 500 index fund would have to own numerous oil and coal companies. That was until Amy created a conscious alternative: a fund based on her index of 400 large companies, each of which met her stringent SRI ethical criteria.

To honor Amy Domini's breakthrough *Time* magazine named her one of the 100 most influential people in the world in 2005 and one of twenty-five "Responsibility Pioneers" in 2009.[8] At the Broadmoor Hotel in Colorado Springs, Colorado, in 2006, where Domini addressed the SRI industry during its annual SRI in the Rockies conference, she laughed when someone called her "the Bob Dylan of SRI."[9]

But her fund is a sort of rock star, too. The Domini Social Equity Fund owns shares of Apple, Intel, Bristol Myers Squibb, and JPMorgan Chase. In 2009, the Domini Social Equity Fund surged 35.56 percent, easily besting the S&P 500's growth of 26.46 percent. In 2011, however, the Domini fund grew 0.74 percent whereas the S&P 500 increased 2.11 percent. (Unless noted, the source of the mutual fund information cited in this chapter is the fund website as of December 31, 2011. The year 2011 was a poor one for the stock market, including the SRI sector. To keep matters in perspective, I have also included data from recent years when SRI funds outperformed the market.)

If you want to invest outside of the United States, consider the Domini International Social Equity Fund. Top holdings include France's Sanofi, Japan's Fujifilm, and the UK's BT (British Telecom) Group. In 2010, the Domini International Fund rose 11.25 percent, beating the European MSCI (the Domini International Fund's benchmark), which grew 8.21 percent. But in 2011, it was the European MSCI that outperformed the Domini International Fund by a similar margin.

"Active Investing"

In recent years, however, the two Domini funds have morphed from strict index funds into an approach called "active investing."[10] As Amy Domini explained to those of us in the audience at the 2006 SRI in the Rockies conference, this new Domini model marries the purity of SRI "screens," that is, the criteria by which a company's responsibility is evaluated, with new ways to achieve financial performance—without compromising on human values. Here's how it works. Domini analysts first apply sixty-five SRI screens to measure a firm's social, environmental, and governance policies. The corporations that qualify then go to a sub-manager who specializes in financial analysis. So both the Domini Social Equity and International funds only hold shares of companies that meet the Domini company's social and financial criteria.

Amy Domini's lifelong commitment to social justice is also reflected in her company's commitment to shareholder activism. In 2010, Domini & Co. lobbied AT&T, Goldman Sachs, and JPMorgan Chase to increase political accountability, and it tackled the issue of harmful chemicals with Coca-Cola and Southwest Energy.[11] The Domini funds and other SRI investors recently persuaded Toyota Motor to pressure a Toyota supplier to cut ties with Burma's brutal military regime.[12] Many SRI investors believe applying the pressure of shareholder activism is a better way to change corporate policy than simply selling your shares in a company that behaves badly.

"There is no such thing as values-neutral business," says Amy Domini. "You run the business for the profit or you honor the triple bottom line of people, planet, and profit."[13]

There are several outstanding providers of SRI mutual funds. Consider SRI pioneers like the Calvert family of funds, with seventeen SRI funds; Pax World, which, among other funds, offers a high-yield international bond fund; Everence (formerly MMA Praxis,) which sells SRI small cap, international, and index funds; and Parnassus, with six SRI funds. The Appleseed Fund, another SRI favorite, recently added a new category to the stocks that SRI funds typically avoid. The fund announced it would now shun large banks such as Citigroup, Bank of America, and others that triggered the subprime crises by investing in credit derivatives. The move invited some to ask whether such banks were the new "sin" stock.[14]

If you want to stay clear of stocks, Domini and Calvert, as well as Pax World, offer bond funds.

Working with a Financial Advisor

Many investors take the "do-it-yourself" approach, creating an account with a discount broker and making their own investment decisions. If you are confident in your understanding of investing, have a limited amount to invest, or both, this can be a good choice. However, when your portfolio grows to a size that is beyond your ability to manage, consider working with an advisor. Most require that a minimum amount be maintained in your portfolio.

When you work with an advisor, however, be sure to follow this core principle of Conscious Money: *Never, ever* give your power away to any investment professional, or nonprofessional, for that matter. This applies to hired investment advisors and customer service personnel at your bank. Giving away your power is an unconscious choice.

Let me clarify this point. When you buy a mutual fund or work with an investment advisor, you are paying for expert advice and giving the advisor or fund manager "discretionary authority" to act on your behalf. That is as it should be. Giving away your power is different. It means being unconscious about how you choose to invest, failing to fully examine your investment choices and options, or forgetting that it's your money and you can fire the fund manager or investment advisor at any point.

The first step toward embodying your power is to absolutely refuse to be afraid of or embarrassed or shamed by anyone handling your money. I write this because unfortunately more than a few have been known to do such things. This is unacceptable. In fact, swindlers seek out people who are vulnerable in these ways because they are easier to manipulate.

Always demand clarity. You want to work with people who explain matters in clear and simple terms. Should a potential advisor (or anyone else) fail to do so, be prepared to assert yourself. You might say, "Please explain that in layman's terms." If they persist, consider working with someone else. No investment advisor should intimidate you with jargon.

When working with an advisor, stay highly conscious about your money. There are too many sad stories about investors, from the beginners to the experienced, who said, "My advisor is taking care of my money, so I don't have to worry about it," only to discover that they lost a substantial amount. Even when you find an advisor you trust, you must remain vigilant. That means assessing the risks of investing, regularly monitoring your money, knowing the basics of business, and sharing your thoughts and concerns with your advisor.

Questions to Ask a Potential Investment Advisor

The following are some questions you can ask an investment advisor you are considering working with:[15]

1. How long have you worked as a financial advisor?
2. What certifications do you hold? Some credentials include Certified Financial Planner (CFP), Accredited Investment Fiduciary (AIF), and Chartered Financial Consultant (ChFC), although there are also good advisors who do not possess them. Chartered Financial Analyst (CFA) is considered the most difficult credential to acquire.
3. Are you registered with the SEC, the state where you practice, or the Financial Industry Regulatory Authority?
4. How did the stocks you recommended to your clients perform last year? In the past quarter?
5. May I call a few of your clients for a reference?
6. How are you compensated? By the hour? (Most advisors are paid by a percentage of the portfolio they manage, ranging from a low of 0.5 percent to 1 percent to a high end of about 2 percent.)
7. If you enroll me in a mutual fund, will you receive a commission? The issue here is transparency. There are many "no-load" mutual funds that don't charge commissions or fees. But there's nothing

wrong with the advisor getting a commission, provided the investor knows about it. If you have a small portfolio, it may be the only way your advisor earns any money—and it will not be very much.

8. How do you feel about SRI, green, and renewable investments? Are you knowledgeable and qualified to invest in these areas?
9. Do you have a specialty, such as high-tech companies or the financial sector? (Consider choosing an advisor whose specialties are of interest to you.)
10. Do you work with young families or people ready to retire? (Choose an advisor whose clients are similar to you.)
11. How much input do your clients have in the stocks you buy and sell for them? Do you solicit their ideas?

I am grateful to Jason Voss, whom you met earlier and will soon meet again, for suggesting I add this excellent, though frank, question: What were some of your biggest investing errors and what steps have you taken to avoid them in the future?

You want to work with an advisor who owns up to making mistakes (anyone who denies making them is highly questionable). Just observing how a potential advisor reacts to this question will tell you a great deal.

There is one more question you should be prepared to ask, and it is an important one: "If I instruct you to sell some or all of my positions, how will you proceed? Do you or your company have any guidelines about such situations?"

You are ultimately responsible for your money. You want an advisor who recognizes this. It is the responsibility of your financial advisor to guide you in the best way she or he knows how, and that may include attempting to persuade you to buy, sell, or hold stocks that your advisor believes are in your best interest. But what if you disagree? Decide in advance how the two of you will work together and put that agreement in writing. That way, you'll avoid situations like this one:

During the last market crash an investor we'll call Bill wanted to sell his positions. But his advisor, Sally, strongly disagreed. Bill went along with Sally's recommendation. But there came a point when he could no longer bear the losses in his portfolio. Bill then insisted on selling. Sally finally agreed. But at that point it was about the worst possible time to sell. When Bill's stocks were sold, he lost a lot of money. Soon the market roared back. Bill was very disappointed. If Bill had firmly demanded to sell early on despite Sally's disagreement, if Sally had agreed sooner, or if Bill had stayed the course and stayed in the market, he would have lowered his losses. But like many of us, he got scared and got out.

By thinking ahead about the ups and downs of the market, anticipating your emotional reaction to those gyrations, and coordinating your strategy with your advisor in advance, chances are you will fare better. To do that, however, you must know your investment philosophy—and stick with it.

Discuss Your Investment Philosophy with Your Advisor

Be prepared to discuss and share your investment passions, values, and priorities with your advisor. He or she will probably *not* ask you about them, but since this is important to you, take some initiative. Furthermore, in chapter 4, you discovered that Conscious Capitalists outperform the stock market in general. It may surprise you to consider that this is something that your advisor may not know (even though many studies have shown it to be so). Since Conscious Money is now part of your "investment philosophy," be ready to speak up.

Discuss with your advisor investing in companies that:

- Treat their employees well
- Advance scientific discovery
- Have a superb record on the environment

- Excel in high technology
- Promote organic or local agriculture or both
- Are committed to renewable energy

Ask also where she or he stands on common approaches like "buy and hold," that is purchasing investments and staying with them for the long haul, and "profit discipline," which advocates selling a portion of your stock holdings when a stock increases a lot in value.

As a do-it-yourself investor, know where you stand on these strategies, too. In recent years, the wisdom of "buy and hold" has been questioned after many people lost a lot of money. Like everything else about investing, contradictions abound. Buy and hold might be the perfect strategy for one decade and a disastrous approach for the one that follows. That is one of the many reasons why you and your advisor must review your investments at least twice a year.

After two recent market crashes, investors are well aware of the downside of various maxims that do not address one ancient and fundamental rule of investing: "Buy low; sell high."

One way to balance "buy and hold" and partly address "buy low; sell high" is through the notion of "profit discipline," which holds that it is wiser to regularly take profits by selling a certain percentage, perhaps one-half, of the stocks that have significantly increased in value. The risk you assume is that your stocks will continue to rise and you will miss out on further appreciation. When you take regular profits, you reduce and may even avoid the need to make a decision when the market is falling and fear is high. During times of panic, investors do not tend to make the best choices. Profit discipline during uncertain markets is an excellent potential strategy for you to investigate.

As you grow clear about how and where you want to invest, the chances of creating a productive, satisfying, and financially successful partnership with an investment advisor expands greatly. Each highly qualified advisor listed below has a solid reputation for working with clients who seek socially responsible, green, and conscious investments:

- First Affirmative Financial Network, FirstAffirmative.com, is an SRI-oriented consortium of one hundred financial advisors in twenty-nine states who work with clients in forty-eight states. The firm's official portfolio minimum is $50,000 but its advisors are free to serve clients whose assets are smaller.
- Trillium Asset Management, TrilliumInvest.com, is the oldest and largest independent advisor devoted exclusively to sustainable and responsible investing. Minimum portfolio is $2 million, but Trillium also manages the Green Century Balanced Fund, whose minimum investment is $1,000.
- SRI pioneer Natural Investments, NaturalInvestments.com, has advisors in Colorado, Hawaii, California, Washington, Oregon, Kentucky, South Carolina, and New York. The portfolio minimum is $30,000. Individual advisors, however, may require larger minimums. Natural Investments offers an hourly rate for investors with smaller portfolios who manage their own money.

As you move forward in your conscious investing practice, remember that you have every right to work with an advisor you trust and with whom you feel comfortable. Many people are competing for your business, and you possess the power to choose the best one for you.

"Green" Investing

Perhaps you know exactly how you want to invest. You care about the Earth and want to align your Conscious Money with companies that make this a cleaner, greener planet. If so, green investing might be for you even if you are a beginning investor, and certainly if you are a more experienced one. I am grateful to Michael Kramer of Natural Investments for the following story.

Green investor Bennett Dorrance, age forty, awakened his investing consciousness two decades ago when a mentor told him to look behind the "numbers" of business at the people who run a company. Later, he followed his passion for sustainable products, healthy living, and the environment with investments in Whole Foods and other stocks, but Bennett says he had "never heard the term SRI" until he began working with Natural Investments advisor Michael Kramer.[16]

Growing up in a family business, Bennett experienced "a weight of responsibility" about using money to make a difference in the world, which boosted his interest in green investing. Today he's exploring companies with beneficial salmon fishing practices, discovering ways to fight deforestation in the tropics, and learning more about renewable investing. Bennett feels a "sense of completeness" that his values and investments are well aligned.

Like Bennett, you may seek to follow your passion and values into green investing. However, before getting started there are a few important factors to consider.

Remember the rule about diversifying your portfolio. Most authorities recommend limiting any major sector of an investment portfolio to 5 or 10 percent. Consider an even smaller percentage if you favor certain kinds of green investing, since many green technologies are still in the experimental stage. One important area of green investing, renewable energy, which includes wind and solar energy, is extremely volatile.

But if you are determined to be a green investor, I have excellent news. Not all green investing involves renewable energy, and not all green investing is risky. Consider investing in leading SRI mutual funds, like Domini, Calvert, Pax World, Parnassus, and Everence (which sells Praxis Mutual Funds). Each of these SRI leaders already stringently assesses corporate environmental performance, which means you will own very green and responsible stocks. This is an excellent option for beginning investors who want to go green.

You might also consider buying an SRI fund that is particularly geared to green stocks, such as Green Century Funds, which believes "companies that are responsible toward the environment may be more likely to act ethically and maintain the trust of their shareholders." It offers two mutual funds: The Green Century Balanced Fund holds stocks and bonds including Apple, Costco, and IBM. The Green Century Equity Fund buys the socially and environmentally responsible stocks on the MSCI KLD 400 Social Index (formerly the Domini Social Index), including Proctor & Gamble, PepsiCo, and Intel.

Portland, Oregon's, Portfolio 21 buys "companies designing environmentally superior products, using renewable energy, and developing efficient production methods." The fund's transparent website discloses why a stock is sold in its "Portfolio Manager's Commentary" feature. The Gabelli SRI Green Fund holds a Morningstar rating of four stars (out of a possible five). Top holdings include Cree, Inc., a pioneer in green lighting, and Novozymes, a leader in green chemicals, biotech, and bioenergy, which often appears on the Sustainable Business 20 list of top green companies.

The Natural Investments "Heart" Chart

If you seek to invest in green or socially responsible mutual funds, you may want to further examine the companies included in each fund. Fortunately, there is a resource to help you do so. In theory, a green mutual fund could have holdings in a solar panel maker that emits toxins, or works with a supplier that manufactures its product in a developing country under poor working conditions. For example, although solar is booming in China, that nation's toxicity standards could pose concerns for conscious investors. Natural Investments, the socially responsible advisor listed above, is designed to help you sort out such issues with a rating system that evaluates about fifty SRI mutual funds on the breadth and depth of environmental, social, and governmental criteria used to select the underlying investments. Log onto NaturalInvestments.com, locate the "Heart Rating" button, and you can see that some SRI funds are awarded only three hearts (instead of stars), while others earn a top five-heart rating. The heart rating is also published regularly in *Green Money Journal* and *LOHAS Journal*.[17]

With the help of an SRI-savvy advisor or by researching your own green mutual funds, you can create a diversified portfolio of assets that are green yet reasonably steady.

Renewable Energy

The spiritual heart of all green investing is the desire to honor and protect this planet. A key factor in achieving that purpose is rethinking humanity's source and use of energy. We have recently witnessed, through accidents and natural disasters, the terrible costs of oil, coal, and nuclear energy. With that in mind, along with the destructive environmental impact of fossil fuels, the importance of renewable energy only increases. Renewable energy such as solar, wind, or geothermal is derived from natural sources that are clean and so plentiful that they are almost limitless. It is virtually carbon-free, but when it comes to investments, it is certainly *not* risk-free. Renewable energy is an extremely unpredictable investment, because the value of renewable stocks has repeatedly surged and plummeted in recent years.

In search of more information about clean green energy, I drove to Boston one sizzling August day to meet with Matt Patsky, CEO of Trillium Asset Management, the top sustainable investment advisor in the United States. Matt is also the former comanager of the Winslow Green Growth Fund, and therefore an expert in renewable energy.

"Grid parity is the Holy Grail of renewable energy," says Patsky, whose cropped salt-and-pepper hair and steady presence suggest fiftyish maturity.[18] Grid parity refers to the electrical grid; there will be parity, or equality, when renewable energy delivers electricity for about the same cost as coal and natural gas. Once parity is achieved, renewable energy stocks will be more likely to stabilize and perhaps prosper.

The day the United States achieves grid parity is not that far away, Patsky feels. "Every day, renewable energy advances on two fronts. First, the technology continually improves. Second, the prices for solar and wind are consistently dropping."

This may surprise some people. Conventional wisdom holds that Europe is "way ahead" of the United States in renewable energy. "Many of the best green companies reside across the pond," as Kiplinger Personal Finance puts it.[19] But geography, argues Matt Patsky, gives the United States a huge advantage and is helping to close the gap. In the deserts of Arizona, New Mexico, and California, sun power is nearly limitless and desert real estate inexpensive.

Renewable Energy Is Growing (And Might or Might Not Earn You Profits)

Growth in renewable, green energy is not just happening in Europe and the United States, however. People and institutions around the world are placing their money in green energy alternatives. In 2008, the green energy movement reached an important benchmark. For the first time, global investors allocated more money to wind, solar, biofuel, geothermal, and other renewable sources than to oil, gas, and coal.

That year, global green energy investment reached a record $140 billion, versus $110 billion for electrical power generated by fossil fuels, reports the United Nations Environmental Programme. Clearly, as the agency's executive director Achim Steiner noted, "renewable energy now has reached a tipping point where it is as important—if not more important . . . than fossil fuels."[20]

Renewable energy sources now account for a surprising 25 percent of global electrical capacity. Global wind power averaged 27 percent annual growth for several years during the first decade of the twenty-first century. Grid-connected solar energy grew an average of 60 percent each year for a decade. Global governments have pledged nearly $200 billion in tax breaks, clean technology, and green incentives.[21] These combined trends are propelling renewables into the mainstream energy picture.

Andreas Schreyer, founder of the Green Investor newsletter, says renewable energy is "nothing short of reinventing . . . the infrastructure powering our world." The newsletter's Green Portfolio Index is a valuable tool for green investors.[22]

Andreas notes that "the renewable energy investment space is extremely fragmented. . . . Some technologies . . . have peaked and are on the decline. Others are decades away."[23] In other words, renewable energy, highly conscious though it is, may still be too volatile an investment for many conscious investors. The year 2011 was especially tough on renewable energy investors. On the other hand, renewable energy could be a very good investment in the next few years if the sector has "bottomed out," as they say in the investment business. Even so, if you are inclined to take a risk on renewable energy, remember the advice offered early in this chapter: "Invest a little—and then maybe a little more?"

Jack Robinson, founder of the Winslow Green Growth Fund and a thirty-year veteran of environmental investing, voices a similar view. His comments about green investing apply to green renewables, too. "There has never been a time when there are so many green investment opportunities. But just because it's green doesn't mean it's a good investment."[24]

A tall, fit, sixty-seven-year-old, Jack is the son of "back to the earth" parents who grew their own food during World War II and published a book titled The "Have-More" Plan, which is still in print. "But you can't just follow your heart," he says. "You need a disciplined approach, a skill set in financial analysis and common sense."

Winslow Green Growth Fund, which has experienced its own share of volatility, looks for "small companies with big, green ideas; enviable business models; and a proven management team." The fund's holdings include United Natural Foods and Acuity Brands, one of the world's leading providers of green lighting.

A few years ago, Jack got interested in WaterFurnace Renewable Energy, a geothermal firm in Fort Wayne, Indiana. Geothermal uses underground pipes to pull heat up from the earth and pump it into residential and commercial heating systems. Since Wall Street mostly ignores geothermal, Jack pronounced the stock "undervalued." Later, WaterFurnace debuted on the SustainableBusiness.com short list of the "World's 20 Most Sustainable Companies." Later, it was a top holding in the Green Growth Fund.[25]

You can also invest in green, renewable energy with an Exchange Traded Fund (ETF), a new investment vehicle born in the 1990s.[26] ETFs can be a good option for intermediate or experienced investors, including renewables investors. An ETF is a basket of stocks or bonds (although some track commodities or currencies) with a theme, such as retail or healthcare. Quite a few are dedicated to green energy. ETFs are similar to mutual funds in that they are comprised of many different stocks. However, unlike mutual funds you can trade ETFs at any time of the day like a stock. In addition to that flexibility and liquidity, most agree their best feature is low cost. There are more than one thousand ETFs.[27]

There are so many renewable energy ETFs that researching them may seem overwhelming. To get started, I suggest focusing on the following three. Each has a somewhat different focus:[28]

• PowerShares WilderHill Clean Energy ETF holds US-based renewable firms like First Solar.

- PowerShares WilderHill Global Clean Energy Portfolio is based on global renewables such as Germany's SolarWorld.
- PowerShares WilderHill Progressive Energy favors technologies that improve the use of conventional energy sources. Holdings include Corning, Inc.

Most investors still prefer mutual funds. New Alternatives Fund invests at least 25 percent of assets in what the fund calls "alternative energy," including renewable energy and fuel cell and hydrogen technologies. Half of its holdings are outside of the United States, mostly in Europe.

The volatility of renewable investing has only increased in recent years. The US leader in solar energy, First Solar, has seen its stock plummet from $160 to about $25 in just one year. But unstable stocks can reward courageous investors handsomely when good companies fall with the rest of the market. One famous and savvy investor made his first move into solar. Warren Buffett purchased a $2 billion First Solar "energy farm" in California, which some analysts view as a bullish sign for the solar industry.

Cutting Coal Emissions

Despite the expansion of renewable energy in recent years, it still accounts for only 8 percent of overall energy use in the United States.[29] Like it or not—and there is much to dislike—50 percent of the country's electrical energy is coal-fired. Coal will be with us for a long time—and so will the imperative to clean up coal production and limit its harmful effects. This means new technologies designed to help the coal industry modernize and become more efficient will be in demand. "Although renewable energy stocks have the most sex appeal," writes Rona Fried, founder and CEO of Progressive Investor (which issues the "Sustainable Business 20" list of the world's leading green companies), the efficiency/conservation sector outperformed renewable energy in some recent years.[30]

One example of energy efficiency is Boston-based Energy Network Operations Center (EnerNOC). EnerNOC is the epitome of the smart grid. While EnerNOC doesn't transform coal into clean green energy, it drastically cuts coal emissions by providing an efficient method for managing electricity demand with digital technology.[31]

Picture a sultry summer day. You turn up the air conditioner, sit back, and relax. So do your neighbors and fellow local citizens. Consequently, the electrical grid strains to power all those units. EnerNOC puts together a network of small to midsize companies that voluntarily cut energy use by switching on their own generator or dimming the lights. This redirects the unused power to utilities and other grids. As a result, EnerNOC helps reap extra energy from cleaner sources and reduces dependence on undesirable sources such as older plants, which emit more toxins and are more likely to be fired up when the grid is overtaxed. The smart grid boosts efficient energy usage and the savings get passed on to customers. EnerNOC is another example of an energy-related company whose stock took a beating in 2011 and may therefore be worth considering as a possible investment—particularly if you are a patient, cautious investor.

EnerNOC is also a wonderful story about two entrepreneurs. Tim Healy and David Brewster dreamt up their brainchild as MBA students at Dartmouth's Tuck School of Business and founded EnerNOC in 2001.[32] The young men pitched their idea to thirty-seven venture capitalists, the people who finance new companies. Only one expressed any interest, but fortunately, that was enough. Tim and David eventually raised $28 million. In 2007, EnerNOC achieved what most entrepreneurs can only dream of: it became a public company, that is one that sells stock to investors like you or me. Today Tim and David's vision is helping change the world.

My choice to invest in EnerNOC came through an intuitive insight. Let me tell you more about the role of intuition in investing.

Intuitive Investing

Learning to merge feeling and logic in investing is a demanding task, but the rewards of success are well worth the required effort. So intuition can play a key role in your Conscious Money strategy. Jason Apollo Voss, author of *The Intuitive Investor*, has mastered the challenge and has much to teach you and me. In his book, I read that Jason receives accurate investment guidance while meditating. That intrigued me enough to inquire more deeply into his investment background and track record.

Jason is around forty years of age with cropped sandy hair and fashionable scruff. Days after graduating from the University of Colorado at Boulder in 1998 with an MBA in finance, he started a job with the Davis Appreciation and Income Fund (DAIF) in Santa Fe, New Mexico.[33] During Jason's period as a fund comanager—from 2000 through 2005, spanning both good and bad years for the market—DAIF outperformed the NASDAQ index by 77 percent, the S&P 500 by 49.1 percent, and the Dow Jones Industrial Average by nearly 36 percent. No wonder the *Wall Street Journal*, *Barron's*, and *Bloomberg Businessweek* sought young Mr. Voss's advice. At age thirty-five, Jason left DAIF and compiled his intuitive investing strategies into a book.

Most of the wealth Jason created for investors and for himself came not from factual analysis, he says, but by "knowing how to use my right brain and its creative and intuitive functions."[34] The message of *The Intuitive Investor* is that intuition, not rational data, is the real source of investment success—and one we should learn to practice.

That is an inviting premise, provided you honor this important warning: no novice should actually make an investment solely based on intuition. Intuitive investing requires a strong investment background. It takes many years of experience to integrate feelings and analysis to become an expert intuitive investor like Jason.

That said, anyone can make a practice of employing intuition to illuminate and clarify their investment questions. In an exercise at the end of the chapter, we'll test our intuitive leanings against objective financial data—without putting any money at risk.

Feelings Are Key to Conscious Wealth in Investing: They Deliver Intuitive Input

As I understand what Jason Voss says, feelings are key to growing Conscious Money because they:

1. Deliver valuable intuitive information
2. Alert you with "a funny feeling" that things "just aren't right"
3. Inform you, with feelings like anxiety, that you don't have enough information[35]

Understanding information, says Jason, is the most crucial skill of intuitive investing. But we collect that information, he adds, from both the rational brain and the feeling brain. We then often make a big mistake by discounting our feelings. We must instead weigh our feelings, because, as Jason says, "an investment is actually an emotional act."[36]

I first thought that was a curious statement, but when I considered it more deeply it made a lot of sense. Investing is about the future. But, as Jason asserts, "there is no such thing as a future fact."[37] Every fact has already happened. The investment industry clearly agrees: it consistently issues this caveat: "Past performance is no guarantee of future results." Since the future is unknowable, Jason is right: Investing is an emotional act.

Jason does not advocate ignoring logic, but rather examining your feelings for insights that can balance rational thinking. He summarizes, "[In] the right brain . . . creativity and intuition robustly help to fill in the gaps left by numbers and words."[38] He also recommends we draw on that intuitive power and combine it with good listening skills, especially when business leaders speak.

Activate Your Intuition When CEOs Talk about Their Companies

It takes a lot of self-awareness to honor our intuition. Jason suggests that investors, as part of their stock research, activate their intuitive listening skills as they watch or listen when CEOs speak publicly. When I interviewed Jason Voss, I learned that we should be particularly aware of—and avoid buying stock in—the companies of leaders who exhibit these "CEO danger signals":[39]

1. Beware of hubris of any sort. A leader should be confident, not arrogant. Ask yourself: "Is this the sort of person I'd invite to my home?"
2. Be alert to overbearing CEOs. Such bullies may turn out great earnings for a year or more, due to brutal cost cutting, but fail to inspire people and grow the business. "Never have I seen a CEO of that sort succeed for three to seven years," says Jason.
3. Watch out for excessively analytical CEOs. An "intelligent and heart-centered CEO who takes care of the company will earn you money," he says. I ask Jason which type might that be? "The Statesman," he swiftly replies.

I've had occasion to engage this and other advice from Jason in my own investing dilemmas as the following story illustrates. I've broken with traditional form a bit here, writing it in the present tense to communicate my feelings in a more immediate way.

It's a miserable day on Wall Street. I scan my stocks. Amidst the red ink are two bright green figures. As I focus, my heart skips a beat: one stock is up 94 percent overnight! I have no idea why. Recovering, I finally do what I've vowed to do for a decade. I enter 1,000 (half of my holding) and hit the "sell" button. I realize this sounds impulsive, but for me, it is the right move. For years, whether my stocks were up or down, I suffered selling paralysis. So I promised to discipline myself to take profits. Even if I make a mistake (and the stock continues to rise), I reasoned, at least I've protected my profit.

Now I see the news story. My stock, a small socially responsible firm that I deeply admire, is acquired by a competitor. I know from my research the company is well run and financially strong. So I've covered the rational bases. It's a responsible firm that I believe will do well long term. A year or so earlier, I read a story speculating that the company was ripe for a takeover. That made no logical sense, however, since it was common knowledge the founders refused to sell. But somehow, as Jason might say, it "activated my intuitive listening" and the story stuck with me.

I held on to the stock. First because I love the company; second because of an intuition that the company might be up for sale some day. My "felt sense" fit perfectly with the more rational "ripe for a takeover" story that I had earlier dismissed. Even though I did not realize I was making an intuitive investment choice, I was honoring my feelings, which returned the favor with a nice little success.

Intuitive investing requires a lot of practice and follow-up research. It's a good idea to practice regularly. There's an exercise at the end of the chapter you can use to do so—no risk involved. Check your intuitive "hits" against the ideas of investment analysts by looking up a stock on Yahoo Finance or a similar site. Discuss your thoughts with fellow investors or an advisor. If you have an account with a discount broker, advice is available at no cost. Intuition will help you grow your investments by engaging the whole brain and merging both feeling and analysis.

Exercises

Tune In to Conscious Investing

Pick a time when you will be undisturbed for ten minutes. Reflect on this statement: "I align my Conscious Money with investments that are as conscious as I am and with initiatives that contribute to life and the greater good." Record any feelings, insights, concerns, fears, or questions in your journal.

Intuitive Development for Investors

We'll now practice investing intuition. But you won't lose money because you are not acting on your insights. The aim of this experiment is to see what would have happened had you done so. Expensive stock trading seminars invite you to test their methods and see how much money you would theoretically earn. We are engaging a similar principle.

Part One: Tune In to Intuitive Investment Guidance

1. Choose a time when you will not be disturbed for fifteen to twenty minutes.
2. In your Conscious Money journal, formulate an investing question. Keep it simple and specific. Ask one question, like: "Should I invest in Verizon?" Do not make either/or inquiries like: "Should I buy Verizon or AT&T?" Or try a real estate question, such as "Should I go to a few open houses on Sunday?"
3. Now ask a more general question: "How do I feel right now about committing to (just choose one) a stock, bond, real estate venture or other investment?" Did your stomach sink? That's fine. You want to clearly experience how fear feels.

4. In your journal, note the date that you asked your specific and general questions. Take notes about your feelings. Documenting your feelings helps you remember them so you can use them as a basis for comparison in the second part of this exercise.

5. Over the next week or so, notice any news stories, conversations, memories, or additional feelings that arise. Record the most noteworthy ones and their dates in your journal.

Part Two: Honor the Rational Brain and Check Your Intuition

Watch how your feelings correlate—or not—with the information that comes to you from the investing universe:

1. Actively research your question on sites like Yahoo Finance. Note any information that confirms or contradicts your intuitive leaning. Add notes in your journal along with the date.

2. Ask your financial advisor what she or he thinks.

3. Watch the market; see what happens.

4. Be patient. Wall Street's herd mentality may work to your advantage.

5. How do you feel when the data seems to confirm your intuition or appears to disprove it? There's no right or wrong in this exercise. The idea is to just observe and note your feelings.

If you receive the answers you expect when practicing intuition, it may mean that you are accessing your mind and not your intuition. Intuition can be surprising.

Should I take that great job? No. What do you mean "no"?

But that is not always the case. Intuition can come as a quiet yes or a silent resonance you experience in the center of your chest. When it happens again and again you might take it as a signal validating a certain choice or direction.

Options

Reflections

- Regularly check in to see how you feel about any investments you are considering making.
- Repeat this chapter's first exercise, "Tune In to Conscious Investing." Depending on your level of possible future investing activity, that could mean weekly or even daily repetition for a while. Intuition requires lots of practice; intuitive investing is no exception to the rule.
- Review the exercises in the "Passion, Values, and Priorities" section of this chapter before any meeting with an investment professional.
- Remember, there are times when investing need not be a top priority. It is okay to place some or all of your money in a bank or money market fund during stressful transitions, especially when markets are uncertain.

Resources

- Catch the business news online, in the paper, or on television. Gather ideas about companies or industries to further research—or avoid entirely.
- Follow the stock market on Yahoo Finance, Google Finance, the *Wall Street Journal*, TheStreet.com, or The Motley Fool.
- To expand your investing know-how, join an investment club or start your own. Get ideas, background, and software from Better Investing at BetterInvesting.org.
- Be familiar with several SRI, green, and renewable-energy funds. Check out these websites for the funds' top holdings and recent returns.
- Pick up Green America's "Guide to Socially Responsible Investing," which sells for $11.95 but is free to members. Visit them at Green America.org to learn more.

- Research a renewable energy source that interests you, be it solar, wind, conservation, geothermal, or biofuel.
- Be aware of ETFs that specialize in your chosen renewable, like Market Vectors Solar Energy or the PowerShares Global Wind.
- Whether you're a green investor or a sustainability advocate, *Green Money Journal*, whose tagline is "From the Stock Market to the Supermarket," is an inspiring and informative resource.

Right Actions

- Build a savings fund of three to six months of income before investing.
- List three stocks that interest you and begin to follow them.
- Research one or more of the recommended financial advisors listed on page 208.
- Interview at least three individuals as potential investment advisors before deciding who is right for you.
- When you meet with an investment advisor, carefully observe whether she or he explains your options and respects your priorities and input.
- When you are ready to do so, take small deliberate steps to put your money to work, beginning with a very small portion of the whole.
- Even if you work with an advisor, consider creating a brokerage account for investments that you self-manage.
- Follow Jason Voss on his blog: JasonApolloVoss.com.

Conscious Money Affirmation

I consider myself a conscious investor because I ask,
"Which investments reflect my values and consciousness?"

8

The Promise of
Global Consciousness

Most conscious individuals earn, spend, and invest Conscious Money in their own country, state, and community. At the same time, it is important to recognize that we are also becoming global citizens. To involve yourself in the world at large, however, whether socially or financially, you need a global perspective. This chapter explores the international dimension of Conscious Money, as well as the opportunities and responsibilities of global citizenship. Yet, we must not forget that the best way to be accountable globally is often with local action.

Wherever you live, work, invest, or do business, be it in Europe, Africa, Latin America, Australia, the Middle East, North America, or Asia, you must balance auspicious possibilities for adventure, fulfillment, and the growth of your Conscious Money with a clear intention to confront and help resolve tough global challenges. Finding that balance calls for the wisdom, understanding, and creativity that can only be sourced through values and consciousness.

Today's global economy is increasingly integrated and interconnected. The financial climate of Europe or Asia influences people in North and South America—and vice versa. The human community is ever more global too. People are instantaneously linked in real time via cellphone, laptop, or tablet. We witness news events, from weather disasters to royal weddings, as shared events, reminding us that we are all in the same boat.

These common experiences reflect and underscore the growing sense that we participate in a collective consciousness that is moving toward unifying the people of this planet. Despite our many differences, humanity is evolving toward a similar groupthink or global cohesiveness.

Millions and millions of people the world over pursue spirituality in ways that have the potential to expand human consciousness. A decade ago, *Time* magazine reported that ten million Americans meditate.[1] But a 2007 US government survey showed the figure was then twenty million—and is probably growing still.[2] Although it is impossible to determine how many people meditate globally (and I have diligently tried), every major world religion—Christianity, Judaism, Buddhism, Hinduism, Sikhism, Islam, and many more—advocates contemplative practice akin to meditation, and all are designed to expand human awareness.

People can and do expand their consciousness in many other ways, such as yoga. As with meditation, it is very difficult to estimate the number of yoga practitioners. *Yoga Journal* put the figure of US yoga fans at 16 million in 2008. But it has clearly expanded since then. In the birthplace of yoga, India, whose population exceeds 1.2 billion, millions more practice yoga. In recent years, growing numbers have become yoga fans, or yogis, in Europe, North America, South America, Australia, and Africa. In *The Science of Yoga*, bestselling author William J. Broad, a *New York Times* reporter and lifelong yoga practitioner, says more than 250 million people practice yoga worldwide, citing international yoga organizations and the Yoga Health Foundation.[3]

Between yoga, meditation, and the wide range of other contemplative activities, including but not limited to prayer, martial arts, and journaling, it is reasonable to conclude that Earth indeed is home to hundreds of millions of conscious individuals.

People the world over desire many similar things, including financial security. They also honor many of the same values. So, the question of how to merge money and meaning naturally arises, although not immediately. As people attain greater material well-being, many may decide to spend thoughtlessly at first. (That certainly occurred in the developed world.) Choosing Conscious Money on a larger scale, such as at the national level, requires a collective consciousness and commitment to reject financial distortions like bribery or corruption. Such change becomes possible as people observe the unhappy consequences of unconscious money, appreciate the benefits of more conscious financial behavior, and demand the financial infrastructure to encourage it. Along the way, individuals start to ask how they might spend more mindfully, perhaps expressing values like sustainability. In Latin America, for example, although poverty persists, many have earned middle incomes for some time and there is a strong interest in conscious consumption, as you will see later in this chapter. As the collective forces of money, values, and consciousness converge and strengthen in the world economy, we are beginning to see Conscious Money emerge globally.

Conscious Money as a global movement rests on the truth of unity: Earth is our collective home. As we enjoy its blessings, we must also accept the responsibilities of shared planetary stewardship. The European Union, in its willingness to post guarantees for financially troubled Greece, Italy, and Portugal in 2011, was expressing the truth of Unity: "We are all in this together." Although few are confident that Europe's financial issues are fully resolved, there can be no disparaging of the valiant efforts European governments have made to preserve the European Union. In continuing to meet that responsibility, Europe acts to stabilize not just its own economy, but the world's.

In this global community, Conscious Money can play a powerful role in promoting peace and prosperity. When individuals from different nations, even unfriendly ones, do business or forge beneficial economic bonds, they must get to know each other as people. In an early example of this in the 1980s, when the United States and the former Soviet Union had not yet agreed to limit nuclear weapons, many people, myself among them, embraced the motto "World Peace through World Trade." Similarly, the global friendships that emerge from travel, study, and work abroad; exchange programs; international conferences; internships; and volunteering, help heal frayed emotions, foster common economic interests, and reduce the potential for conflict. That is love in action.

By contrast, the impulse toward isolationism is a product of fear, which freezes the flow of prosperity, thereby dampening economic growth. When we recognize—and take responsibility for—the ways in which we share the same humanity, consciousness, and many of the same economic interests, opportunities for equitable trade and shared financial blessings grow exponentially.

As Conscious Money expands globally, we can see the world anew, envisioning fresh opportunities for ourselves, our children, and our grandchildren to live, work, and invest in a world of peace and prosperity. It's not economics alone, but economics supported by shared consciousness that lays the groundwork for this scenario.

Prosperity and Conscious Money

In 2011, the Arab world exploded in demonstrations against autocratic leaders of long standing. The "Arab Spring" brought down the governments of Tunisia, Egypt, Libya, and Yemen. Syria crushed protestors with deadly force, but even that did not stop people from risking their lives for freedom.

I believe the thirst for freedom is a marker of the search for higher consciousness. When external freedom is denied through the power of brute force by despotic leaders, slavery, censorship, and other forms of oppression, people naturally focus on removing those barriers to their freedom. But once people secure basic human and economic rights, the ongoing search for greater freedom expands in a new direction: toward liberating themselves from the prisons of *internal* conditioning, where negative thoughts, emotions, and unconscious patterns reside. Freeing ourselves from this brand of imprisonment is the work of self-mastery—and a powerful step toward conscious choice and Conscious Money, as we have seen.

Today, despite continued inequities, glaring injustices, and distressing environmental developments, an initial level of economic well-being and social freedom is within reach for hundreds of millions of people, particularly in Latin America, Asia, Eastern Europe, and some of the more prosperous countries of Africa and the Middle East, expanding the potential for Conscious Money in truly global proportions.

The truth about prosperity, however, cannot be revealed in mere economic metrics, however handy they might be. "The gross national product does not allow for the health of our children, the quality of their education, or the joy of their play," said Robert F. Kennedy in 1968. "It does not include the beauty of our poetry . . . our wisdom . . . our compassion . . . it measures everything, in short, except that which makes life worthwhile."[4]

True prosperity requires a complex set of human factors that encompass human values and consciousness. Determining and measuring the factors that sustain prosperity is the work of the London-based Legatum Prosperity Index, a global database that defines prosperity as wealth *and* well-being.[5] The Index's findings often defy traditional thinking about who is prosperous and who isn't. For example, the United States, often deemed the world's wealthiest nation, ranks as only the tenth most prosperous. Ranked number forty-six on the Prosperity Index, the former Soviet republic of Kazakhstan, which is hardly considered well-to-do, is more prosperous than oil-rich Saudi Arabia, which ranks number forty-nine. The people of sub-Saharan Africa are more optimistic about entrepreneurship than those of many richer countries.[6]

The Prosperity Index evaluates 110 countries, comprising 90 percent of the world's population, on eight foundational factors of prosperity:

economy, entrepreneurship and opportunity, governance, education, health, safety and security, personal freedom, and social capital.[7]

Except for "economy," which might be construed as purely financial, these building blocks of prosperity gauge or reflect values and the cultivation of higher consciousness. For example, education raises human awareness: higher education levels generally point to greater possibility of conscious choice. Entrepreneurship requires hope, a core human value. Security frees the human spirit to engage in productive activity, including economic activity. Social capital, which the Index defines as cohesive community and family networks, relies on the value of trust, the lack of which is highly detrimental to prosperity. The Prosperity Index demonstrates that money, values, and consciousness are powerfully intertwined in the dynamic history of our evolution here on Earth.

Some people dismiss worldwide economic growth as "more meaningless materialism" spreading around the globe. To some extent this can be true. On the other hand, prosperity generally delivers more opportunities. And greater opportunity means more choice. As choices increase, then the question arises: will those choices be conscious or unconscious? In real numbers, however, there is little doubt that as prosperity blossoms more people are making more Conscious Money choices.

Conscious Money Is Global

There was a time when the financial power of the United States, Europe, and Japan ruled global finance. Today these economies are labeled "mature," because they grow at a slower pace than they once did. This is a normal process for global capitalism. In the 1980s and 1990s, the world cheered the Asian "Tigers:" Hong Kong, Singapore, South Korea, and Taiwan, whose gross national products surged nearly 10 percent or more.

Today the economies of China, India, and Brazil are growing 8 to 10 percent each year, compared with about 3 percent on average in Europe and the United States. At some point, it is generally agreed, China will replace the United States as the world's largest economy.

In the areas where many people are more prosperous, Conscious Money is already becoming an established phenomenon. Of course, each region possesses a unique character shaped by culture, history, politics, and religious traditions. Yet today, so many people and cultures are beginning to embrace the principles of Conscious Money that it is impossible to fully describe even the major global trends. Nevertheless, I will offer a sampling of some highly visible ways in which the themes of Conscious Money are playing out in Europe, Asia, and Latin America.

Conscious Capitalism was born in Europe and, as I tell my American friends, in the States we call it socialism. But there is no confusion about Europe's commitment to address Conscious Money issues like global warming and social equality with the values of justice and sustainability. A 2010 study by the European Social Investment Forum shows that Europe accounts for approximately $6.5 trillion of the approximately $10 trillion global market in Socially Responsible Investing. From 2008 to 2010, Europe's commitment, as measured in total SRI assets, nearly doubled.[8]

Europe is equally passionate about green spending. In Germany, 44 percent of adults are values-driven consumers, as identified by the Lifestyles of Health and Sustainability (LOHAS) demographic, versus 25 percent or less in the United States.[9] Germany is the second largest organic food market (after the United States), as well as a global leader in generating solar and wind energy.

In Asia, Hindu, Buddhist, and Shinto traditions are alive in wise monetary principles. Buddhism espouses Right Livelihood, which asks: what is the ethical or right way for me to earn a living? It is a core principle of the Noble Eightfold Path. The Japanese principle of *shobaido*, which is similar to corporate social responsibility, advocates doing business in a just or correct manner.

As Asian incomes rise, shoppers honor sustainability at the grocery store. Organic food sales in China and Japan alone represented a $2.3 billion market by 2010.[10] In Singapore, Malaysia, and Taiwan, demand for organics rose 30 to 40 percent during some years of the past decade. Thai Buddhists appreciate the harmony of organic farming.[11] China's Commerce Ministry reports that more than 300 million Chinese city dwellers purchase certified safe or organic produce.[12] The total Asia-Pacific organic food market will exceed $5 billion by 2015, predicts market researcher Datamonitor.[13]

No matter where you live, you probably earn your Conscious Money in the workplace. Conscious companies like the *Times* of India, winner of an International Spirit at Work Award, encourage their people to catalyze their "latent divinity" with yoga, meditation, and breathing work.[14] Such practices also enhance creativity and performance, boost an individual's potential to earn more Conscious Money, and foster health and well-being.

Indian officials are growing increasingly concerned about health. India faces a rise in heart disease and diabetes as its middle class eats more junk food and exercises less, says Dr. Anbumani Ramadoss, India's Health Minister from 2004 to 2009. "Yoga can go a long way in reducing such diseases as hypertension and diabetes," he adds.[15] Perhaps officials should encourage yoga in the workplace, as the *Times* of India does.

Sustainable Global Investment: Asia and Africa

Conscious investors can be humanity's greatest defense against unconscious business. When global investors refuse to own greedy companies and lobby business leaders to address Conscious Money priorities, their power will match or exceed that of government regulators. Investors will succeed where others fail because they are one stakeholder that even unconscious corporations cannot afford to ignore. Corporate policy changes when investors demand it.

Investment is critical to economic development. A pioneering group of African investment professionals and sustainable investors believes Africa will attract billions of investment dollars when it creates a positive investing climate where conscious principles are honored. The Africa Sustainable Investment Forum, or AfricaSIF, was launched in Johannesburg and Cape Town in 2010 to achieve that ambitious goal by fostering consciousness raising, trust building, and transformation.[16]

As Asia welcomes greater abundance and investment capital, concerns about the environment have boosted interest in sustainable investing. In 2001, ASrIA, a nonprofit entity devoted to sustainable Asian investing, was founded.[17]

Latin America's Conscious Workplaces and Shoppers

In Latin America, traditional capitalism is under siege, as populist, antibusiness leaders assume power. But many people are eager to explore a more conscious brand of free enterprise. The Great Place to Work (GPTW) Institute, which compiles *Fortune*'s "100 Best Places to Work" lists, surveyed 2.8 million Latin American employees at 1,900 companies to create the 2011 "100 Best Companies to Work for in Latin America" list.

In Latin America, multinational firms like IBM scored high on GPTW's list, as did 3M and Spanish telecom giant Telefónica. This is hardly surprising. But smaller local companies emerged as great workplaces too, such as Columbia's 395-person transportation firm Gases de Occidente and Brazil's Chemtech, a 1,204-employee IT company, demonstrating that small- to medium-size firms are "great places to work" all over the world.[18]

As a mindful shopper, you might assume that conscious consumers emerged in Europe or the United States, but more than a decade ago Brazil's Helio Mattar, a former CEO and government minister, founded São Paulo's Akatu Institute for Conscious Consumption. Around that time, 44 percent of Brazil's consumers already wanted big companies to adopt ethical standards and to contribute to society.[19] Now, Mattar estimates that between 50 and 80 percent of consumers throughout Latin America are "conscious," including many low-income people who are not well educated.[20] The media, including the Internet, says Mattar, have raised social awareness among all income groups. Higher levels of consumer consciousness, he believes, keeps the pressure on business to become more conscious.

Humanity's Challenges Are Global Challenges

As Asia, Latin America, the Middle East, and Africa move toward fulfilling their economic potential, billions of people will escape poverty and know better lives. But there are costs as well as benefits to economic growth. Today, humanity's greatest challenges are global and our shared environment, say many, tops the list, along with the quest to eradicate poverty and expand human rights. What some see as a conflict between growing prosperity and environmental calamity explodes in the trend toward inexpensive cars now marketed to middle-class drivers in China and India.

Working mom Shweta Kumari, a Mumbai, India, software developer, is excited about the Nano, which is a tiny car manufactured by India's Tata Motors. At $2,500 she can afford it. In fact, it's half the price of the cheapest car around. The Nano pollutes less than a motorbike or scooter, according to Tata Motors. With her new Nano, "I can drop my kid at school, go to work, and go shopping," said Kumari, who shares a car with her husband.[21]

But some environmentalists are extremely worried. "Low-cost cars will be disastrous," says Anumita Roychowdhury, associate director of New Delhi's Centre for Science and Environment.[22]

Steve Howard of Britain's The Climate Group takes a different view. "It's an elitist view that only a small percentage of the population should own cars," says Howard, who thinks that "technology, moral pressure, regulatory pressure, and high oil prices will push even premium carmakers" to manufacture less-polluting, more efficient engines.[23]

Howard's optimistic view is based on the belief that the automotive industry will balance the opportunity of an expanding car market with greater responsibility for the detrimental impact more cars will have on the environment. There is some evidence for this view, since automakers are manufacturing more hybrid and electric cars—and consumers are buying them. But notice that Howard thinks "moral pressure" is an important part of the equation. As global citizens, it is our job to exert that pressure. We can do so as investors by owning stock in visionary carmakers. We can act locally by spending our Conscious Money to share a car, not own one, or we can apply our collective will locally by lobbying for better bike parking and bike access to public transportation. In fact, we must all become activists of some sort because of the common threat we all face.

Global Warming

The United Nations final report in a series of several on global warming, drafted by 2,500 top scientists, proclaimed that: (1) global warming is "unequivocal"; (2) humans are primarily to blame for climate change; and (3) the situation is deteriorating. Scientists once feared that temperatures would increase five to seven degrees by 2050.[24] Now they feel certain it will happen and a new report shows that global warming is getting worse. In November 2011, the US Department of Energy confirmed that the world churned out 6 percent more greenhouse gases in 2010 than in 2009: 512 million metric tons of carbon is the biggest amount ever released.[25]

Global warming is the world's "greatest humanitarian challenge," states a Global Humanitarian Forum report based on data from the World Bank, the World Health Organization, and the United Nations. Tragically, most of the death and destruction will occur in the developing world, the report concludes. "But it's the developed world that has precipitated global warming," said the late Wangari Maathai, a Kenyan environmentalist and Nobel Peace Prize winner.[26]

Global warming is also an economic catastrophe. It will cost trillions of dollars, wreak havoc on industries from construction to aviation and beyond, and decimate prosperity. Industries that ignore warnings to mitigate their environmental impact will be severely hit.

The only bright spot in a dismal scenario is that when governments adopt greener policies, the results are clearly visible. The developed countries that endorsed the 1997 Kyoto Protocol (and cut emissions to 8 percent below 1990 levels) saw a real drop in emissions. In 1990, the developed world released 60 percent of greenhouse gases, says John Reilly, codirector of MIT's Joint Program on the Science and Policy of Global Change. Now it's "probably less than 50 percent," he says.[27] That evidence is a clear and vivid reminder that the actions of individuals and governments *do* make a difference. It should inspire us all to keep the faith that we possess the wherewithal to transform this planet and that we shall do so through our collective global consciousness.

Green building is another force for global good. We're quick to blame cars for toxic emissions, but 38 percent of greenhouse gases are from buildings, says the US Green Building Council.[28] The World Green Building Council, with representatives from Europe, the Americas, Africa, the Middle East, and Asia, is committed to reducing global warming by transforming the building industry into a sustainable sector. Half the world's new building in the next decade will be in Asia, says the World Council.[29]

In a world of opportunity and responsibility, where individuals and organizations are free to pursue prosperity in a global economy, we are also required to take on issues like poverty and the environment—and to do so both locally and globally. But the way we act locally on issues like global warming, for example, can often have the greatest global impact. As Conscious Money grows increasingly relevant on an international stage, we can look for innovative and exciting ways to make a difference.

Possibilities for Individual Action

As this interconnected world of ours grows more conscious and its people make more financial choices that better mirror their deeply held values, individuals like us are free to explore new ways to live, earn, invest, create, and contribute that we may never before have considered.

Conscious Money Global Career Building

Though the United States and Europe no longer assert the same economic prowess as they once did, many of their citizens share in the optimism for a new world that's truly global in scope. While US baby boomers may have traveled abroad as tourists, their children are avid internationalists. They're eager to work overseas, speak a second language fluently, and get to know a foreign culture by living amongst its people. Most universities encourage and some require a year of study abroad. The stereotype of the self-centered American—flowered shirt and linguistically challenged—is fast fading. In its place is a savvy and open-minded individual whose heart is set on a genuine overseas journey including new, lifelong friends and day-to-day adventures.

This passion for overseas experience has been quietly brewing for a decade or more. But it accelerated during the Great Recession as frustrated job seekers, aware of the new shifts in the global economy, sought opportunity and success abroad. As new economies in Asia and Latin America ascend, the Middle East explores democracy, and Africa seeks more trade and investment, corporations everywhere hunt for sophisticated people with global experience.

So, whether you are a young person eyeing an internship abroad, a volunteer eager for international service, or a shopper hunting for greener global products, the world is welcoming your vision and your international outlook.

Work experience overseas can boost your Conscious Money earning potential and lead to top leadership positions. In fact, 75 percent of Fortune 100 CEOs worked abroad for at least two years.[30] When today's thirty-year-olds achieve larger leadership roles, that percentage will be even higher.

But what's most amazing about that 75 percent statistic is how swiftly times have changed. In just ten years, the percentage of "C-level" executives (those whose job title includes the word "chief," like chief financial officer) with overseas experience has rocketed from 48 to 71 percent.[31]

In fact, twenty years ago, conventional wisdom held that an overseas post threatened a career. The fear was "out of sight, out of mind." Now business seeks out the cultural sophistication that smooths global deal-making. Foreign experience also enhances your awareness of complexities and broadens your perspective so that you're more flexibile, rather than limited by absolutist thinking.

However, it is not wise to seek an overseas assignment just to advance your career. If you are not the right type of person, that move may prove to be detrimental instead. Indeed, the failure rate for international assignments is high. People who succeed abroad generally have "a global mind-set," says Mary B. Teagarden, professor of global strategy at the Thunderbird School of Global Management in Glendale, Arizona.[32] Such people enjoy variety and novelty, are resilient, and willing to take risks, she adds. The same is true for young people seeing global experience. In fact, today's job market is highly receptive to job seekers whose résumés boast international internships.

Interning Abroad:
A Smart Investment of Your Conscious Money

Today new college graduates and others are willing to invest their Conscious Money as a strategy to gain job skills, experience, and overseas savvy—especially during a recession.

In 2008, Marquette University graduate Matthew Moughan faced the worst job market in decades. After a six-month search and no leads, he turned to Intrax Internships Abroad, which found him a summer internship at London's Electronic Shipping Solutions. The company later hired Matthew, then twenty-four years old, as a project manager. Intrax Internships Abroad charges $5,000 to $8,000, which covers visa help, housing, weekend trips, insurance, and orientation. Matthew borrowed the money from his parents. "It was a smart move, career-wise," he says.

From 2001 to 2008, the total number of US students who went abroad as interns doubled from seven thousand to fourteen thousand.[33]

Sarah Block graduated from Syracuse University during the recession and soon decided to gain overseas work experience. Masa Israel, which helps Jewish graduates find work and internships in Israel, secured her a marketing position at Tel Aviv's Radvision, a specialist in video networking infrastructure. Five months later, she returned stateside, where prospective employers often inquired about her experience abroad. She soon found employment at Godfrey Q & Partners, a San Francisco advertising agency. "I think it gave me an edge," Sarah said.[34]

For nearly a decade, Abroad China, with offices in Reston, Virginia, has placed more than one hundred young professionals and university interns in China each year. Abroad China's local staff eliminates a lot of the uncertainties "so interns can focus on cultural and business experiences." Interns need not possess Chinese language skills, but they must have a bachelor's degree or be enrolled in an accredited college or university. Abroad China places interns in multinational firms or Chinese companies located in Beijing or Shanghai. Interns can start at any time of the year.[35]

Angel Rich enjoyed an "enlightening and beneficial" internship working at China's VSS, the sole security service provider for the Beijing 2008 Olympics.[36] At VSS, she created the company motto and mission statement, while receiving extensive training as a Risk Assessment Expert.

Opportunity, however, was not simply given to her. Initially, her Chinese employer was reluctant to give her very much to do. Determined to make the most of her overseas venture, Angel took the initiative to describe her marketing expertise to a top executive with VSS's British partner. Soon after, her marketing skills were put to work.

Back in the United States after her internship, Angel interned with the Financial Industry Regulatory Authority. After evaluating offers from numerous well-known companies, Angel accepted a full-time position with Prudential Financial as a Global Market Researcher. "I would definitely say the China internship opportunity has increased my value in the workplace," she concludes.

Abroad China's Janet Zhou notes that potential employers are less interested in the specific job that the intern held than in the China experience in general. "It is really about taking on the challenge," she reasons.[37]

The Power of Conscious Philanthropy

This book describes how the threads of consciousness weave through the world of money. When you spend mindfully, earn creatively, and invest consciously, the energy of Conscious Money heals your relationship with money. Giving of yourself or your money or both in a caring, thoughtful way is the culmination of your Conscious Money practice.

When we witness the natural disasters that have caused devastation in Haiti, Pakistan, Japan, and many other areas, even if only on television, it rouses the compassion and commitment that are the hallmarks of global consciousness and the dimension of Conscious Money called philanthropy.

Americans donated more than $298 billion in 2011, reports the Giving USA Foundation in a 2012 study. Even though total contributions fell due to the lingering impact of recession, individual giving held steady—it makes up 73 percent of the total donated.[38] It is inspiring to learn that in times of hardship, people opened their hearts and wallets.

The way you look at money and people or abundance and scarcity plays a decisive role in your experience of satisfaction as a conscious donor. That is true whether you contribute your money, time, energy, skills, or love.

Fund-raiser and philanthropist Lynne Twist, author of *The Soul of Money*, has much to teach conscious contributors of all types.[39] She acquired a great deal of wisdom about money and life during the decades when she worked in places like India, Ethiopia, and Bangladesh with the people, she said in a 2010 workshop, "that I used to call poor . . . I would never call them poor again . . . They are whole and complete people, living in the ebb and flow of financial circumstances."[40]

Perhaps part of what Lynne Twist is teaching us is that when we experience contribution as an energetic exchange that is equally satisfying and therefore beneficial for donor and recipient, we understand the truth of conscious giving. It is a sacred activity without space for emotions like guilt, shame, or feeling sorry for the person or cause to which you contribute. It is instead the evocation of acceptance and dignity in giving and receiving.

Conscious philanthropy contains the wisdom that giving to others is best accomplished from a place in which you honor and care for yourself as well. Be sure to include yourself, givers are often advised, in the circle of compassion.

Lynne Twist led the Hunger Project for twenty years and later launched the Pachamama Foundation. In both cases, her job was, and is, to cultivate contributions from wealthy people. Here, too, she gained many insights that are enormously useful to people on the path of Conscious Money—especially if that path requires raising funds for your own organization or as a volunteer.

Labeling people "rich," Lynne said in the same 2010 workshop, treats them as if "they are their private plane, stock options, or net worth." That does them a great disservice, she explains. In truth, they are simply human beings who are "living in the ebb and flow . . . of financial circumstances." Of course, these are the exact words Lynne uses to describe people with fewer financial resources. Excessive wealth, Lynne cautions, creates its own tyranny even if it comes in a designer package. Rich or poor, she teaches us, the labels are equally demeaning.

Lynne's conscious neutrality, her divine nonchalance, and inner peace about money make her one of the great money teachers—as well as one of the world's most successful fund-raisers.

Volunteers Rule

In 2010, despite tough economic times for many, more than 26 percent of American adults, or sixty-three million people, volunteered, says the Corporation for National and Community Service, which valued their service at an impressive $173 billion.[41] Nearly 30 percent of baby boomers volunteered in 2010, contributing three billion hours of service.[42] For those baby boomers and their elders, volunteering is a call that many now feel ready to answer.

Donating money is important; it's very important. But for many people, including those who may be unable to contribute financially, giving must not be defined only in monetary terms. Growing numbers want to donate their skills, time, or strength to a worthy project. Almost all volunteers who do so report that their experience is a fulfilling one. That is the case whether they contribute to small local nonprofit agencies or internationally renowned global organizations

An American Icon Turns Fifty

Some who heard President Kennedy's "Ask not what your country can do for you, but what you can do for your country" speech in 1961 are responding some fifty years later. The average Peace Corps volunteer is twenty-eight years old, but hundreds of volunteers have joined after retiring. Volunteers must be at least eighteen years old, but there is no upper age limit. In fact, the percentage of volunteers over age fifty has been steadily climbing and is currently at 7 percent.[43]

Connie Genger of Billings, Montana, joined the Peace Corps in her sixties. As a volunteer in Morocco, she drew on decades of work experience to support a woman's association in launching its business. "When I left Morocco at the age of sixty-five, I was the oldest volunteer," she says. A year later, the Peace Corps in Morocco welcomed a woman in her early eighties.[44]

Like Connie, volunteers commit to two years of service and three added months of training, mostly in the host country. It can be lonely and living conditions can be harsh, admits Connie. But, she adds, the "high moments" make it all worthwhile. The loneliness factor drops a lot when couples, who now represent 7 percent of all volunteers, join together.

Pat and Ardella Moran of Wyoming had a lifetime of local service behind them when, as "empty nesters," they sought international adventure. The Peace Corps landed them in St. Lucia. "The Carribean?" they asked. "Is this a dream?"

The Morans soon encountered the reality behind pretty tourist posters. Beautiful places have their own special needs. Pat put his skills to work on two community-building projects and Ardella worked for the Ministry of Health at a community HIV/AIDS clinic. Once settled into a daily routine, the couple met a local woman who sparked the Morans' involvement with a youth organization where Ardella taught life skills and Pat taught carpentry to thirteen- and fourteen-year-olds.

"We were . . . treated as family," Pat says. After a day at the beach with the young people he and Ardella served, he recalls, "We would look at each other and say, 'This is the Peace Corps? The toughest job you'll ever love.'"[45]

Volunteer Travel

More than fifty-five million Americans combine volunteering with vacation, which some call "voluntourism," says the newsletter *VolunTourist*.[46]

As consciousness expands, people seek meaningful adventure. Global Vision International (GVI) finds volunteer jobs for 3,500 people per year in sixty countries. Since 1997, GVI has sent volunteers to organizations like the Jane Goodall Institute, Rainforest Concern, and the Whale and Dolphin Conservation Society, winning a 95 percent approval rating from its volunteers.[47]

Volunteering on the Job

Your ability to contribute as an individual is greatly enhanced when you work for a conscious employer. Big companies often loan their executives to nonprofit organizations; other firms support inventive in-house philanthropies.

Whole Foods cofounder and coCEO John Mackey once told me, "I've never seen anything excite our people as much as the Whole Planet Foundation (WPF)." I later understood why he said so: nearly one third of Whole Foods team members have contributed a total of more than $3 million to the Foundation with payroll deductions. The Foundation's aim is to alleviate poverty through microcredit in communities that supply products to Whole Foods stores.[48]

By 2012 WPF had committed more than $26 million in funds and some 200,000 clients had received loans averaging $235 each. The Foundation works in 50 countries. Ninety-two percent of the recipients are women. The beauty of microfinancing is that a small amount of money can transform the life of an entrepreneur. To date, 95.5 percent of loans have been repaid.[49]

Team member Katherine Nilbrink of Durham, North Carolina, contributes because she has seen poverty all over the world. Microfinancing is a way to "get people out of the cycle of poverty in practical, functional ways with dignity," she says.[50]

The Foundation's frugal philanthropic model:

- Eliminates overhead, which is covered by Whole Foods Market, so that 100 percent of the money raised goes to beneficiaries
- Raises funds from customers, team members, and suppliers
- Requires team members to raise their own funds to travel to the countries served by WPF
- Maximizes the power of partnerships. WPF streamlines operations by working with top-notch agencies like Global Vision International.

Team member Michael Mormino is delighted with the recipes the volunteers bring home. "When I sit down to a bowl of spicy Guatemalan Chicken Stew, I think about people in those communities sitting down to the same meal," he says. "It's like we're sharing a dinner table even though we're miles apart."[51]

In 2011, WPF expanded operations to India, Kenya, and Peru. In 2012, the foundation plans to expand to Brazil and is considering projects later in Haiti, Ghana, Tanzania, Thailand, and Turkey. If your goal is a great job, profit sharing, stock options, plus volunteer opportunities, Whole Foods is hiring.

Do-It-Yourself Volunteer Travel

There are plenty of other ways to volunteer overseas. If you are not fond of formal programs or structured travel, or if your life is too busy to fit someone else's schedule, you can still find unique volunteer travel opportunities to fulfill your deepest philanthropic instincts.

In Telluride, Colorado, where I lived for more than twenty years, Sharon Shuteran is a familiar figure and a beloved one, provided you stay out of trouble: she's the county judge.[52] Every October, however, Sharon, an expert skier, mediator, and a mom, becomes an adventurous volunteer traveler. The first leg of a long journey lands her in mountainous Bhutan, "only" twenty-seven hours, including bus travel and an overnight from her final destination, the village of Trongsa, where she joins a team of skilled medical professionals.

On arrival day, Sharon begins interviewing patients and families, while her team sets up the operating room. Later, she collapses into sleep. For the next week or so, an international team of three surgeons, two anesthesiologists, nurses, speech therapists, Sharon, who serves as a multi-tasking local coordinator, and her Bhutanese colleague Kezang Drupka will see seventy patients through successful cleft palate surgeries as part of the Bhutan Cleft Care Project (BCCP), an independent project that gets a portion of its funding from US-based Smile Train.

For her friends, Sharon posts heartwarming stories of patients, ranging from three months to seventy or more years in age, who travel a day or two on foot followed by a two- or three-day bus trip to BCCP's makeshift clinic. With good cheer, she describes twelve-hour days, amusing misunderstandings, and her own humorous mishaps photographing the exquisite landscape. The heroes, says this inveterate adventurer, are the doctors, nurses, and medical staff who calmly confront exasperating water shortages, malfunctioning equipment, and power outages. Equally heroic, she says, are the families who go to such great lengths to get help for their loved ones. Sharon and her entire dedicated team will return next year to do it all over again.

Seeds for Development

One of the most rewarding ways to volunteer is to send the Universe a prayer of your willingness, and then keep your heart open for the offers that arrive. This approach yielded remarkable results for Alison Hall, founder of Seeds for Development.[53]

In 2007, Alison was leading a happy life. An IBM marketing manager, she commuted to London once or twice a week. On other days she telecommuted from her home in Surrey, where she tended her beloved garden. Still, on some level, Alison longed to make more of a difference. At a global women's conference in Oslo, inspiration struck. One of the speakers was Ugandan businesswoman Josephine Okot, founder and managing director of Victoria Seeds, whose goal is to be the Uganda farmer's "most trusted seed source." Josephine, the 2007 YARA Prize Laureate for pioneering Africa's green revolution, described to the audience her enterprise's humanitarian mission: to transform impoverished people into successful seed farmers. Uganda farmers, she explained, endure pests, drought, and disease.

The words struck a chord for Alison. "This I understand," she thought. "I grow vegetables, too. But if my tomato crop fails, I can go to the store. What do they do?"

With that insight, Alison's career of service in microfinance and volunteer travel was born. She soon established Seeds for Development, a UK-registered charity, which raises funds that are advanced to Ugandan farmers who raise crops for high quality seed, which they then sell to Victoria Seeds. Once or twice a year, Alison travels to Uganda, meets with farmers and seals their new loan deals with an in-person handshake.

Every cent that Seeds for Development's donors contribute goes directly to the farmers. Alison and her colleagues pay all of their own expenses. Founded in 2007, Seeds for Development now supports more than 700 farming families.

Local Giving

"Think globally, act locally" is not just an adage; it's a strategy. There are of course numerous worthy grassroots organizations that need your service and your Conscious Money, from the local homeless shelter, soup kitchen, or food distribution center to community outfits that collect used clothes and charities devoted to children, education, healthcare, or specific illnesses.

If you feel overwhelmed by a long list of options, one way to begin is find a local need that's also a good fit with your personal passion. If you follow your heart, you will probably find it easier to remain interested and committed. Some areas to explore include:

Catholic Charities	Food	Medical care	Transportation
Children	Goodwill	Outdoors	Tutoring/
Clothing	Housing	Salvation Army	teaching
Disabled	Hospices	Shelters	Women
Elders	Hospitals	Teens	

Perhaps you want to contribute your time or Conscious Money to a nonprofit that raises money or serves people confronting a serious illness like heart disease or cancer. Many people are moved to give to a charity that benefits an illness that a loved one has faced. You might focus on a specific cancer, such as breast, prostate, lung, or colon, or on a disease like cystic fibrosis, multiple sclerosis, or muscular dystrophy.

People who have survived harsh situations to live fruitful lives are a powerful inspiration for those confronting debilitating issues like domestic violence, sexual abuse, or handgun violence. Women who volunteer to work domestic violence hotlines at places like the Domestic Violence Center of Greater Cleveland or San Francisco's WOMAN (Women Organized to Make Abuse Nonexistent) typically receive extensive training. To serve on the National Domestic Violence Hotline, you must live in Austin, Texas, and pass an exam based on your training.

Global Warming: Acting Locally

When it comes to global warming, the admonition to "act locally" may be the only way to make a real difference, say environmentalists. "Saving the planet must begin at the local level," conclude Jim Schumacher and

Debbie Bookchin in a *Huffington Post* blog.[54] And in Europe, they add, a local decentralized movement succeeds without help from individual countries or the European Union.

Boris Palmer, mayor of Tübingen, Germany, who took office at age thirty-four, promptly got rid of the official car, a luxurious, gas-guzzling Mercedes, and replaced it with a Japanese-built Prius. He was soon branded a traitor for spurning a German-made car. But the ever steadfast Palmer persisted in persuading the 190 thousand citizens of Tübingen to endorse his plan to cut 70 percent of the city's greenhouse gas emissions by 2020. Later, Palmer ditched the Prius for a Swiss-made electric bike. When the mayor really needed a car, he picked it up at the citywide car-sharing program for an hourly cost of 1.5 Euros, about two dollars. Tübingen's "wildly successful" project is 100 percent citizen-sponsored.

But if your town is not Tübingen, how do you confront global warming?

Sierra Club's "Cool Cities"

Stateside, you can "act locally" in the Sierra Club's volunteer-led Cool Cities project. With its partner the US Green Building Council, Cool Cities aims to "save money, create jobs, and help curb global warming." The Cool Cities website invites individuals to get involved with a local Cool Cities group or start their own Cool Cities initiative in a US or Canadian city.[55]

Cool cities are the antidote to global warming and pioneers in climate change policy: more than one thousand cities and counties have signed the US Conference of Mayors Climate Protection Agreement, which endorses the Kyoto Protocol's goal to cut carbon emissions below 1990 levels by 2012. The Mayors' compact is "the only climate protection agreement of its kind among US elected officials," states the US Conference of Mayors.[56]

Individuals like you are making a concrete difference in the environments of cities like Florissant, Missouri, where the efforts of Cool Cities volunteers and local citizens are cutting city energy use and saving $80,000 per year. Cool City San Jose, California, invites its citizens to: (1) lead by their own actions; (2) act locally to reduce greenhouse gases; and (3) challenge their place of business to follow suit.[57]

Volunteers in Cool City Ottawa, Ontario's Green Bin program collect food scraps and organic waste from 240 thousand households. Great, you might say, but what's that got to do with global warming? The garbage collected would otherwise end up in a landfill where it would generate methane gas, which is twenty-three times more harmful than carbon dioxide. Thanks to Green Bin's volunteers, those organic scraps are productively composted instead.[58]

Similarly, the Environmental Protection Agency's "Act Locally" initiative connects volunteers to local opportunities in recycling, food recovery, and waste cleanup. Just enter your zip code in the EPA's link to Earth 911's "Recycling Hotline" to find centers for "all types of recycles." For people undaunted by the toughest jobs, the EPA's "Superfund Community Toolkit" shows you how to tackle hazardous-waste cleanup. The EPA's "Waste Not, Want Not" initiative links you to the US Department of Agriculture's practical guidelines for collecting wholesome surplus food to feed the hungry.[59]

There are of course many respected environmental groups—from the National Audubon Society to Greenpeace International—that offer excellent volunteer opportunities. Sort through your options with the Natural Resource Defense Council's list of direct links to other environmental groups at nrdc.org/reference/environgroups.asp. Some people wonder how effectively nonprofits use their contributions. The website Fundraiser Insight gives high marks to the World Wildlife Fund, National Geographic Society, the National Wildlife Federation, Greenpeace, Audubon, and Friends of the Earth. Check out their ratings at fundraiserinsight.org/articles/environmentalfundraising.html.

Start Your Own Environmental Group

If you can't find a group that speaks to your issue, consider creating your own. The environmentalist site EcoHearth.com offers uncomplicated advice from blogger Francisco Ramos, summarized here:[60]

1. *Research.* Start brainstorming and do your homework. Figure out what's missing in your community. Don't duplicate the efforts of others: join forces. It's often easier and quicker to start a chapter of a national organization, like the Sierra Club Cool Cities initiative cited earlier, which provides grassroots leaders with resources and a game plan.

2. *Focus.* Prepare to articulate your group's purpose in a few memorable words or a key phrase. To accomplish that goal, explore your issue with classic questions: who, what, when, where, and why. Add a timeline stating when you'll achieve your goals. For example, you might aim to create "a 500-vehicle bike sharing program in the city center by 2014 to cut traffic and greenhouse gases by 7 percent."

3. *Attract members.* Build awareness and support by finding a sympathetic cosponsor (who might also share his or her email and phone lists). Schedule your first meeting at a community center, coffeehouse, or other meeting room. Get the word out via email, social networks, posters, flyers, and sites like Craigslist. Invite key local officials connected to your issue. If you want a bike sharing program, for example, ask a representative from the local transportation agency to attend.

4. *Get organized.* A clear, concise meeting agenda demonstrates focus and organization. Win over attendees with strong research and information. Describe your mission and goals. Explain why people should be concerned about the issue and how the community will benefit. Collect feedback from participants. Assign and delegate tasks and due dates. Schedule your next gathering.

5. *Recruit leaders.* Create a board of directors composed of people with the connections, skill, talent, and time to get your group on the map. The board's job is to raise funds, establish a budget, and help with public relations and event promotion.

"Starting a local environmental organization is a great way to give back to society," writes Ramos, "and leave a better world for future generations." And whether your local issue is the environment, hunger, or domestic violence, the organizational steps described above work equally well.

You might think that by acting locally in a program like Cool Cities or launching your own group, you are focusing your engagement exclusively on the principle of responsibility rather than capitalizing on opportunity. But that is not the case, because there is no better way to invest in your leadership potential. Lessons learned on the front lines as a grassroots activist will serve you throughout your life and open doors to leadership in business, politics, and the community.

Exercises

Where on Earth Do I Feel Attracted?

As the power of Conscious Money permeates the global economy, it invites us to explore parts unknown for work, fun, service, and other pursuits. Most of us are so busy with day-to-day life that we don't allow ourselves to dream. Let's do so now because our dreams are the first draft of our future.

This is the first of three exercises that tap into higher consciousness and explore the rich potential of global adventure. Completing this pleasurable exercise can lift your spirits and open your Being to many possibilities beyond what is familiar. Take a few deep breaths. Listed below are five types of travel that may help you to discover your own travel desires:

- Sacred sites: Machu Picchu (Peru), Angkor Wat (Cambodia), Chartres (France)
- Economic centers: Shanghai (China), São Paulo (Brazil), Bangalore (India)
- Adventure: Patagonia (Chile), Baffin Island (Canada), Kilimanjaro (Tanzania)
- Intrigue: Amman (Jordan), Bahia (Brazil), Hong Kong (China), the Baltic States
- Remote: Bhutan, Greenland, Trans-Siberian Railway, Tasmania (Australia)
- Traditional: Hawaii, the South of France, Tuscany, Alaska

For each category above, list a few places that appeal to you. Connect to the energy of these places. Research them. Allow yourself to be curious, fearful, or excited about each possibility. Invite the Universe to send you guidance about the places that attract you.

What on Earth Would I Do?

If traveling to sightsee is not your idea of fun, or you've already done enough, you may want to consider more purposeful motives for renewing your passport. Review these reasons to travel, noting any that speak to you:

- Volunteer
- Invest
- Work
- Study
- Learn a language
- Grow personally or spiritually
- Vacation
- Find a business supplier
- Seek outdoor adventure
- Start a new life
- Meet a mate
- Start a business
- Intern
- Seek healing

In your Conscious Money journal add more of your own ideas. Choose your top three reasons to travel, and write down some notes about each.

Connect the Dots to Global Travel

Fold a sheet of paper in two. On the left, list three places in the world to which you feel powerfully drawn. On the right, list three reasons that might inspire you to travel. Without thinking too much about it, connect a place with one of your purposeful desires.

Here's what my connections would look like: I'd love to learn Portuguese in Bahia, Brazil; volunteer in Cape Town, South Africa; and study the investment landscape of Taipei, Taiwan.

Which places and purposes inspire you? Note any insights in your Conscious Money journal.

The Global Breath Meditation

The wisdom of Conscious Money reflects the harmony of giving and receiving that is expressed in the act of breathing. By infusing the power of intention into your breath, you can expand your capacity to give and receive love, energy, and money—at a global level—and express appreciation for this harmony.

With each breath, you invoke the flow of life. Inhale and you receive the gift of life and the power of Spirit. Exhale and you send that gift out into the world. Inhaling mirrors the "in-come" of money. Exhaling is a metaphor of financial "out-flow." By consciously choosing to breathe, you invoke the rhythm of the Universe and the balance of Conscious Money.

1. Breathe and imagine your financial resources in perfect harmony. Exhale in ease and trust. Repeat the invocation for a few more breaths.
2. With a series of slow conscious breaths, enlarge your awareness to encompass your home, your town, state, country, and beyond.
3. Send your awareness to countries around the world one continent at a time. Let the borders dissolve in the shared humanity that unites us all. Picture the entire planet thriving in peace and prosperity.

4. Feel the kindness, trust, and goodwill of the people who make peace and prosperity possible.

5. Expand this global meditation, a few breaths at a time, to all of the planet including the pristine cradle in which our world rests.

Options

Reflections

- Think globally: honestly consider whether your actions help or hinder the planet.
- Ask yourself: "What is my mission as a global citizen?" Describe your thoughts and feelings in your journal.
- Dream globally: choose three places to visit, live, or explore more deeply. Sense the gifts each dream destination might hold for you.
- As you prepare to act locally, think about how you wish to contribute in your local community.
- Tune in to the ebb and flow of money in your life by observing your breath. As you are present to the intake and outflow of your breath, allow it to be a metaphor for receiving and then gently releasing your money into circulation through giving to others as well as yourself.
- Recall any difficult travel experiences from the past. Note any travel fears. Think of someone you consider a great global citizen. Recall his or her stories of adventure abroad. Let yourself be inspired.
- Describe in your journal a new and desirable global adventure.

Resources

- Choose a region, such as Latin America, Asia, or Africa. Follow the regional news and explore opportunities to travel or volunteer there.

- Study a language spoken in your region. Consider free courses on Japanese-Online.com, MasterRussian.com, or CyberItalian.com. Or try Rosetta Stone. Practice with native speakers or fellow students.
- Whether for yourself or the young people in your life, research global destinations that will offer great experience and opportunity during the next decade.
- In light of global warming, rethink your housing, transportation, and energy options with help from Green America's *Green American* magazine, online at GreenAmerica.org.
- Expand your investing horizons. Research SRI in Europe on the site Eurosif.org, in Asia at Asria.org, and/or in Africa at Africasif.org.
- Find complete lists of "Great Places to Work" in Latin America, Japan, and Europe at GreatPlacetoWork.com. Start by clicking on "Best Company Lists" on the right side of the home page.
- Research the Pachamama Foundation at PachamamaFoundation.org, or the Whole Foods Foundation at WholeFoodsMarket.com.
- Visit VictoriaSeeds.com and SeedsforDevelopment.org for more information on how to support the Ugandan farmers.

Right Action

- Seek expansive life or work opportunities on a global stage.
- Discuss an overseas assignment with your employer, or consider which companies in your field regularly send people abroad.
- Contribute your heart as well as your Conscious Money by volunteering.
- Volunteer in your local community on an issue that you passionately care about, such as hunger, affordable housing, green energy, tutoring, or reading to the elderly.
- Consider starting your own local activist organization and take inspiration on how to do it from the advice on pages 251–252.

- Create a unique do-it-yourself volunteer job as Sharon Shuteran and Alison Hall did.
- For the ultimate guide to volunteer travel, read the revised *Volunteer Vacations* by Bill McMillon.

Conscious Money Affirmation

The world is my oyster: I am a responsible global citizen.

Conclusion

Throughout this book you have had the opportunity to create a strategy—designed to carry your Conscious Money practice into your future—by committing to the options presented at the end of each chapter. Now open your journal and write a sentence or two about where you stand right now in your Conscious Money practice. Include any breakthroughs you've enjoyed. Also acknowledge any barriers that may have thus far prevented you from experiencing or living the principles of Conscious Money to your fullest satisfaction.

To assess your current Conscious Money strategy, carefully consider the following steps:

1. In your Conscious Money journal, write a paragraph or two describing how your Conscious Money strategy has evolved over time, keeping in mind the core principles of values, consciousness, and self-mastery discussed in the early chapters.
2. What developments have occurred in your life and financial life since you launched your Conscious Money strategy?
3. Have you noticed any changes in your thoughts and feelings about money?

4. Describe your answers to questions two and three in your journal.
5. Record any advances, even small ones, in your financial circumstances. Remember that even if your financial circumstances remain exactly the same, you are making enormous progress if you are experiencing greater well-being and more positive thoughts and emotions.

Now try a quantitative assessment: on a scale from one to ten, with ten being the highest state, numerically rate where you stand right now in terms of your Conscious Money practice. Then choose a number that represents where you want to be in six months, one year, or another time frame that you choose. For example, perhaps you have just classified your practice at a level of six. Maybe you want to be operating at a level that feels more like eight. To recall how to get there, you might revisit the section titled "Building a Conscious Money Strategy" in chapter 1, which describes the process of moving from one level to a higher one, from level six, for example, to level eight.

At some point you may wander off the path of Conscious Money. This is simply part of life and can happen to anyone. To get back on track, return to the simple questions that form the foundation of your strategy: "Where am I now?" and "Where do I want to be?" Then you might take a bit of time to seek new direction and fresh inspiration by reviewing the chapter options, reaffirming your commitments or choosing new ones that better fit your current circumstances. In so doing, you are encouraging yourself to be inspired anew.

The Power of Conscious Money

As you grow more conscious about finance, you realize that Conscious Money is more valuable than precious metals, paper currency, or electrons darting across your online banking page. You come to see that money is energy in motion. Remember, "current," as in a current of electricity, comes from the same root as "currency." Contributing our energy, time, and love can be as powerful, or perhaps more powerful, than giving money, as the stories of volunteers in chapter 8 illustrate. For me, that insight illustrates the truth of money as energy, especially positive energy. The Soul of Money is appreciation, says intuitive Kathleen Loughery, founder of the website GuidanceEnergy.com.

In a sense, money is what we make of it. In a Conscious Money practice, the energy of our values and awareness infuses finance with meaning. Decide that you want your money to be conscious, positive, and harmonious—and those choices will help foster fulfillment and abundance. This is how and why positive emotions generate Conscious Wealth.

Money is the power of human consciousness in motion.

As we choose the path of Conscious Money, we know decisively that finance, while still important, takes second place to the consciousness that creates it and the values that guide it.

Hundreds of millions of people around the world are increasingly aware of their consciousness and spirituality. As the old economic system continues to deteriorate, we all yearn for new global systems that better match the current state of human evolution and better deliver the blessings of abundance.

You are part of this change. When you embrace the power of Conscious Money, you are transforming global economics. As you act on fresh opportunities that mirror your values and your frequency, something wonderful, even magical happens, not just for you, but for all of humanity. Conscious people alone can create conscious financial systems. Your choices and actions help melt away millennia of perceived separation between the ethereal realms of Spirit and the mundane world of commerce. As consciousness permeates finance, it lays the groundwork for the transformation of humanity.

Therein lies the power of Conscious Money.

Notes

Introduction

1. "out of balance" Mark Murray, "NBC Poll: Despite National Pessimism, Obama Tops GOP Foes," msnbc.com, November 7, 2011, accessed May 21, 2012. http://www.msnbc.msn.com/id/45196665/ns/politics-decision_2012/t/nbc-poll-despite-national-pessimism-obama-tops-gop-foes/#.T7qsQY5OHFB.

2. *"That's like profiting from tobacco stocks"* Cliff Feigenbaum quote from author interview and correspondence, April 2004.

Chapter 1: The Fundamentals of Conscious Money

1. *As Hill tells it* Napoleon Hill, *Think and Grow Rich* (Hillsboro, OR: Beyond Words Publishing, 2011), 3.

2. *"Thought"* and *"Definite Major Purpose"* Ibid., 10.

3. *Hill advises the would-be wealthy* "Napoleon Hill 'Think and Grow Rich' #1 Definiteness of Purpose," YouTube video, 10:33, from a 1960s televised performance, posted by "PrimeauProductions," February 17, 2009, accessed January 23, 2012, http://www.youtube.com/watch?v=kYO0ydiJG3E.

Chapter 2: Making Conscious Money Choices

1. *Felix Adler spoke of self-mastery* "The Art of Self-Mastery," *New York Times*, November 14, 1898, http://query.nytimes.com/gst/abstract.html?res=9E02EFD81438E 433A25757C1A9679D94699ED7CF&scp=145&sq=Felix+Adler&st=p.

2. *"mastery is not about perfection"* George Leonard, *Mastery* (New York: Plume, 1992), 140. I am grateful to Jeff Klein for sharing this quote.

3. *Abundance thinking unlocks* Nana Naisbitt story and quotes from author interview and correspondence, March 2011.

4. *extensive coverage* "In the Media," CPM Institute website, last modified 2008, http://www.cpminstitute.com.

5. *"Consider this vision: you wake up in the morning"* Srikumar Rao, *The Personal Mastery Program: Discovering Passion and Purpose in Your Life and Work*, "You Can Have Your Ideal Life," session 1, track 2 (Louisville, CO: Sounds True, 2008), six compact discs.

6. *Srikumar Rao was born in Mumbai* Background information on Srikumar Rao from "Bio" on the website CPMInstitute.com, last modified 2008; from Rao, *Personal Mastery Program*, session 1, track 2, "You Can Have Your Ideal Life"; and from Carolina A. Miranda, "Change Agent: B-School Buddhism," *Time*, April 2, 2006, http://www.time.com/time/magazine/article/0,9171,1179373,00.html.

7. *"somewhat down and downright miserable"* Correspondence between Dr. Srikumar Rao and author, November 2010.

8. *"a very spiritual lady"* Interview with Dr. Srikumar Rao by Prasad Kaipa, "The New Age of Capitalism," *ISB Insight* (December 2008), 21, http://www.areyoureadyto succeed .com/ISBInsight_December_2008.pdf.

9. *three of his core concepts* Rao, *Personal Mastery Program*, "You Can Have Your Ideal Life," session 1, track 2; "Deconstructing Your Reality," session 2, tracks 1–7; and "Mental Chatter Is Not Your Enemy," session 3, track 2.

10. *"mental models"* Rao, *Personal Mastery Program*, "You Can Have Your Ideal Life," session 1, track 2.

11. *The problem comes, the professor says* Rao, *Personal Mastery Program*, "Understanding Mental Models," session 2, track 2.

12. *"My coworkers try to undermine"*   Srikumar Rao, *Are You Ready to Succeed?* (London: Rider, 2006), 34.

13. *"creates our reality"*   Rao, *Personal Mastery Program*, "The Creative Power of Thought," session 1, track 6; and "Constructing Alternative Realities," session 2, track 6.

14. *"a whole lot of stuff"*   Rao, *Personal Mastery Program*, "Mental Chatter Is Not Your Enemy," session 3, track 2; and "The Creative Power of Thought," session 1, track 6.

15. *"You're stuck with it"*   Rao, *Personal Mastery Program*, "Mental Chatter Is Not Your Enemy," session 3, track 2.

16. *"a tiny fraction of one percent"*   Rao, *Personal Mastery Program*, "The Voice of Judgment," session 1, track 7.

17. *"a quantum improvement"*   Rao, *Personal Mastery Program*, "Homework: Focused Intent," session 3, track 4.

18. *"My boss really has my best interests at heart"*   from Rao, *Personal Mastery Program*, "Living Your Alternative Reality," session 2, track 7.

19. *It's absolutely essential*   from Rao, *Personal Mastery Program*, "Constructing Alternative Realities," session 2, track 6.

20. *"You'll be amazed"*   Rao, *Personal Mastery Program*, "Living Your Alternative Reality," session, 2, track 7.

21. *Brandon Peele . . . "I wanted to make a lot of money"*   Amy Wu, "Emotional Striptease, and Other Paths to Ethics," *New York Times*, March 7, 2004, http://www.nytimes.com/2004/03/07/business/business-emotional-striptease-and-other-paths-to-ethics.html?pagewanted=all&src=pm.

22. *Charles Marcus . . . "was forced to fire people"*   Ibid.

23. *the reality you want*   Rao's description of "mental screen savers" and specific questions from Rao, *Personal Mastery Program*, "Crafting Mental Screensavers," session 1, track 8.

24. *188 companies . . . 85 to 90 percent*   Daniel Goleman, "What Makes a Leader?" *Harvard Business Review*, January 2004, http://hbr.org/2004/01/what-makes-a-leader/ar/1; Cary Cherniss and Daniel Goleman, *The Emotionally Intelligent Workplace* (San Francisco: Jossey-Bass, 2001), xv.

25. *Byron Stock . . . "applied" Emotional Intelligence*   Byron Stock's background, workshop descriptions, participant results, and quotes from a series of interviews with Stock conducted by the author between 2006 and 2010.

26. *distinguish between fear and anxiety* Definition of fear, anxiety, and the destructiveness of anxiety from Jason Apollo Voss, *The Intuitive Investor* (New York: SelectBooks, 2010), 37, 39.

27. *"what masquerades as fear is anxiety"* Ibid., 40.

28. *There are several steps in Jason's method* Ibid., 38.

29. *your fear was probably justified* Ibid., 40.

30. *Penney Peirce . . . "the frequency of energy you hold"* "Frequency & Transformation," Penney Peirce website, accessed March 9, 2012, http://www.penneypeirce.com.

Chapter 3: Money Shadows and Higher Consciousness

1. *The following excellent advice* Gary Moore, "Pursuing Ponzi Protection from Financial Wolves in Sheep's Clothing," Morgan Stanley Capital International website, January 26, 2009, http://www.financialseminary.org/articles/pursuing_ponzi_protection.

2. *Amy Foster . . . knew that her life purpose was* Amy Foster story and quotes from interview and correspondence with author, August 2011 and March 2012.

3. *"I came to realize . . . I was living on borrowed money"* Ibid.

4. *"Spiritual intelligence"* Stephen R. Covey, *The 8th Habit: From Effectiveness to Greatness* (New York: Free Press, 2004), 53.

5. *Cindy Wigglesworth . . . is a former Exxon human resources executive* Quotes from Cindy Wigglesworth, her bio, SQ self-assessment tool, its questions and interpretive results, and the definition of Spiritual Intelligence are from interviews and correspondence with Cindy Wigglesworth by the author from 2007 through 2010.

6. *mainstream organizations such as Hewlett-Packard* Ian Wylie, "Hopelessly Devoted," *The Guardian* (UK), December 9, 2005, http://www.guardian.co.uk/money/2005/dec/10/workandcareers.careers?INTCMP=SRCH.

7. *Jeff Klein . . . a successful conscious business leader* Jeff Klein story and quotes are from author interview and correspondence, June 2011.

8. *"Everyone carries a Shadow"* Website of astrologer Rebecca Eigen, whose practice focused on Jung's shadow work. "The following are some favorite quotes by Dr. C. G. Jung." This quote is the third in the list and is attributed to the book *Psychology and Religion*, 76, http://www.shadowdance.com/cgjung/cgjung.html.

Chapter 4: The Trademarks of Conscious Capitalism

1. *"the social responsibility of business"* Milton Friedman, "The Social Responsibility of Business Is to Increase Its Profits," *New York Times Magazine*, September 13, 1970, http://www.colorado.edu/studentgroups/libertarians/issues/friedman-soc-resp-busi ness.html.

2. *studied twenty-eight companies* Raj Sisodia, David Wolfe, and Jagdish Sheth, *Firms of Endearment: How World-Class Companies Profit From Passion and Purpose* (Upper Saddle River, NJ: Pearson Prentice Hall, 2007).

3. *1,025 percent—versus 122 percent* "A Groundbreaking New Book," *Firms of Endearment* website, last modified 2007, http://www.firmsofendearment.com/.

4. *"great places to work"* Amy Lyman, "The Trust Bounce," The Great Place to Work Institute (2009), http://resources.greatplacetowork.com/article/pdf/trustbounce.pdf. During this terrible decade for the stock market, *Fortune*'s "100 Best Companies to Work For" grew 6.8 percent, while the S&P 500 rose 1.04 percent (or a factor of nearly six).

5. *"the paradox of profit"* John Mackey has described the paradox of profit at several public and private Conscious Capitalism gatherings and in "Conscious Capitalism: Creating a New Paradigm for Business," *John Mackey's Blog*, November 9, 2006, http://www2.wholefoodsmarket.com/blogs/jmackey/2006/11/09/conscious-capitalism -creating-a-new-paradigm-for-business/.

6. *"sweet spot for conscious business"* Vanderbeck and Eisenman described the advantages of midsize companies in "Getting Investors' Support for Conscious Capitalism," and Stagen did so in "Entrepreneurship and the Cultivation of Consciousness," both speeches delivered at Catalyzing Conscious Capitalism (C3), the first annual Conscious Capitalism conference in Austin, Texas (November 7–9, 2008), hereafter called "First C3 Conference."

7. *a net of 2.2 million jobs* Rachel Layne, "GE Study Finds Recession's Job Creators Still See Sales Gain," *Bloomberg News*, October 6, 2011, http://www.bloomberg .com/news/2011-10-06/ge-study-sees-midsized-firms-adding-sales-even-as-economy -slows.html.

8. *"Top 25 Medium-Size Businesses to Work For"; estimated sales and number of employees* "Best Medium Businesses to Work for 2011: #14 Eileen Fisher," *Entrepreneur* online, last modified 2012, http://www.entrepreneur.com/gptw/89.

9. Eileen Fisher's company benefits, stated values, vendor policies in China, auditing firms, and environmental practices from a presentation by Eileen Fisher salesperson Lisa Ann Schraffa to the Boston chapter of the Association for Spirit in Business, May 2008. Eileen Fisher's personal role as a leader in developing the SA8000 accountability standard and the company as one of its first signatories is discussed in a lively, in-depth piece: Jennifer Lewin, "Eileen Fisher Case—Brand-Linked Workplace Standards," a case study by Lewin, then a New York University MBA student, 2003 (and subsequently updated by Eileen Fisher Social Consciousness Director Amy Hall). Accessed March 25, 2012, http://www.csrnyc.com/humanrightsworkplace /eileenfishercase.html.

10. *27.5 million small businesses* All SBA facts and figures are from "Frequently Asked Questions," SBA Office of Advocacy, last modified January 2011, http://www.sba.gov /sites/default/files/sbfaq.pdf.

11. *"It burned really well"* Stefan Lovgren, "Coffee-Based Log Burns Cleaner—But No Starbucks Smell," *National Geographic News*, October 25, 2004, http://news.national geographic.com/news/2004/10/1025_041025_java_log.html.

12. *His Java-Log Firelogs emit up to 78 perent less* "Java-Log Firelogs: A Greener Firelog," Pine Mountain Brands website, last modified 2009, http://www.pinemountain brands.com/pages/java_log__firelogs/20.php.

13. *"There's no Starbucks smell"* Lovgren, "Coffee-Based Log Burns Cleaner."

14. *hotbed of creativity* The four SBA bullets on innovation in green small businesses are from Anthony Breitzman and Patrick Thomas, "Analysis of Small Business Innovation in Green Technologies," Small Business Research Summary, SBA Office of Advocacy, no. 389 (October 2011), http://www.sba.gov/advocacy/7540/28811.

15. *Pangea is a pioneer in green innovation* Joshua Onysko and the Pangea story are based on several interviews and correspondence with Onysko conducted for this book by researcher Trudi Irons, 2007. IDEO design work from, "Pangea Organics," *@issue Journal* 13, no. 1, last modified 2012, http://www.cdf.org/issue_journal/pangea _organics-5.html.

16. *$700 billion in recent small business loans* The SBA figures on loans to small business and small business survival rates are from "How Are Credit Conditions for Small Firms?" Frequently Asked Questions, SBA Office of Advocacy, last modified January 2011, http://www.sba.gov/sites/default/files/sbfaq.pdf.

17. *SoulCycle, a fitness business* The SoulCycle story is based on "About Soul," SoulCycle website, accessed March 9, 2012, http://www.soul-cycle.com/about.cfm.

18. *Callie Micek . . . "I knew it was not just a job"*   Interview with Callie Micek, conducted for this book by researcher Joy Molony, July 2011.

19. *no layoffs*   TCS's no layoff policy was described by its CEO, Kip Tindell, on *CBS News Sunday Morning*, CBS, March 9, 2011.

20. *"It's just good business"*   and other Costco-related quotes, Steven Greenhouse, "How Costco Became the Anti-Wal-Mart," *New York Times*, July 17, 2005, http://www .nytimes.com/2005/07/17/business/yourmoney/17costco.html?pagewanted=al. *The Simply Hired website*   Simply Hired, "Average Costco Salaries," accessed March 28, 2012, http://www.simplyhired.com/a/salary/search/q-Costco; "Average Sam's Club Salaries," accessed March 28, 2012, http://www.simplyhired.com/a/salary/ search/q-Sams+Club.

21. *Costco stock rose . . . while Wal-Mart*   Barbara Farfan, "2010 Stock Results from the Largest Publicly Traded US Retail Chains," About.com Retail Industry, accessed March 28, 2012, http://retailindustry.about.com/od/statisticsresearch/a/2010-Stock -Results-From-The-Largest-Publicly-Traded-U-S-Retail-Chains.htm.

22. *"a dialogue about the Good"*   Nikos Mourkogiannis, "The Power of Purpose and the 'Y' Movement," presentation at the First C3 Conference.

23. *"Purpose is where you're going"*   Roy Spence's quotes, descriptions of Herb Kelleher and Southwest Airlines, the percentage of Americans who have flown, and Southwest's purpose are from his talk, "It's Not What You Sell; It's What You Stand For," at the First C3 Conference.

24. *Pierre Omidyar . . . "We believe people are basically good"*   George Anders, "Business Fights Back: eBay Learns to Trust Again," *Fast Company*, November 30, 2001, http://www.fastcompany.com/magazine/53/ebay.html.

25. *considerably less than 1 percent of eBay transactions*   From numerous sources, including "eBay Identity Theft Hits Close to Home," *CNN Technology*, February 18, 2002, http://articles.cnn.com/2002-02-18/tech/ebay.identity.theft.idg_1_ebay-users -ebay-bid-kevin-pursglove?_s=PM:TECH.

26. *Agilent did so with heart*   Agilent's conscious layoff policies from Daniel Roth, "How to Cut Pay, Lay Off 8,000 People, and Still Have Workers Who Love You," *Fortune*, January 22, 2002, http://www.danielroth.net/archive/2002/01/how_to_cut_pay_.html.

27. *"The 100 Best Corporate Citizens"*   "GMCR Named One of the '100 Best Corporate Citizens,'" *Green Mountain Coffee Café* (blog), March 2, 2010, http://blog.green mountaincoffee.com/blog/sandy/gmcr-named-one-of-the-100-best-corporate-citizens.

28. *"Best Medium Company"* "Green Mountain Coffee Roasters Ranked #9 on List of 'Best Medium Companies to Work for in America,'" *Business Wire*, June 29, 2004, http://www.businesswire.com/news/home/20040629005087/en/Green-Mountain -Coffee-Roasters-Ranked-9-List.

29. *Ryan Dreimiller . . . "I'm less distracted"* "Continuous Learning: A Catalog Full of On-Site Courses," Green Mountain Coffee Roasters website, last modified 2009, accessed March 9, 2012, http://www.gmcr.com/continuous-learning.html.

30. *Josh Martin . . . "I've never been told no"* Ibid.

31. *"humane, collaborative, and economically vibrant"* Gerry McDonough, "Organizational Culture: The Bedrock of Conscious Capitalism," at the First C3 Conference.

32. *Terri Kelly . . . considers herself fortunate* Terri Kelly quotes and her description of W. L. Gore & Associates corporate culture and values are from her presentation "Nurturing a Vibrant Culture to Drive Innovation," at the First C3 Conference.

33. *Why can't an entire company run like this?* Founding philosophy of W. L. Gore & Associates and Bill Gore quotes from 1985 interview with Bill and Vieve Gore by John Naisbitt and Patricia Aburdene, cited in John Naisbitt and Patricia Aburdene, *Re-inventing the Corporation* (New York: Warner Books, 1985), 9, 24, and 26.

34. *"You are only a leader when someone follows you"* Terri Kelly, "Nurturing a Vibrant Culture to Drive Innovation," at the First C3 Conference.

35. *profit surged to nearly 80 percent* from Brian Gaar "Profits up 79% at Whole Foods," *Austin American-Statesman*, February 9, 2011, accessed March 29, 2012, http://www.statesman.com/business/area-employers/profits-up-79-at-whole-foods -1244344.html.

36. *86 percent of Green Mountain employees agree* "Employee Benefits," accessed March 29, 2012, http://www.gmcr.com/csr/CreatingAGreatPlaceToWork/Employee Benefits.aspx; *employee trips to coffee plantations* from Green Mountain spokesperson Sandy Yusen in interview and correspondence with researcher Joy Molony, January 2011.

37. *"Conscious Capitalism is the new story"* R. Edward Freeman, "Creating Value for Stakeholders," presentation at the First C3 Conference.

38. *"Conscious Capitalism contributes to life"* Marianne Williamson, closing remarks at Catalyzing Conscious Capitalism: Exploring the Edges of Conscious Leadership conference, Lake Arrowhead, California, October 19–22, 2010.

Chapter 5: The Joy of Mindful Spending

1. *"benefit a good cause"* Telis Demos, "Thrifty Is the New Frugal," *Fortune,* April 20, 2009, http://money.cnn.com/2009/04/20/pf/citigroup_kerschner_thrifty.fortune /index.htm.

2. *39 percent of shoppers* "More Consumers Believe Sustainability Claims—But Many Still Skeptical," describes the results of GfK Roper Consulting's 2010 "Green Gauge US Report," *Environmental Leader: Environmental & Energy Management News,* September 22, 2011, http://www.environmentalleader.com/2011/09/22/more-consumers -believe-sustainability-claims-but-many-still-skeptical/.

3. *81 percent, care more* Tom Crawford, "10 Green Trends for Consumers in 2010," from the blog of UK sustainability brand firm Clownfish, January 21, 2010, http://www.clownfishmarketing.com/discussion/10-green-trends-consumers-2010.

4. *Of conscious consumers polled, 80 percent* "Unlocking the Power of Renewable Energy Certification to Build Credibility with Consumers," a brief study by the Natural Marketing Institute and the Center for Resource Solutions, June 23, 2009, http://www.resource-solutions.org/pub_pdfs/NMI%20Case%20Study%200609.pdf.

5. *more than 40 percent* Ibid.

6. *"We're seeing a shift"* Demos, "Thrifty Is the New Frugal."

7. *"The roots of Fair Trade . . . preserve the land."* Paul Rice quote from author interview and correspondence, April 1, 2012, facilitated by Fair Trade USA spokesperson Katie Barrow.

8. *"It means a lot to know"* Carolyn Long story and quotes from author interview and correspondence, December 2010.

9. *62 percent of consumers . . . "Fair Trade Finder"* Fair Trade USA, "Fair Trade Products Just a Click Away with New 'Fair Trade Finder' Application," press release, October 4, 2011, http://www.fairtradeusa.org/press-room/press_release/fair-trade-products-just -click-away-new-fair-trade-finder-application.

10. *The Conscious Money of millions* Information on farmers helped by Fair Trade, number of countries involved and which ones, global sales of $4.5 billion, number of US retailers, total FT products sold in the United States, and types of products from "Fair Trade Global Sales Figures Looking Up," Fair Trade USA blog, May 26, 2010, http://fairtradeusa.org/get-involved/blog/fair-trade-global-sales-figures-looking; and from

"Fair Trade Certified 2011 Media Kit," Fair Trade USA. A PDF of the press kit can be found at http://www.fairtradeusa.org/press-room/press_release/archive/ 2012/01.

11. *FT sales were flat in 2010*   Fair Trade USA "Holiday Greetings and Gratitude from Fair Trade USA," Letter from President and CEO Paul Rice (blog), December 24, 2011, accessed March 30, 2012, http://fairtradeusa.org/blog/holiday-greetings-and -gratitude-fair-trade-usa. Fair Trade USA estimate of 2011 sales from spokesperson Katie Barrow in correspondence with author, March 2012.

12. *sixty thousand locations . . . ten thousand FT products*   Fair Trade USA, "Fair Trade Certified 2011 Media Kit."

13. *popular items and stores where you can find them*   Ibid.

14. *certified more than 100 million . . . more than half*   Fair Trade USA, "Introduction and Highlights," *2010 Almanac*, 21, Alter Eco USA website, http://www.altereco -usa.com/media/images/Almanac_2010_0.pdf.

15. *at least 30 percent*   "Corporate Social Responsibility: Where We're Going in FY '10," Green Mountain Coffee Roasters website, last modified 2009, http://www.gmcr.com /csr/PromotingSustainableCoffee/WhereWeAreGoingInFY08.aspx.

16. *If you start your day at Starbucks*   "Responsibly Grown Coffee," Starbucks website, last modified 2011, http://www.starbucks.com/responsibility/sourcing/coffee; *Starbucks offers FT-certified*   "Fair Trade Certified™ French Roast," Starbucks website, last modified 2012, http://www.starbucks.ie/coffee/dark/french-roast.

17. *"In the hyper-caffeinated world"*   Information on Dean's Beans from Dean Cycon interviews and correspondence conducted for this book by researcher Trudi Irons, 2008–2011.

18. *Dunkin' Donuts was the first*   "Dunkin' Donuts to Sell New Espresso Beverages Using Fair Trade Certified™ Coffee," Organic Consumers Association website, April 25, 2003, http://www.organicconsumers.org/starbucks/050703_fair _trade.cfm.

19. *rival or exceed FT standards*   "Direct Trade," Stumptown Coffee website, last modified 2011, http://stumptowncoffee.com/direct-trade/; "Relationship Coffee," Sustainable Harvest website, accessed March 9, 2012, http://www.sustainableharvest .com/relationship-coffee/; and Planet Friendly PR, "Sustainable Harvest Earns SCAA's 2006 Sustainability Award," press release on Coffee Geek website, April 11, 2006, http://coffeegeek.com/resources/pressreleases/sustainableharvest.

20. *Ireland's Insomnia Coffee Company . . . British national retailer Marks & Spencer's*   Fairtrade Foundation, "7 Million Farming Families Worldwide Benefit as Global Fair-

trade Sales Increase by 40% and UK Awareness of the Fairtrade Mark Rises to 57%," press release, August 10, 2007, http://www.fairtrade.org.uk/press_office/press _releases_and_statements/archive_2007/aug_2007/global_fairtrade_sales_increase_by _40_benefiting_14_million_farmers_worldwide.aspx.

21. *Virgin Airlines serves an estimated twelve million cups*   "What We're Doing," Virgin Atlantic website, last modified 2012, http://www.virgin-atlantic.com/en/gb/allaboutus /environment/ouractions.jsp.

22. *"Social change consumers" spend $45 billion*   Stefanie Olsen, "eBay to Unveil Fair-Trade Marketplace," CNET News, May 20, 2008, http://news.cnet.com/8301-11128 _3-9949104-54.html?tag=mncol;1n.

23. *"Our technology gives workers a voice"*   Data and descriptions of Good World Solutions, its Fair Wage Guide, and Labor Link from Fair Trade USA, "Good World Solutions Expands Technology to Connect Companies with Workers in Global Supply Chains," press release, November 22, 2011, http://www.fairtradeusa.org/press -room/press_release/good-world-solutions-expands-technology-connect-companies -workers-global-su. For more information on Good World Solutions, including its Fair Wage Guide, consult its website, http://www.goodworldsolutions.org/about-us/.

24. *Ten Thousand Villages*   "Global Shopping with a Conscience," Mompreneur International, July/August 2009, 30, http://www.themompreneur.com/documents/MGN _07_08_2009.pdf; "2010 World's Most Ethical Companies," *Ethisphere Magazine*, 2010, http://ethisphere.com/past-wme-honorees/wme2010/.

25. *"You never change things by fighting the existing reality"*   From the website of the Buckminster Fuller Challenge, which awards $100,000 each year to support the development and implementation of a strategy with significant potential to solve humanity's most pressing problems, accessed March 9, 2012, http://challenge.bfi .org/About.

26. *"Toxic ingredients applied to the skin"*   Courtney Helgoe, "Beauty Beware," *Experience Life*, December 2009, 59.

27. *ingredients are not reviewed by the FDA*   Andrew Schneider, "How Safe Are Cosmetics? New Bill Wants to Find Out," *AOL News*, July 21, 2010, http://www.aolnews .com/2010/07/21/how-safe-are-your-cosmetics-new-bill-wants-to-find-out/; See also, "Myths on Cosmetics Safety" (third myth) on the Environmental Working Group's Skin Deep Cosmetics Database website, last modified 2012, http://www.ewg.org /skindeep/myths-on-cosmetics-safety/.

28. *US personal care industry polices itself*   "FDA Authority over Cosmetics," US Food and Drug Administration website, last modified January 22, 2012, http://www.fda

.gov/Cosmetics/GuidanceComplianceRegulatoryInformation/ucm074162.htm; See also, "Myths on Cosmetics Safety" (third myth), Environmental Working Group (EWG) Skin Deep Cosmetics Database, last modified 2012, accessed March 9, 2012, http://www.ewg.org/skindeep/myths-on-cosmetics-safety/.

29. *Nearly 80 percent of the 10,500 ingredients* Leann Brown with Travis Mitchel, "Not in My Cosmetics: The Series," *Environmental Working Group Enviroblog*, November 23, 2009, http://www.enviroblog.org/2009/11/not-in-my-cosmetics-the-series.html.

30. *FDA has only banned eleven ingredients* Market Shift: The Story of the Compact for Safe Cosmetics and the Growing Demand for Safer Products, a report from The Campaign for Safe Cosmetics, November 2011, 5, http://safecosmetics.org/downloads/MarketShift_CSC_Dec2011.pdf.

31. *more than 500 cosmetic products* "Myths of Cosmetic Safety" (third myth), EWG Skin Deep Cosmetics Database.

32. *an independent coalition* The birth of The Campaign for Safe Cosmetics, number of groups, and notable members from "Who We Are," *Market Shift*.

33. *More than one in five . . . 80 percent* "Research," The Campaign for Safe Cosmetics website, last modified 2011, http://safecosmetics.org/article.php?list=type&type=29.

34. *22 percent of personal care products* "Myths of Cosmetic Safety" (third myth), EWG Skin Deep Cosmetics Database.

35. *phase out the controversial chemical 1,4-dioxane* Amy Westervelt, "As Report Reveals Toxic Ingredients in Baby Shampoo, Johnson & Johnson Goes Public with Plans to Clean Up Products," *Forbes*, November 1, 2011, http://www.forbes.com/sites/amywestervelt/2011/11/01/as-report-reveals-toxic-ingredients-in-baby-shampoo-johnson-johnson-goes-public-with-plans-to-clean-up-products/.

36. *When EWG tested twenty teens* Rebecca Sutton, PhD (EWG staff scientist), "Adolescent Exposures to Cosmetic Chemicals of Concern," *The Environmental Working Group*, September 2008, http://www.ewg.org/reports/teens.

37. *banned for use . . . twenty of thirty lipstick brands* US Consumer Product Safety Commission, "CPSC Announces Final Ban on Lead-Containing Paint," press release from the Office of Information and Public Affairs, September 2, 1977, http://www.cpsc.gov/cpscpub/prerel/prhtml77/77096.html; "A Poison Kiss: The Problem of Lead in Lipstick," The Campaign for Safe Cosmetics, October 11, 2007, http://safecosmetics.org/article.php?id=327.

38. *Five years later . . . FDA* Dina ElBoghdady, "400 Lipsticks Found To Contain Lead FDA Says," *The Washington Post*, February 14, 2012, accessed March 30, 2012,

http://www.washingtonpost.com/business/economy/400-lipstick-brands-contain-lead
-fda-says/2012/02/14/gIQAhOyeDR_story.html.

39. *"a proven neurotoxin"* Stacy Malkan of The Campaign for Safe Cosmetics quoted in "Don't Pucker Up: Lead in Lipstick," ABCNews.com, October 12, 2007, http://abc news.go.com/GMA/story?id=3722013#.Txhvrm9SScg.

40. *63 percent of girls seven to ten* From a Mintel study cited in Owen Bowcott, "Makeup and Marketing: Welcome to the World of 10-Year-Old Girls," *The Guardian* (UK), September 7, 2004, http://www.guardian.co.uk/uk/2004/sep/08 /childprotection.schools.

41. *One quarter of American shoppers* Helgoe, "Beauty Beware," 57. The author cites the Natural Marketing Institute spokesperson Gwynne Rogers.

42. *Dr. Bronner's Magic Soaps . . . sued* Organic Consumers Association, "Dr. Bronner's Magic Soaps Files Lawsuit against Major 'Organic' Cheater Brands," press release, April 28, 2007, http://www.organicconsumers.org/articles/article_11855.cfm.

43. *these brands to be authentically organic* Organic Consumers Association, "Carcinogenic 1, 4-Dioxane Found in Leading 'Organic' Brand Personal Care Products," press release March 14, 2008, http://www.organicconsumers.org/bodycare/Dioxane Release08.cfm.

44. *Dr. Bronner's Magic Soaps is settling* from interview and correspondence with Dr. David Bronner by researcher Joy Molony, February 2012.

45. *Natural Products Association Seal of Approval* "The Natural Seal: Home Care & Personal Care," Natural Products Association website, accessed January 25, 2012, http://www.npainfo.org/index.php?src=gendocs&ref=NaturalSealMain.

46. *Whole Foods "Premium Body Care"* "Premium Body Care™ Standards," Whole Foods website, last modified 2012, http://wholefoodsmarket.com/stores/departments /premium-body-care.php; A list of 400 chemicals that Whole Foods bans is also available on its website: http://wholefoodsmarket.com/vendor/wholebody/unacceptable _pbc.pdf.

47. *"Get rid of every lotion"* Ann Garrity story from Helgoe, "Beauty Beware," *Experience Life*, December 2009, 57; "Organic Diva Story," Organic Diva website, accessed March 9, 2012, http://www.organicdivas.com/story.html.

48. *Horst Rechelbacker sold his natural beauty line* "Our Founder," Intelligent Nutrients website, last modified 2010, http://www.intelligentnutrients.com/our-vision/our -founder.

49. *In 1985, German biochemist* "Dr. Jurgen Klein Biography," Dr. Jurgen Klein website, last modified 2010, http://www.drjurgenklein.com./biography/index.php. See also Anna Chesters, "A Brief History of Jurlique," *The Guardian*, December 5, 2011, accessed March 30, 2012, http://www.guardian.co.uk/fashion/fashion-blog /2011/dec/05/brief-history-of-jurlique.

50. *Jane Iredale mineral makeup* "What Makes Our Make-up Different?" Jane Iredale website, last modified 2012, https://janeiredale.com/us/en/mineral-makeup/our-difference.htm.

51. *Suki's 100 percent synthetic-free* "Science of Suki," Suki website, accessed March 9, 2012, http://www.sukiskincare.com/v7/pages/about+suki+our+science; "Founder & Owner of Suki, Inc., Suki Kramer's Exclusive Interview with Nature's Basin," *Nature's Basin* (blog), August 13, 2012, http://blog.naturesbasin.com/2010_08_01_archive.html.

52. *Inara is a 100 percent organic-certified* "Welcome to Inara," Inara website, last modified 2005, http://www.inaraorganic.com/homepage.htm.

53. *Dr. Hauschka* "Our History: A Timeline," Dr. Hauschka Skin Care website, last modified 2012, http://drhauschka.com/about-dr-hauschka-skin-care/our-history/; and "Can't Buy Me Love: How Luxury Organic Skin-Care Company Dr. Hauschka Has Infused Sustainability into Its Financial Structure," *Fast Company*, December 2007, http://www.fastcompany.com/magazine/121/cant-buy-me-love.html.

54. *Thus far the Campaign has identified* Information on companies deemed safe by The Campaign for Safe Cosmetics in "Appendix A: Champion Companies" and "Appendix B: Innovator Companies," *Market Shift*, November 2011, 14–15, http://safecosmetics.org/downloads/MarketShift_CSC_Dec2011.pdf.

55. *the US organic food and drink market grew nearly* Organic Trade Association, "US Organic Industry Valued at Nearly $29 Billion in 2010," press release, April 21, 2011, http://www.organicnewsroom.com/2011/04/us_organic_industry_valued_at.html.

56. *Global organic sales reached $59 billion* Claire Videau, "Organic Monitor Predicts More Investment in European Organic Sector," FoodAndDrinkEurope.com, February 24, 2011, http://www.foodanddrinkeurope.com/Financial/Organic-Monitor-predicts -more-investment-in-European-organic-sector.

57. *78 percent of families said* Organic Trade Association, "Seventy-Eight Percent of US Families Say They Purchase Organic Foods," press release, November 2, 2011, http://www.organicnewsroom.com/2011/11/seventyeight_percent_of_us_fam.html.

58. *Local Harvest, a comprehensive sustainable food website* The descriptions of CSAs, food co-ops, and farmers' markets are from the Local Harvest website, modified 2011,

http://www.localharvest.org. See the website for searchable food co-ops, CSAs, and farmers' markets. *More than 800 consumer existing food co-ops* Local Harvest website, accessed March 25, 2012, http://www.localharvest.org/search.jsp?m&ty=3&nm=.

59. *5,000 CSA farms* Local Harvest website, accessed March 25, 2012, http://www.local harvest.org/search-csa.jsp?lat=39.0&lon=97.0&scale=3&ty=6&co=1&nm=.

60. *2.2 million farms . . . 98 percent of them family-owned* Robert A. Hoppe and David E. Banker, "Structure and Finances of US Farms: Family Farm Report, 2010 Edition," EIB-66, US Dept. of Agriculture, Economic Research Service (July 2010): 6, http://www.ers.usda.gov/Publications/EIB66/EIB66.pdf.

61. *between 2002 and 2007* US Department of Agriculture data reported in John Tozzi, "Entrepreneurs Keep the Local Food Movement Hot," *Bloomberg Businessweek*, December 18, 2009, http://www.businessweek.com/smallbiz/content/dec2009/sb20091217 _914398.htm.

62. *criteria that define "local" can vary* Steve W. Martinez, "Varied Interests Drive Growing Popularity of Local Foods," *Amber Waves* (US Department of Agriculture), December 2010, http://www.ers.usda.gov/AmberWaves/December10/Features/Local Foods.htm.

63. *In 2011, there were 7,175 markets* US Department of Agriculture, "More than 1,000 New Farmers Markets Recorded across Country as USDA Directory Reveals 17 Percent Growth" news release, August 5, 2011, http://www.usda.gov/wps/portal /usda/usdahome?contentid=2011/08/0338.xml.

64. *John Mackey . . . "the local tomato"* John Cloud, "Eating Better than Organic," *Time*, March 2, 2007, http://www.time.com/time/magazine/article/0,9171,1595245,00.html.

65. *two to five times higher* General Accounting Office, "Indoor Pollution: Status of Federal Research Activities," report to the Ranking Minority Member, Committee on Government Reform, House of Representatives, August 1999, 4, http://www.gao.gov /archive/1999/rc99254.pdf.

66. *A four-year study* Muriel Cozier, "Household Cleaners Can Harm," *ICIS Chemical Business* (weekly), June 5, 2006: 5, http://business.highbeam.com/435238/article -1G1-147468785/household-cleaners-can-harm.

67. *Household cleaning products are the third leading substance* Alexandra Gorman, *Household Hazards: Potential Hazards of Home Cleaning Products* (Missoula, MT: Women's Voices for the Earth, 2007), 8, http://healthychild.org/uploads/file/Hazards Report.pdf.

68. *the most common cleaning product accidentally swallowed* "Chemical Encyclopedia: Chlorine," Healthy Child website, accessed March 9, 2012, http://healthychild .org/issues/chemical-pop/chlorine/.

69. *the University of Washington analyzed* Anne C. Steinemann, University of Washington, "Scented Consumer Products Shown to Emit Many Unlisted Chemicals," press release, October 26, 2010, http://depts.washington.edu/exposure/press_release.html.

70. *nearly 90 percent of them are women* Gorman, *Household Hazards*, 7. Independently verified with US Department of Labor statistics.

71. *Sam Katz . . . sprayed the same cleaners on his child's bathtub.* Marcelle S. Fischler, "A Safe House?" *New York Times*, February 15, 2007, http://www.nytimes.com/2007 /02/15/garden/15clean.html?pagewanted=all.

72. *childhood wheezing and asthma* Gorman, *Household Hazards*, 12. See also the study's endnotes, 42–44.

73. *thirteen million missed school days per year* US Environmental Protection Agency, "Managing Asthma in the School Environment," IAQ Tools for Schools, EPA website, last modified December 7, 2011, http://epa.gov/iaq/schools/managing asthma.html.

74. *fifty-five million people . . . half of those schools* US Environmental Protection Agency, "Indoor Air Quality," Healthy School Environment Resources, EPA website, last modified February 7, 2012, http://cfpub.epa.gov/schools/top_sub.cfm?t_id=45&s_id=4.

75. *New York State has responded* Fischler, "A Safe House?"

76. *By 2011, Illinois, Connecticut* "Many States Require Green Products," *CleanLink: The Professional Cleaning Industry's Online Resource*, May 4, 2011, http://www.clean link.com/cleanlinkminute/details/Many-States-Require-Green-Products--26432.

77. *more than twenty pounds of household hazardous waste* US Environmental Protection Agency, "Solid Waste: Household Hazardous Waste," Pacific Southwest Waste, EPA website, last modified June 7, 2011, http://www.epa.gov/region9/waste/solid/house.html.

78. *thirty-two million pounds of household cleaners* "Fragile: Handle with Care," Maryland Department of Natural Resources, accessed January 27, 2012, http:// www.dnr.state.md.us/bay/protect/home.html.

79. *69 percent of streams contain detergent* US Geological Survey, "Pharmaceuticals, Hormones, and Other Organic Wastewater Contaminants in US Streams," USGS Fact Sheet FS-027-02, June 2002, http://toxics.usgs.gov/pubs/FS-027-02/pdf/FS-027 -02.pdf.

80. *three hundred Stop & Shop supermarket locations*   Fischler, "A Safe House?"

81. *By 2010, 42 percent of consumers*   Packaged Facts, "US Market for Green Household Cleaning Products Enters Forefront of Consumer Consciousness with Shift toward More Eco-Friendly and Sustainable Lifestyles," press release, May 24, 2010, http://www.packagedfacts.com/Green-Household-Cleaning-2554249/.

82. *Half of eighteen- to twenty-nine-year-olds say*   Describing the results of a Global Market Insite survey, "Consumer Survey Finds Doing Good is Good for Business," GreenBiz.com, September 13, 2005, http://www.greenbiz.com/news/2005/09/13/consumer-survey-finds-doing-good-good-business.

83. *Mintel International forecasts*   Jessica Kwong, "Keeping Your Home Clean and 'Green,'" Forbes.com, March 8, 2010, http://www.forbes.com/2010/03/08/method-clorox-green-technology-ecotech-cleaning.html.

84. *The merits of green cleaning*   Gabrielle Lennon story from Jeffrey Hollender, "Profits with Purpose: Seventh Generation," *45 Social Entrepreneurs Who Are Changing the World*, Fast Company website, last modified 2012, http://www.fastcompany.com/social/2008/profiles/seventh-generation.html.

85. *All of the company's products*   Seventh Generation ingredient list from Fischler, "A Safe House?"

86. *Childhood friends . . . during the 2001 recession*   Margaret Heffernan, "Soap Stars," *Reader's Digest*, October 2009, 76–77. *100 percent recycled plastic bottles*   Method Firsts, 2008, accessed http://methodhome.com/methodology/our-story/method-firsts/. *Method quickly grew into a $100 million business*   Method description from Kwong, "Keeping Your Home Clean and 'Green.'"

87. *Method and Seventh Generation registered double-digit sales*   Andrew Martin and Stephanie Clifford, "For a Few, Focus on Green Products Pays Off," *New York Times*, April 21, 2011, http://green.blogs.nytimes.com/2011/04/21/rebound-for-product-makers-with-green-focus/.

88. *Monica Nassif, a former marketing executive*   Product story from Thomas Lee, "Mr. Muscle Marrying Mrs. Meyer," *StarTribune* (Minneapolis, MN), April 28, 2008, http://www.startribune.com/business/18351899.html; See also "Monica Nassif Caldrea and Mrs. Meyer's Clean Day," Ladies Who Launch website, January 19, 2010, http://www.ladieswholaunch.com/magazine/monica-nassif-mrs-meyers-clean-day/5167.

89. *at least 95 percent natural ingredients*   "Where Green Meets Clean," "Products" page, Green Works website, last modified 2011, http://www.greenworkscleaners.com/products/ingredients/.

90. *first product ever endorsed by the Sierra Club*   Felicity Barringer, "Clorox Courts Sierra Club, and a Product is Endorsed," *New York Times*, March 26, 2008, http://www.nytimes.com/2008/03/26/business/businessspecial2/26cleanser.html.

91. *Some Sierra Club chapters have criticized*   Associated Press, "Some in Sierra Club Feel Sullied by Clorox Deal," *MSNBC* online, July 16, 2008, http://www.msnbc.msn.com/id/25708115/ns/us_news-environment/t/some-sierra-club-feel-sullied-clorox-deal/#.Txh6NG9SScg.

92. *"safe and effective and PhD toxicologists"*   Fischler, "A Safe House?"

93. *"Federal law doesn't require full disclosure . . . 300 to 400 raw ingredients"*   Ibid.

94. *Today Clorox*   "Ingredients Inside," last modified 2011, http://www.theclorox company.com/products/ingredients-inside. *Earthjustice*   "Clean Up Their Act," http://earthjustice.org/features/campaigns/cleans-up-their-act-companies-that-haven-t-disclosed-chemicals-in-cleaning-products.

95. *254 million registered vehicles . . . 50 percent of air pollution*   Research and Innovative Technology Administration, "Table 1-11: Number of US Aircraft, Vehicles, Vessels, and Other Conveyances," US Department of Transportation, Bureau of Transportation Statistics, accessed March 9, 2012, http://www.bts.gov/publications/national _transportation_statistics/html/table_01_11.html; US Environmental Protection Agency, "Sources of Pollutants in the Ambient Air—Mobile Sources," *Air Pollution Control Orientation Course*, January 29, 2010, http://www.epa.gov/apti/course422/ap3a.html.

96. *29 percent of US greenhouse gas emissions*   US Department of Transportation, "Transportation's Role in Reducing US Greenhouse Gas Emissions," Federal Transit Administration, 2010, http://www.fta.dot.gov/12347_12128.html.

97. *Zipcar, the industry leader in car sharing*   All Zipcar data from "Car Sharing Takes Off," CNBC, video interview with Zipcar CEO Scott Griffith, 7:29, June 2, 2009, http://video.cnbc.com/gallery/?video=1139125735; and "Zipcar Media Backgrounder," (download) Zipcar website, last modified 2012, http://zipcar.mediaroom.com/index .php?s=23.

98. *200 car share programs in 600 US cities*   John Addison, "Car Sharing Competition: Hertz and Enterprise Chase Zipcar," *Clean Fleet Report*, accessed March 9, 2012, http://www.cleanfleetreport.com/fleets/car-sharing-competition-hertz-and-enterprise-chase-zipcar/.

99. *"people want to be more sustainable"*   "Car Sharing Takes Off," CNBC interview with Zipcar CEO Scott Griffith.

100. *Why stop at cars?* Sharing story from Nancy Trejos, "Recession Lesson: Share and Swap Replaces Buy and Grab," *Washington Post,* July 17, 2009, http://www.washington post.com/wp-dyn/content/article/2009/07/16/AR2009071604201.html.

101. *In 1970, nearly 9 percent* US Census Bureau, "Means of Transportation to Work for the US: 1960–1990," 1970 Census of Population, Characteristics of Population, United States Summary, accessed March 9, 2012, http://www.census.gov/hhes /commuting/files/1990/mode6790.txt.

102. *about 5 percent* Brian S. McKenzie, "Public Transportation Usage among US Work-ers: 2008 and 2009," *American Community Survey Briefs,* US Census Bureau, October 2010, http://www.census.gov/prod/2010pubs/acsbr09-5.pdf; Brian S. McKenzie and Melanie Rapino, "Commuting in the United States: 2009," *American Community Survey Reports,* US Census Bureau, September 2011, http://www.census.gov/prod /2011pubs/acs-15.pdf.

103. *10.3 billion rides* Kenneth Musante, "Mass Transit Surge: Most Riders Since 1957," CNNMoney.com, June 11, 2008, http://money.cnn.com/2008/06/11/news/mass _transit/index.htm.

104. *twenty billion fewer miles* "Americans Drive 1.4 Billion Fewer Highway Miles," CNN(US), June 18, 2008, http://articles.cnn.com/2008-06-18/us/driving.cutbacks_1 _americans-highway-trust-fund-record-gas-prices?_s=PM:US.

105. *Andy Clarke . . . Scott Jaeger* Biking and bike sales rise with high gas prices from Wendy Koch, "Bike, Scooter Sales Pick Up Speed," May 9, 2011, *USA Today,* http://www.usatoday.com/money/economy/2011-05-09-scooter-bike-sales-boom _n.htm.

106. *2,400 EV charging systems* CarStations website, last modified 2011, http://car stations.com/.

107. *new charging stations appear so rapidly* Interview with David Raboy, CEO of Car Stations.com, conducted for this book by researcher Joy Molony, January 2012.

108. *national average for a round-trip commute* Gary Langer, "Poll: Traffic in the United States," *ABC News,* February 13, 2005, http://abcnews.go.com/Technology/Traffic /story?id=485098&page=1#.TyGpXZhOHFC.

    Note from author: The 32-mile round trip is calculated from the poll's finding that the average one-way commute is sixteen miles. This figure appears at the top of the second (digital) page of this long unpaginated story.

109. *the world's second largest EV market* Pike Research, "China Will Lead Electric Vehicles Sales in Asia Pacific by 2015," press release, October 6, 2011, http://www

.pike research.com/newsroom/china-will-lead-electric-vehicle-sales-in-asia-pacific-by -2015. Pike Research predicted the US would be the world's second largest EV market, from Larry Dignan, "Plug-in Electric Vehicles to Hit 3.2 Million by 2015," SmartPlanet, September 1, 2010, http://www.smartplanet.com/blog/smart-takes/plug -in-electric-vehicles-to-hit-32-million-by-2015/10356.

110. *Mini Cooper . . . Smart ForTwo* MiniUSA website, accessed March 31, 2012, http:// www.miniusa.com/minie-usa/; Brad Berman, "Smart ED" (Review) PluginCars .com March 9, 2010, accessed March 30, 2012, http://www.plugincars.com/smart -ed/review.

111. *By 2011, Toyota alone had sold* Toyota USA Newsroom, "Toyota Sells One-Millionth Prius in the US," press release, April 6, 2011, http://pressroom.toyota.com/article _display.cfm?article_id=2959.

112. *"Hybrids are merely a way-station" . . . Not so* "The End of Hybrids? Not So Fast," HybridCars.com, May 5, 2010, http://www.hybridcars.com/news/end-of-hybrids- not-so-fast-27906.html.

113. *Ford Fusion hybrid "drives better"* James R. Healey, "A Fusion of Winning Qualities," *USA Today*, February 6, 2009, 4B, http://www.usatoday.com/printedition/money /20090206/drive06_st.art.htm.

114. *Sonata represents "solid value"* Chris Shunk, "2011 Hyundai Sonata Hybrid: Decent Fuel Economy, Better Looks, Solid Value," Autoblog.com, October 5, 2011, http:// www.autoblog.com/2011/10/05/2011-hyundai-sonata-hybrid-review/.

115. *Honda Civic hybrid "Honda's Prius"* Ben Stewart, "2012 Honda Civic vs. 2011 Toy- ota Prius: Hybrid Mileage Test," *Popular Mechanics*, May 9, 2011, http://www .popularmechanics.com/cars/reviews/comparisons/2012-honda-civic-vs-2011-toyota -prius-hybrid-mileage-test.

116. *average mileage per gallon surged from forty-eight to ninety-three* "RechargeIT.org: A Google.org Project," Google.org, accessed March 9, 2012, http://www.google.org /recharge/.

117. *90 percent of global ethanol* Sam Shrank and Farhad Farahmand, "Biofuels Regain Momentum," August 30, 2011, a report by Worldwatch Institute, http://www.ends europe.com/docs/110831a.pdf.

118. *reduces tailpipe emissions* "Alternative and Advanced Vehicles," Alternative Fuels and Advanced Vehicles Data Center, US Department of Energy, accessed March 31, 2012, http://www.afdc.energy.gov/afdc/vehicles/emissions_e85.html.

119. *some cars run on pure ethanol . . . "processing the plants into fuel consumes a lot of energy"* from "Biofuels: The Original Car Fuel," *National Geographic*, accessed February 16, 2012, http://environment.nationalgeographic.com/environment/global-warming/biofuel -profile/.

120. *ethanol . . . made from nonfood agricultural waste* "Cellulosic Ethanol" (Texas) State Energy Conservation Office, accessed April 1, 2012, http://www.seco.cpa.state.tx.us /re_ethanol_cellulosic.htm.

121. *53 percent of the world's biodiesel* Shrank and Farahmand, "Biofuels Regain Momentum."

122. *Biodiesel "essentially eliminates" sulfur oxides and sulfates* "Biodiesel FAQs: How Do Biodiesel Emissions Compare to Petroleum Diesel?," the National Biodiesel Board, last modified 2012, http://www.biodiesel.org/what-is-biodiesel/biodiesel-faq's. *"the only alternative fuel"* "Biodiesel Basics: Is Biodiesel the Same Thing As Raw Vegetable Oil?, " the National Biodiesel Board, accessed April 1, 2012, http://www .biodiesel.org/what-is-biodiesel/biodiesel-basics.

123. *57–86 percent* "Biodiesel Industry Launches First Ever National Advertising Effort," press release issued by the National Biodiesel Board, June 15, 2011, accessed April 1, 2012, http://americasadvancedbiofuel.com/news.htm.

124. *one quarter of world transportation energy demands* *Technological Roadmap: Biofuels for Transport,* International Energy Agency, 2011, 5, http://www.iea.org/papers/2011 /biofuels_roadmap.pdf.

125. *airlines recently won the right* Louise Downing, "Biofuels from Algae, Wood Chips Are Approved for Use by Passenger Airlines," Bloomberg, June 9, 2011, accessed January 26, 2010, http://www.bloomberg.com/news/2011-06-09/biofuel-from-algae -wood-chips-approved-for-airlines-ata-says.html.

Chapter 6: The Wealth of Creativity

1. *96 percent of Generation Y* Lisa Belkin, "When Whippersnappers and Geezers Collide," *New York Times*, July 26, 2007, http://www.nytimes.com/2007/07/26/fashion /26work.html?pagewanted=all.

2. *one third of Americans* Cited on Richard Florida's website, "Richard Florida Books: Overview," accessed February 27, 2012, http://www.creativeclass.com/richard_florida /books/the_rise_of_the_creative_class.

3. *Michael Gelb . . . "Corporate executives today tend to be"* Janet Rae-Dupree, "Da Vinci, Retrofitted for the Modern Age," *New York Times*, June 1, 2008, http://www.nytimes .com/2008/06/01/business/01unbox.html.

4. *Forbes estimated that J. K. Rowling* Julie Watson and Tomas Kellner, "J. K. Rowling and the Billion-Dollar Empire," Forbes.com, February 26, 2004, http://www.forbes .com/maserati/billionaires2004/cx_jw_0226rowlingbill04.html.

5. *wealthier than the queen* "JK Rowling 'Richer than Queen,'" BBC News, which cites the *Sunday Times* "Rich List" as its source, April 27, 2003, http://news.bbc.co.uk /2/hi/2979033.stm.

6. *creativity can potentially earn you* Lynne Sausele story and quotes from author interview and correspondence, May 2011.

7. *Thomas Edison . . . go fishing* from Michael J. Gelb and Sarah Miller Caldicott, *Innovate Like Edison* (Dutton, 2007), 118, 121.

8. *Gail McMeekin . . . is blessed with a steady flow of ideas* Gail McMeekin story and quotes from author interview and correspondence, May 2011.

9. *IBM asked 1,500 global chief executives* IBM Corporation, *Capitalizing on Complexity: Insights from the Global Chief Executive Officer Study 2010* (Somers, NY: IBM Corporation, 2010), ftp://public.dhe.ibm.com/common/ssi/pm/xb/n/gbe03297usen /GBE03297USEN.PDF.

10. *Samuel Palmisano . . . "Events, threats, and opportunities" . . . "a more important leadership quality"* "A Note to Fellow CEOs," *Capitalizing on Complexity*, 4.

11. *having the skills companies need* The bulleted list of skills, including the quotes "continuous rapid-fire shifts and adjustments," "fresh thinking," and "deeply held values, vision, and convictions," are from Frank Kern, IBM's Senior Vice-President of Global Business Services, "What Chief Executives Really Want," *Bloomberg Businessweek*, May 18, 2010, http://www.businessweek.com/innovate/content/may2010 /id20100517_190221.htm.

12. *Companies . . . host meditation classes* Mara Der Hovanesian, "Zen and the Art of Corporate Productivity: More Companies Are Battling Employee Stress with Meditation," *Bloomberg Businessweek*, July 28, 2003, http://www.businessweek.com/magazine /content/03_30/b3843076.htm.

13. *When 3M* The story of 3M's creative crisis, the Post-it Note quote cited in the text by a 3M veteran, and 3M's fall in the rankings of innovative companies is from Brian Hindo, "At 3M, a Struggle between Efficiency and Creativity," *Bloomberg Businessweek*,

June 11, 2007, http://www.businessweek.com/magazine/content/07_24/b4038406 .htm.

14. *"One reason why bosses might not want"* . . . *"hard-nosed approach"* "A Dark Art No More," a fourteen-page special report on innovation, *The Economist,* October 13–19, 2007, 10.

15. *topped Microsoft in profit* Amy Lee, "As Apple's Profits Surpass Microsoft's, All Eyes Are on iPad," *The Huffington Post,* April 29, 2011, accessed April 1, 2012, http:// www.huffingtonpost.com/2011/04/29/microsoft-apple-profit_n_855605.html.

16. *Apple had surpassed Exxon Mobil* From numerous sources, including Scott DeCarlo, "The World's 25 Most Valuable Companies: Apple Is Now On Top," *Forbes,* August 11, 2011, http://www.forbes.com/sites/scottdecarlo/2011/08/11/the-worlds-25-most -valuable-companies-apple-is-now-on-top/.

17. *highly engaged people grew profits by 19.2 percent* Towers-ISR, *The ISR Employee Engagement Report,* 2006, cited in David MacLeod and Nita Clarke, "Engaging for Success: Enhancing Performance through Employee Engagement," a report commissioned by the government of the United Kingdom, July 2009, 36, http://www.bis .gov.uk/files/file52215.pdf.

18. *59 percent of engaged employees "strongly agreed"* "Gallup Study: Engaged Employees Inspire Company Innovation," *Gallup Management Journal,* October 12, 2006, http://gmj.gallup.com/content/24880/Gallup-Study-Engaged-Employees-Inspire -Company.aspx.

19. *Arthur Levinson . . . "Hire innovative people"* Jena McGregor, "The World's Most Innovative Companies: The Leaders in Nurturing Cultures of Creativity," *Bloomberg Businessweek,* May 4, 2007, http://www.businessweek.com/innovate/content/may2007 /id20070504_051674.htm.

20. *40 percent of the executives agreed* IBM Corporation, *Expanding the Innovation Horizon: The Global CEO Study 2006* (Somers, NY: IBM Corporation, 2006), ii, 22, http://www-935.ibm.com/services/us/gbs/bus/pdf/ceostudy.pdf.

21. *20 percent of their time . . . half of Google's new products* Megan Barnett, "Marissa Mayer: I Thought Google Had a 2% Chance of Success," *CNNMoney,* October 3, 2011, http://management.fortune.cnn.com/2011/10/03/marissa-mayer-google/.

22. *"nurture cultures that value creative people"* Jena McGregor, "World's Most Innovative Companies," *Bloomberg Businessweek,* April 17, 2008, http://www.businessweek.com /magazine/content/08_17/b4081061866744.htm.

23. *Apple, Yahoo . . . host in-house meditation*   Der Hovanesian, "Zen and the Art of Corporate Productivity."

24. *Marc Benioff . . . of Salesforce.com*   Courtney Pannell and Sarah Lynch, "Zen Meditation: Marc Benioff, CEO of Salesforce.com, 44," ForbesLife Special Report on Hobbies, in Pictures: Hobbies A-Z, Forbes.com, accessed April 1, 2012, http://www.forbes.com/2009/06/16/hobbies-billionaires-celebrities-lifestyle-hobbies-09_slide_27.html.

25. *"more than a corporate meditation program,"*   Google's Search Inside Yourself (SIY) initiative, "Google Searches," *Shambhala Sun*, September 2009, 35–41.

26. *creative economy . . . comprised of four categories*   *Creative Economy Report: A Feasible Development Option, 2010* (New York and Geneva: United Nations Development Programme and United Nations Committee on Trade and Development, 2010), 7–9, http://www.unctad.org/en/docs/ditctab20103_en.pdf.

27. *2002 to 2008 . . . global creative economy doubled . . . surged 14 percent*   "Scope of This Report," *Creative Economy Report 2010*, xix.

28. *The developing world is a major player*   "Ten Key Messages," *Creative Economy Report 2010*, xxiii.

29. *Nigeria's $2.75 billion film industry*   "Creativity and Culture-Linked Industries Are More Resilient to Crisis," *New Horizons*, UNDP Turkey Monthly Newsletter, Issue 64, April, 2011, accessed April 1, 2012, http://www.undp.org.tr/Gozlem2.aspx?WebSayfaNo=3048.

30. *Steve Jobs . . . "the best thing that could ever have happened"*   "Steve Jobs 2005 Stanford Commencement Address," presented June 12, 2005, *The Christian Science Monitor*, October 6, 2011, http://www.csmonitor.com/USA/2011/1006/Steve-Jobs-s-2005-Stanford-commencement-address.

31. *Da Vinci filled seven thousand pages . . . Edison jotted down*   Michael Gelb, *How to Think Like Leonardo da Vinci* (New York: Delta, 2004), 57; Bruce Rosenstein, "Tap into Your Inner Edison," *USA Today*, October 29, 2007, 2012, http://www.usatoday.com/money/books/2007-10-28-innovate-like-edison_N.htm.

32. *Lawler Kang . . . has a different take*   Lawler Kang story and quotes from author interview and correspondence, July 2011.

Chapter 7: The Rewards of Conscious Investing

1. *A value stock "tends to trade"* "Value Stock," *Investopedia*, accessed March 9, 2012, http://www.investopedia.com/terms/v/valuestock.asp#axzz1jlCOuFyd.

2. *Growth stocks are shares* "Growth Stock," *Investopedia*, accessed March 9, 2012, http://www.investopedia.com/terms/g/growthstock.asp#axzz1jlCOuFyd.

3. *Karen Gross . . . joined a ten-woman investment club* Fortune Cookie story and Karen Gross quotes from author interview, March 2012, and correspondence with Karen and the club members, February 2012.

4. *During tough economic times* Expansion during recession and current size of US SRI industry from the Forum for Sustainable and Responsible Investment (formerly the Social Investment Forum), "Report: Socially Responsible Investing Assets in US Top $3 Trillion," press release, November 9, 2010, http://ussif.org/news/releases/press release.cfm?id=168.

5. *Conventional investment wisdom* Alyce Lomax, "Responsibility Won't Wreck Your Returns," The Motley Fool, March 18, 2011, http://www.fool.com/investing /general/2011/03/18/responsibility-wont-wreck-your-returns.aspx.

6. *SRI "portfolios perform comparably"* The prestigious report is from GovernanceMetrics International and cited in Lomax, "Responsibility Won't Wreck Your Returns."

7. *nearly 70 percent of SRI funds* "Publisher's Note: Financial Transformation," *Green Money Journal* 18, no. 3 (Spring 2010): 3.

8. Time *magazine named her* "About Domini, Milestones," Domini website, last modified 2011, http://www.domini.com/about-domini/Milestones/index.htm.

9. *"the Bob Dylan of SRI"* During Amy Domini's address at the SRI in the Rockies (SRIR) Conference, Colorado Springs, Colorado, October 28–31, 2006.

10. *an approach called "active investing"* Ibid.

11. *lobbied AT&T, Goldman Sachs, and JPMorgan Chase* "Shareholder Activism, Activism Archive," last modified 2011, http://www.domini.com/shareholder-advocacy /History-of/index.htm.

12. *Domini funds . . . recently persuaded Toyota* "Investor Pressure Moves Toyota Affiliate to Divest from Joint Venture with Burmese Regime," Domini News Archive, October

5, 2010, http://www.domini.com/about-domini/News/Press-Release-Archive/Investor
-Pressure-Moves-20101005.doc_cvt.htm.

13. *"no such thing as a values-neutral business"* Amy Domini's address at SRIR, October 2006.

14. *Appleseed Fund . . . shun large banks such as Citigroup* Alyce Lomax, "New Sin Stocks To Avoid," The Motley Fool, July 30, 2010, accessed March 31, 2012, http://www.fool.com/investing/general/2010/07/30/new-sin-stocks-to-avoid.aspx.

15. *questions you can ask an investment advisor* Most of these questions are from the author's personal experience; a few are inspired by "Investment Advisers: What You Need to Know before Choosing One," the US Securities Exchange Commission, accessed May 22, 2011, http://www.sec.gov/investor/pubs/invadvisers.htm and "How to Choose a Planner," the Certified Financial Planner Board of Standards, accessed June 2, 2011, http://www.cfp.net/learn/knowledgebase.asp?id=6.

16. *awakened his investing consciousness* Bennett Dorrance story and quotes from author interview and correspondence facilitated by Michael Kramer, October 2011 and February 2012.

17. *Natural Investments* For more information on the Natural Investment Heart Chart visit the Natural Investments website, last modified 2012, http://naturalinvesting.com/the-heart-rating.

18. *Matt Patsky, CEO* Matt Patsky quotes and remarks on grid parity and solar geography from interview by author, August 2010, and correspondence between Patsky and author in 2010 and 2011.

19. *"best green companies reside across the pond"* "The Brightest Green Fund," *Kiplinger's Personal Finance*, June 2009, http://www.kiplinger.com/magazine/archives/2009/06/winslow-green-solutions.html.

20. *a record $140 billion . . . "renewable energy now has reached a tipping point"* Terry Macalister, "Green Energy Overtakes Fossil Fuel Investment, says UN," *The Guardian* (UK), June 3, 2009, http://www.guardian.co.uk/environment/2009/jun/03/renewables-energy?INTCMP=SRCH. The United Nations Environment Programme report cited in *The Guardian* is *Global Trends in Sustainable Energy Investment 2009* (Paris: U.N. Environmental Programme), 2009, http://www.unep.org/publications/search/pub_details_s.asp?ID=4028.

21. *Renewable energy sources . . . global wind power . . . nearly $200 billion* "Global Trends in Green Energy 2009: New Power Capacity from Renewable Resources Tops Fossil Fuels Again in US, Europe," July 15, 2010, a press release marking the joint launch of

two reports: the United Nations Environmental Programme's *Global Trends in Sustainable Energy Investment 2010* and the *REN21 2010 Renewables Global Status Report* (REN21 stands for Renewable Energy Policy Network for the 21st Century), http://www.unep.org/sefi-ren21/documents/pr/GlobalTrendsInGreenEnergy2009 .pdf, 3–5.

22. *Andreas Schreyer . . . "nothing short of reinventing"* From correspondence between Andreas Schreyer and the author, January 2012; See also "Welcome to The Green Investor," Green Investor website, last modified 2012, http://www.thegreen investor.com.

23. *"extremely fragmented"* Ibid.

24. *Jack Robinson . . . voices a similar view* Robinson quotes, description, and his comments about WaterFurnace and that Wall Street ignores geothermal are from an interview with Jack Robinson conducted by the author in August 2007 and correspondence in July 2011.

25. *"World's 20 Most Sustainable Companies."* For the "SB20" list, visit the "Progressive Investor" on SustainableBusiness.com, last modified 2012, http://www.sustainable business.com/index.cfm/go/progressiveinvestor.main.

26. *an Exchange Traded Fund (ETF)* ETF history and description from Ken Hawkins, "Exchange-Traded Funds: Background," *Investopedia*, accessed March 9, 2012, http://www.investopedia.com/university/exchange-traded-fund/etf1.asp#axzz1jl COuFyd and *Investopedia*, "Definition of Exchange-Traded Fund—ETF," accessed February 29, 2012, http://www.investopedia.com/terms/e/etf.asp#axzz1np03 BhET.

27. *more than one thousand ETFs* The total number of ETFs is widely cited. See Selena Maranjian in "ETFs Can Kick You to the Curb," The Motley Fool, October 12, 2011, http://www.fool.com/investing/etf/2011/10/12/etfs-can-kick-you-to-the-curb.aspx.

28. *focusing on the following three* I was inspired to learn more about ETFs and these three in particular after reading Rona Fried's article, which includes a longer list of green energy ETFs. See Rona Fried, "Reviewing Green ETF Performance for 2009," Seeking Alpha, February 4, 2010, http://seekingalpha.com/article/186721-reviewing -green-etf-performance-for-2009.

29. *renewable energy . . . still accounts for only 8 percent* "Energy in Brief—What Everyone Should Know About Energy: How Much of Our Electricity Is Generated from Renewable Sources?" US Energy Information Administration (part of the US Department of Energy), last modified September 1, 2010, http://www.eia.gov/energy_in_brief/ renewable_energy.cfm.

30. *have the most sex appeal* Fried, "Reviewing Green ETF Performance for 2009."

31. *the epitome of the smart grid* From "Resources," EnerNOC website, last modified 2012, http://www.enernoc.com.

32. *EnerNOC . . . a wonderful story* The story of EnerNOC, how it works, and its entrepreneurial founders is told in Scott Kirsner, "An Entrepreneurial Fairy Tale: Two MBA Students Turn an Idea for Virtual Power Plants into Start-Up," *Boston Globe*, August 12, 2007, http://www.boston.com/business/globe/articles/2007/08/12/an_entrepreneurial_fairy_tale/.

33. *Days after graduating* Jason Voss's description and background from author interviews with Voss, August 2010 and November 2010, and the author's correspondence with him in 2010 and 2011. For additional biographic data, publications that sought Voss's advice, and DAIF performance, see "About," accessed March 9, 2012, http://www.jasonapollovoss.com/web/about/.

34. *by "knowing how to use my right brain"* From Jason Voss, preface to *The Intuitive Investor* (New York: SelectBooks, 2010), xvii.

35. *As I understand* This understanding of Voss's intuitive principles, summarized here in three points, is based on Jason Voss, *The Intuitive Investor* (New York: SelectBooks, 2010).

36. *"an investment . . . emotional act"* Ibid., 13.

37. *"no such thing as a future fact"* Ibid., 12.

38. *"robustly help to fill in the gaps"* Ibid., 11.

39. *It takes a lot of self-awareness* The section "Activate Your Intuition When CEOs Talk about Their Companies," including quotes, is based on an interview conducted with Jason Voss by the author in August 2010.

Chapter 8: The Promise of Global Consciousness

1. *ten million Americans meditate* Joel Stein, David Bjerklie, Alice Park, David Van Biema, Karen Ann Cullotta, and Jeanne McDowell, "Just Say Om," *Time Magazine*, cover story, August 4, 2003, http://www.time.com/time/magazine/article/0,9171,1005349,00.html.

2. *2007 US government survey* "Meditation: An Introduction," National Center for Complementary and Alternative Medicine, last modified June 2010, http://nccam.nih .gov/health/meditation/overview.htm.

3. *US yoga fans at 16 million* "Yoga Journal Releases 2008 'Yoga in America' Market Study," *Yoga Journal*, February 26, 2008, accessed April 3, 2012, http://www.yoga journal.com/advertise/press_releases/10. *more than 250 million people practice yoga* William J. Broad, *The Science of Yoga* (New York: Simon & Schuster, 2012) 2.

   A few years ago the website of Yoga News put the figure at 435 million yoga practitioners worldwide. But the site went dark for a while and then appeared to reemerge under a different format.

4. *"The gross national product does not allow"* Robert F. Kennedy, speech at the University of Kansas, March 18, 1968. The full text is available at http://www.jfklibrary.org /Research/Ready-Reference/RFK-Speeches/Remarks-of-Robert-F-Kennedy-at-the -University-of-Kansas-March-18-1968.aspx.

5. *the London-based Legatum Prosperity Index* General information on the Legatum Prosperity Index from "Home" and "Summary," Legatum Prosperity Index website, accessed March 9, 2012, http://www.prosperity.com.

6. *Kazakhstan . . . more prosperous than oil-rich Saudi Arabia* "The Rankings: Overall Rankings," Legatum Prosperity Index, accessed March 8, 2012, http://www.prosperity .com/rankings.aspx. *people of sub-Saharan Africa are more optimistic* "Freeing the Entrepreneurial Spirit of Africa," in "Summary: Index Insights," Legatum Prosperity Index website. See also, "Arab Spring Countries Could Look to Indonesia and Malaysia," in "Summary: Index Insights," Legatum Prosperity Index website.

7. *eight foundational factors of prosperity* "The Rankings," Legatum Prosperity Index website.

8. *approximately $6.5 trillion* Eurosif, *European SRI Study, 2010* (Paris: Eurosif, 2010), 59, http://www.eurosif.org, 7, http://www.eurosif.org/images/stories/pdf/Research /Eurosif_2010_SRI_Study.pdf. Euro-to-dollar conversions in text calculated January 2012.

9. *44 percent of adults* "LOHAS Anyone?" Allianz Deutschland, February 11, 2009, accessed January 18, 2012, https://www.allianz.com/en/press/news/studies/news _2009-02-11.html; *versus 25 percent or less* "About," LOHAS website, last modified 2010, http:// www.lohas.com/about.

10. *Organic food sales in China and Japan* Malcolm Moore, "China Goes Organic after Scandal of Cooking Oil from Sewers," *The Telegraph (UK)*, August 30, 2010, http://www

.telegraph.co.uk/news/worldnews/asia/china/7971983/China-goes-organic-after
-scandal-of-cooking-oil-from-sewers.html.

11. *rose 30 to 40 percent . . . Thai Buddhists* Dominique Patton, "Organic Food and Farming Sector Booming in Asia," *Decision News Media—Asia Pacific*, December 19, 2006, reprinted on the Organic Consumers Association website, http://www.organic consumers.org/articles/article_3628.cfm.

12. *more than 300 million Chinese city dwellers* "China: Consumers Develop Taste for Organic Foods," AsiaFoodJournal.com, April 3, 2007, reprinted with permission from Organic Monitor, http://www.asiafoodjournal.com/article/china-consumers -develop-taste-for-organic-foods/4186.

13. *will exceed $5 billion by 2015* "Organic Food in Asia-Pacific," Datamonitor, December 2011 (announcement of a published study) Just-Food.com, accessed March 2, 2012, http://www.just-food.com/market-research/organic-food-in-asia-pacific_id131113.aspx.

14. The Times *of India . . . International Spirit at Work Award* "ISAW Award and Conference: ISAW Award Nominees," Association for Spirit at Work, last modified 2007, http://www.spiritatwork.org/index.php/isaw_casestudies.

15. *India faces a rise in heart disease* Reuters, "India: Yoga in the Schools," *New York Times*, December 15, 2006, http://www.nytimes.com/2006/12/15/world/asia/15briefs -indiayoga.html.

16. *A pioneering group of African investment professionals* "Africa Sustainable Investment Forum," AfricaSIF website, accessed March 9, 2012, http://www.africasif.org/.

17. *In 2001, ASrIA, a nonprofit* "Introduction: The Association for Sustainable & Responsible Investment in Asia," ASrIA website, accessed March 9, 2012, http:// www.asria.org/asria/intro.

18. *In Latin America . . . "great places to work"* "2011 Las Mejores Empresas Para Trabajar en América Latina," Great Place to Work website, last modified 2012, http://www.greatplacetowork.net/best-companies/latin-america/latin-america/best -companies-in-latin-america.

19. *44 percent of Brazil's consumers* "Helio Mattar: A Catalyst for Corporate Social Responsibility in Brazil," *Global Giving Matters*, September/October 2004, http:// www.synergos.org/globalgivingmatters/features/0409mattar.htm.

20. *between 50 and 80 percent of consumers* Carin Zissia, "Interview: Helio Mattar, President of the Akatu Institute for Conscious Consumption," Americas Society, Council of the Americas, July 16, 2008, http://www.as-coa.org/article.php?id=1135&nav=res& pid=9.

21. *Working mom Shweta Kumari*   Shweta Kumari story and information on the Tata Nano from "How Green Is My Low-Cost Car? India Revs Up Debate," from Reuters on the Environmental News Network online, June 19, 2008, http://www.enn.com /sci-tech/article/37437.

22. *"Low-cost cars will be disastrous"*   Ibid.

23. *"It's an elitist view"*   Ibid.

24. *United Nations final report . . . on global warming*   Steve Hargreaves, "Global Warming's Trillion Dollar Debate," CNNMoney.com, November 16, 2007, http://money .cnn.com/2007/11/15/news/international/climate_change/index.htm.

25. *US Department of Energy confirmed*   Seth Borenstein, Associated Press, "Biggest Jump Ever Seen in Global Warming Gases," *USA Today*, updated November 9, 2011, http://www.usatoday.com/tech/science/story/2011-11-03/huge-increase-in-global -warming-gasses/51065082/1.

26. *"greatest humanitarian challenge" . . . Wangari Maathai*   John Vidal, "Global Warming Causes 300,000 Deaths a Year Says Kofi Annan Thinktank," *The Guardian* (UK), May 29, 2009, accessed January 2012, http://www.guardian.co.uk/enviroment/2009 /may/29/1.

27. *8 percent below 1990 levels . . . "probably less than 50 percent"*   Borenstein, "Biggest Jump Ever Seen in Global Warming Gases."

28. *38 percent of greenhouse gasses*   US Green Building Council, "Building Design Leaders Collaborating on Carbon-Neutral Buildings by 2030," press announcement, May 7, 2007, http://www.usgbc.org/News/PressReleaseDetails.aspx?ID=3124.

29. *Half the world's new building*   *Tackling Global Climate Change: Meeting Local Priorities* (Toronto, World Green Building Council, 2010), 26, http://www.google.com/search ?client=safari&rls=en&q=Tackling+Global+Climate+change+World+Green+Building+ Council+Special+REport&ie=UTF-8&oe=UTF-8.

30. *75 percent of Fortune 100 CEOs*   Alison Damast, "Interns Head Abroad for Work Experience," *Bloomberg Businessweek*, March 29, 2010, http://www.businessweek.com /bschools/content/mar2010/bs20100329_030399.htm.

31. *In just ten years*   Liz Wolgemuth, "What the Résumés of Top CEOs Have in Common," *US News and World Report*, May 21, 2010, http://money.usnews.com/money /careers/articles/2010/05/21/what-the-rsums-of-top-ceos-have-in-common.

32. *"a global mind-set"*   Phyllis Korkki, "When a Career Path Leads Abroad," *New York Times*, December 4, 2010, http://www.nytimes.com/2010/12/05/jobs/05search.html.

33. *Matthew Moughan . . . "It was a smart move, career-wise" . . . From 2001 to 2008* "Matthew Moughan story" and Intrax Internships Abroad information from Damast, "Interns Head Abroad for Work Experience," which is also the source for the doubling of student interns.

34. *Sarah Block . . . "it gave me an edge"* Ibid.

35. *For nearly a decade, Abroad China* Description of Abroad China from "Young Professional Internship/Study Program," Abroad China, last modified 2011, http://www .abroadchina.net/internship/young.asp.

36. *an "enlightening and beneficial" internship* Angel Rich story and quote from interviews and correspondence conducted for this book by researcher Joy Molony, with assistance from Abroad China, June 2011.

37. *Abroad China's Janet Zhou notes* Interviews and correspondence with Janet Zhou, conducted for this book by researcher Joy Molony, March 2011.

38. *Americans donated more than $298 billion* The Center on Philanthropy at Indiana University (research partner of Giving USA), "Has America's Charitable Giving Climbed Out of Its Great Recession-fueled Trough?" press release, June 19, 2012, accessed July 22, 2012, http://www.philanthropy.iupui.edu/news/2012/06/pr-GivingUSA2012.aspx.

39. *Fund-raiser and philanthropist Lynne Twist* Lynne Twist's background and philosophy from the Soul of Money website, last modified 2011, http://www.soulofmoney.org /about/about-lynne-twist/.

40. *"I would never call them poor again"* Lynne Twist, "The Soul of Money Workshop Video Summary," 1:22:24, posted by Katiyana, May 4, 2011, http://www.soulof money.org/blog/.

41. *more than 26 percent* "What's New," Volunteering in America 2011 Research Highlights, August 2011, http://www.volunteeringinamerica.gov/index.cfm.

42. *Nearly 30 percent of baby boomers* "Volunteering of Baby Boomers (Born 1946–1964)," Volunteering in America website, last modified 2011, http://www.volunteeringin america.gov/special/Baby-Boomers-(born-1946-1964).

43. *Some who heard President Kennedy's* Peace Corps description, age requirements, recruitment of baby boomers, and increase in volunteers over fifty years old from "About Us: Fast Facts," last modified January 13, 2012, http://www.peacecorps.gov /index.cfm?shell=about.fastfacts.

44. *Connie Genger of Billings, Montana* Connie Genger story and quotes from "Woman Finds Peace Corps in Retirement," *KULR-8 News* online, January 8, 2011, http://www .peacecorps.gov/index.cfm?shell=resources.media.medstories.view&news_id=1685.

45. *Pat and Ardella Moran of Wyoming* Pat and Ardella Moran story and quotes from "Stories from the Field," Media Resources, Peace Corps website, last modified September 20, 2008, http://www.peacecorps.gov/index.cfm?shell=resources.media.stories .emptynest.

46. *More than fifty-five million Americans* Justin Taillon and Tazim Jamal, "Understanding the Volunteer Tourist: A Qualitative Inquiry," VolunTourist Newsletter 4, no. 4, Voluntourism website, accessed March 9, 2012, http://www.voluntourism.org/news -studyandresearch44.htm.

47. *Global Vision International (GVI)* "Why Choose GVI?" Global Vision International website, accessed March 9, 2012, http://www.gvi.co.uk/about-us/why-gvi.

48. *nearly one third of Whole Foods team members* "Team Member Giving," Whole Planet Foundation, accessed January 24, 2012, http://www.wholeplanetfoundation.org/get -involved/team-member-giving/. *aim is to alleviate poverty* "About the Foundation" accessed January 27, 2012, http://www.wholeplanetfoundation.org/about/.

49. *WPF had committed . . . in 50 countries . . . 95.5 percent of loans* "Metrics from the Field," Home Page, accessed March 30, 2012, http://www.wholeplanetfoundation .org/; Additional Whole Planet Foundation information from interviews and correspondence with Whole Foods spokesperson, Claire Montaut, research conducted by Joy Molony, January 2011.

50. *Katherine Nilbrink of Durham* "Team Member Spotlight," last modified 2012, http:// www.wholeplanetfoundation.org/get-involved/team-member-spotlight/archives/.

51. *Team member Michael Mormino* Ibid.

52. *In Telluride . . . Sharon Shuteran is a familiar figure* Sharon Shuteran story and quotes from author interview and correspondence, August 2011. In May 2012, I received the sad news that my friend Sharon died unexpectedly. To honor her indomitable spirit, I have chosen to keep this story in the present tense.

53. *founder of Seeds for Development* Alison Hall story and quotes from author interview and correspondence, August 2009 and August 2011. In addition to author's interview and correspondence with Alison Hall, some data on Seeds of Development is from the project's website, http://www.seedsfordevelopment.org.

54. *"begin at the local level"* and *Boris Palmer, mayor of Tübingen*   Jim Schumacher and Debbie Bookchin, "In Europe 'Think Globally and Act Locally' Is More Than a Slogan for Saving the Planet," *Huff Post Green* (blog), http://www.huffingtonpost.com/jim-schumacher-and -debbie-bookchin/in-europe-think-globally_b_552170.html.

55. *Stateside, you can "act locally"*   "About Cool Cities," Sierra Club, Cool Cities website, last modified 2012, http://coolcities.us/about.php?sid=c89e8beb516dcee22386e 666934a4119; For examples of Cool Cities, see also "Featured Cool Cities," last modified 2012, http://coolcities.us/.

56. *"the only climate protection agreement of its kind"*   Lina Garcia, "Over 600 Mayors in All 50 States, Puerto Rico Take Action to Reduce Global Warming," *US Mayor Newspaper*, July 30, 2007, http://usmayors.org/usmayornewspaper/documents/07_30_07 /pg7_600_mayors.asp.

57. *like Florissant, Missouri . . . San Jose, California*   "Florissant, MO" Cool Cities website, October 15, 2005, http://coolcities.us/cityProfiles.php?city=68&state=MO; and "San Jose, CA," June 10, 2005, http://coolcities.us/cityProfiles.php?city=171&state=CA.

58. *Cool City Ottawa, Ontario's Green Bin program*   Ottawa, ON, January 18, 2012, http://coolcities.us/cityProfiles.php?city=1347&state=ON.

59. *"Act Locally" initiative*   EPA-sponsored programs are described in "Act Locally" under "Resources: Protecting the Environment" on the EPA website, last modified June 24, 2011, http://www.epa.gov/epahome/acting.htm. Also see, specific programs mentioned: Recycling Hotline (EPA link to Earth 911), last modified 2012, http:// earth911.com; "Superfund Community Toolkit," Hazardous Waste Clean-Up, last modified, November 9, 2011, http://www.epa.gov/superfund/community/toolkit.htm; and "Waste Not, Want Not" US Department of Agriculture, accessed March 9, 2012, http://www.epa.gov/epawaste/conserve/materials/organics/pubs/wast_not.pdf.

60. *If you can't find a group*   Francisco Ramos, "Eco Action: How to Start Your Own Local Environmental Group," Eco Hearth *Eco Zine*, August 11, 2011, http://ecohearth .com/eco-zine/green-issues/741-eco-action-how-to-start-your-own-local-environmental -group.html.